How to Keep the Law of Moses:
The Step-by-Step Guide to the Old Testament Torah

How to Keep the Law of Moses:
The Step-by-Step Guide to the Old Testament Torah

By Genesis Pilgrim

For my heart & when you awaken:

The man of God walked alone.
Faith compelled him forward.
His body trembled—but not from fear.
He approached the veil of this world in confidence:
Unshakable, the Spirit blazing power within him—
Pushing back with mighty surges upon oblivion.

Therefore, upon the silent mount we think of you:
The most honored laid to rest in solitude—
Showing us the futility of human praise
With human honor withheld at the end of majestic life.

To him whose face shines with the radiance of reflection,
Who spoke face to face with Him whom others flee:
Silence those who seek your subjugation
And shield yourself from their fell purpose.

Remember me.
Grant me holy seclusion in my pilgrimage.
Speak of me to the Master and grant me a place at the door.

Contents

Introductory Vignettes

Introduction

Many in the 21ˢᵗ Century have been misled with "partial" references to the Law of Moses.

The Law is often discussed in pieces and seldom addressed in its fullness. But when one understands the *entire* Law *as written*, it quickly dispels slapdash appeals made by those who attempt to justify themselves by it.

For example, when reading the Law of Moses, we find that the keeping of the sabbath is in fact a very small component of the Law, yet there are many Christian groups who overemphasize the sabbath . . . a true fulfillment of swallowing a camel; yet straining at a gnat.

And, in the cases where people refer to the Law of Moses in its fullness, it is often muddied by unauthorized additions and lists of rabbinical commands—which are in fact prohibited by Moses himself (Deu. 4:2). Perhaps the most fanciful embellishment—and the most hurtful one to the faith of Moses itself—is the position that the "temple" must be rebuilt. Of course, the Law of Moses does not at all order the construction of a "temple," but rather a "tabernacle."

Remarkably, this artificial preoccupation with the "temple" is altogether foreign to Moses, yet it has been used as an effective show-stopper for the reestablishment of the faith of Moses. Whereas God called His people to maintain the tabernacle for all generations; His people answer His call with empty thoughts—stating, "Well, we cannot rebuild the temple because the temple mound is occupied," or, "The New Testament took over for the Old Testament." And, within such thoughts which hold captive ambition, God's holy place of worship remains unestablished—completely absent from the Earth.

Yet, if one follows the God of the Bible, and since the God of the Bible calls forth for His dwelling to be maintained in all generations, then it should be the heart desire of His people to reestablish what has been lost. Shouldn't it? If you are not convinced, read these passages—which command the tabernacle to be maintained perpetually for all generations, in addition to its eternal establishment (Isa. 4:5; 66:18-23; Ezek. 37:26-28; Amos 9:11; Zech. 14:16-21). This is just a small sample of the many verses in the Law which declare its intention to be followed in its entirety for all generations as a "lasting" ordinance.

So, how can those who worship the Lord turn away from the ordinances He has established to exist perpetually through all the ages of humanity?

How is it possible for us to live in a world where His ordinances have altogether vanished?

How can we worship the Lord, yet be indifferent to the special place—the tabernacle—which He commanded to be maintained for all generations?

Of course, those are rhetorical questions, but if anything, I hope this examination of Moses' Law stirs within you deep reflection. I hope you may find yourself on a journey where you answer those questions *for yourself*—determining how they impact your own spirituality. Don't shy away from such questions, but seek answers for yourself.

When I look at the 21ˢᵗ Century world, I am deeply dissatisfied. And, at the center of my spiritual dissatisfaction is the neglect of God's special worship—as He commanded.

Isn't this exactly what the prophet Haggai said, when he challenged the people who neglected the rebuilding of God's house (Haggai 1:4)? (If you are unfamiliar with Haggai 1:4, please read this passage and reflect upon it.)

So, how can one follow the God of the Bible, yet be altogether unconcerned with His holy dwelling place?

Of course, the New Testament teaches in Romans 8 the believer himself is the "temple" of the Holy Spirit, and within him the Spirit dwells.

But the presence of the Holy Spirit within individual believers does not dismiss the necessity of God's house—where the ark is maintained in the most holy place.

Why?

Well, Moses was filled with the Spirit. Joshua was filled with the Spirit. The judges were all filled with the Spirit. Yet, while they were indwelled by the Holy Spirit, the tabernacle was maintained. Therefore, it is inconsistent to say we do not need the tabernacle because New Testament believers are filled with the Holy Spirit. The two concepts are unrelated: The presence of the Holy Spirit within believers does not dismiss the absolute requirement to maintain God's house perpetually in all generations. In this, God's people err—most grievously . . . an error which is challenged by Haggai's words: *Why indeed do God's people live in beautiful houses while the house of our God is in ruins?*

So, in this book, I will help you to approach the Law of Moses in its fullness—helping you to see it *only* as written in the Bible. And, as Haggai's spokesman, I will offer you similar challenges—helping you to see our responsibility within the Law.

My goal in writing this book is to provide clarity . . . complete clarity—offering practical assistance to Bible believers in their walk of faith.

I have found the phrase "keeping the Old Testament Law" to be somewhat shrouded and inaccurate when used by people who have not researched for themselves the depths of the Bible.

So, to be frank, this book will show readers "exactly" what portions of the Old Testament Law they are capable of "keeping" and which portions are beyond their reach—mostly due to the absence of an established, fully administered tabernacle.

Through my writing, you will be drawn closer to your own spiritual goals. If you desire to keep the Law of Moses to your fullest ability, I will help you to probe through the Pentateuch—showing you the very shore to which you can travel. And I will show you exactly what is beyond your reach.

Above all, I want my work to be inspiring—drawing you to an ever-growing appreciation of the Old Testament.

I pray you will be most devout upon the path which God has placed you. May you walk in faithfulness to the commands He has placed upon your heart.

The Lord bless you and keep you,
The Lord make His face shine upon you and be gracious unto you.
The Lord turn His face toward you and give you peace. (Num. 6:24-26)

In Christ,

Genesis Pilgrim

How to Use this Book

The first five books of the Bible are referred to as the "Pentateuch"—the five books of Moses. They are also referred to as the "Torah" or instruction.

My book is not written to "interpret" the Law / Pentateuch / Torah—as many other have attempted to do in contradiction to Deu. 4:2. Rather, my book is designed to help readers to understand *how to* "keep" the Old Testament "Law of Moses"—found within the Bible books of Exodus, Leviticus, Numbers and Deuteronomy.

Thus, this book will serve as a basic guide to these foundational teachings of Bible faith. If you are new to the Bible, this book will help you to build a basic understanding of Old Testament Law. If you have spent years studying the Bible, you will be pleased with the straightforward presentation of the Pentateuch found within this book—helping you to see things in detail.

Step-by-step, I will show you how a person "could" keep the Old Testament Law *in its entirety*—from *start to finish*. That is what makes this book unique. And, through this step-by-step presentation you will gain a full understanding of how the law was *originally designed* to be administered.

So, I recommend you read through this book from start to finish. But if for whatever reason you are reading something which doesn't suit your fancy, skip it and flip to another page.

You can also use this book as a reference tool. Depending on the place in which you find yourself in your spiritual journey, you can frequently refer back to the steps contained within this book—helping you to "do your best" to walk according to the wisdom of the Old Testament Law in whatever stage you find yourself.

I trust this book will be highly educational. And I trust this book will be highly practical—bringing your attention to those areas of the Old Testament Law in which you can currently choose to grow.

Many people have a difficult time comprehending the Bible—especially areas of the Pentateuch. So, if you find you are having a difficult time focusing, I encourage you to be mindful of the surroundings where you are studying.

In my own reflections and studies as I prepared this book, I found it was helpful to fast at times. At many other times I would sit in a silent room and study—secluding myself with the Word of God. And, within that seclusion, I found my mind was drawn into thoughts of the Law.

In other words, if you are hungry to understand the Law, take the path of Moses. Allow yourself some seclusion and a break from many of the other things which excite you. Then your mind will be left to create its own excitement from within as you reflect on the Law. I am convinced this is the missing step which veils many people's understanding of these Bible passages.

So, as you begin reading, I challenge you to find ways in your own life to once again embrace your own *simple spirituality*. Find *seclusion* where you can spend moments alone with God. And, in those moments, you can gain excitement—peering into the perfection of His Word.

How this Book will Assist Your Spiritual Journey

So, here you are.

You have been saved by trusting the Lord Jesus as your savior. You have been following His Word with diligence. And, as you have dedicated your life to the study and observance of Christ's commands, you have been ushered into a realization . . .

The Lord Jesus kept the Law of Moses.

Throughout Christ's teachings, you see that the Law of Moses is foundational. And, when you realize this, you are further ushered into a gratitude and devout observance of the Old Testament Law. Since Christ taught it—being its very source—you are moved to the next step in your faith journey . . .

You desire to follow the Old Testament Law.

Although you know only Christ fully "kept" the Law in its entirety—and is the only one who is "perfect," you nonetheless desire to use the Law as a guide for your feet and a light for your own path (Psa. 119:105). This is noble and good—to seek out God's wisdom through dedication to the principles of His Law. Venturing to understand and apply the whole counsel of God.

So, please allow me to assist you on your journey.

In this book, I will carefully lay out exactly how a 21st Century believer can keep the Law of Moses. In some cases, it may be impossible or impractical to accomplish certain things. But in others, it is possible to work diligently to apply basic principles and guidelines. I will show you everything—helping you to make decisions which fit your own spiritual journey. You can search out the things which are beyond your reach. You can also make plans to tailor other portions to your life—providing you a basic structure to implement the Law of Moses in simplicity.

My book will give you the "bare bones" minimums on all things pertaining to the Law of Moses. I will show you exactly what is required for festivals, sacrifices and other aspects of the Law—*with nothing added*. Thus, within this book you will find an organic, no-GMO approach to the Old Testament Law. I won't be telling you to buy unnecessary things or leading you down a confusing, complicated path. Nor will I be expounding on traditions which were later, and quite wrongly, added to the Law (Deu. 4:2). This book will deal only with the perfect Law as delivered to Moses from the Lord.

I want to help you "see" the Law for yourself.

The Law is simple—and my goal will be to expound it to you in its simplicity. I will accomplish this by presenting the Law of Moses in ten Phases, containing series of steps—each building upon one another. At the end of this book, you will be prepared to declare which "steps" to which you will work to implement.

I invite you to use this book as a tool in your spiritual journey. Jot down your notes on its pages. Or make your own notecards.

Perhaps the best addition you could make to this book would be to add quick reference tabs to allow you to quickly thumb to different sections, ceremonies, offerings, etc. If you do this you will be able to quickly wield the provisions of the Law. So, do not approach this book as a finished product. Use it as a toolbox to coach you to deeper understanding—and it will be faithful in that purpose.

Then, pass on what you learn!

Talk to other people about the simple things you learn within this book. Frankly, people have many misunderstandings about the Law, so this book can perform a good work by helping people to see its simplicity and purpose. I guarantee you will learn many things as you read. You will find yourself considering many new things.

So, put on your robe, belt and sandals. Grab your walking stick. You don't need a passport or a plane ticket, but I am going to show you things you have never seen.

Prepare for a journey.

Tone & Tense

Many people have a difficult time understanding the Torah—especially the ceremonies and sacrifices.

It is my conviction this "difficulty in understanding" is a result of perspective. In other words, when you think of something as being "in the past" it creates a stumbling block.

Think of it this way . . .

Let's say you are reading a passage from Leviticus and you are having a difficult time understanding it. If your perspective is that Leviticus offers only a description of "past" events, your mind will stumble. You will find no reason to push yourself—simply conceding to your lack of understanding. "After all," your mind will reason, "these are just descriptions of things from the distant past."

However, this book will help you to understand by first challenging you to *change your perspective*.

Rather than thinking of the Law of Moses as something "in the distant past," I will challenge you to imagine it is something you are planning to do <u>now</u>.

Therefore, in this book, I will challenge you to imagine you are involved in the planning efforts to fully implement the Law of Moses—in the present.

This approach will allow you to move beyond stumbling blocks. After all, if you were called to implement the Law of Moses <u>now</u>, you would have no choice but to figure it out. If God told you to put the Law of Moses into practice now, you would need to muster the decisiveness to work through all the difficult passages. Setting down the book would not be an option.

In my presentation of the Law, this is my approach. I challenge you to think of the Law of Moses as something which is *imminent*—to see it in the same way Moses saw the Law when it was delivered to him.

Moses had no choice. He needed to understand. Failure was not an option. And, likewise, through this approach, I absolutely guarantee you will see the Law in a new way.

So, stick with the course ahead! See the Law as something *present*. Then the Law of Moses will blossom within your mind. You will become capable of seeing things beyond your previous stumbling blocks.

About the Illustrations

Throughout this book I include many illustrations. They are intended to be simple and non-authoritative. I did not want to provide *perfect* illustrations because my intent is to help you to visualize these things for yourself. So, please approach all illustrations from this perspective.

Many of the concepts contained within the Law are mentally out of reach. My illustrations are included to help you to see a simple portrayal of items—not necessarily exactly as they are, but brief snapshots.

My goal with the illustrations is not to cater to the pretentious—whose artificially high expectations hinder their conceptualization. If it were then I would have hired a professional illustrator. Instead, my goal is to spur you to *use your own mind*—seeing for yourself the ornate details described.

So, when you view my illustrations, take the time to pause. Reflect on the descriptions given. Allow the illustration to provide your mind with a general frame. Then close your eyes and let your own mind help you to see how the basic picture can be enhanced. If you are not in the habit of relating to your own mind in this way, let me invite you to reestablish this basic connection with yourself as you read this book.

One thing which strikes me about the Law of Moses is how it simply captures *natural* items—such as pomegranates, branches—and makes use of *unchiseled* stones for the altar area. In fact, when examining the Law, we see God called the people to have such an approach. Although God Himself is perfect, things within His creation can lack symmetry. Rather than shying away from His creation, God's tabernacle commands us to embrace *variances* found within rocks and things which grow—which is why they were included in the tabernacle area and its art.

This being said, I am pleased with my illustrations as they appear in this book—with their lack of symmetry and imperfections. Furthermore, within these imperfect illustrations I impart to the reader a means of self-reflection in preparation to embrace the Law itself.

If a reader has a difficult time bearing with lack of symmetry in simple book illustrations, how much more would that reader struggle with the presence of the twelve undressed stones standing vigil around the bronze altar itself? So, you see, my simple pictures have a far-reaching purpose in revealing the reader unto himself. Many people—when viewing for themselves the things of God—are hindered by their artificially-created, high expectations (Ezra 3:12). And, by holding such high expectations, the person is stripped of joy which can be found in simple things (Ezra 3:12). Therefore, my simple illustrations wield their simple form as the mirror of the Law, revealing to the reader any pretentions which can be found within his heart—anything which might hinder from acceptance of the Law itself.

Therefore, I leave you with this thought: In your searching out of the Law, be prepared to accept it *as it is*—in perfection when it calls for unblemished animals, and also in its lack of symmetry in embracing nature as it was created. I hope my illustrations help you capture the wonderous beauty contained within the Law of Moses. I invite you to search your heart for pretention, just as God's people searched to remove leaven from their midst. Approach this book with childlike faith and wonder—prepared to see things with wonderous excitement, rather than unreasonable expectation. And, in this heartfelt simplicity, the Law will blossom before you.

The Drill Master

As you prepare to examine my work, I would like to briefly share with you pertinent information about my background . . .

As a U.S. Marine Corps First Sergeant, my job involved viewing publication manuals and working diligently to ensure unit compliance. In other words, my background as a leader has made me a stickler for details—capable of searching diligently to ensure what is done best fits with what is required by the Commandant. Some of the manuals with which I have the most experience include the Marine Corps Order (MCO) P1020.34G—which describes every detail about our uniforms, and the Marine Corps Drill Manual— which describes nearly every detail about how military ceremonies are to be conducted.

But whereas the uniform manual can be followed precisely, the drill manual is a bit trickier.

Why?

Well, depending on where a military ceremony is conducted, you might not have room for everything to *fit*. Think of a ballroom with *limited space*. Or, during a particular ceremony it might be necessary to combine different things. And in those cases, drill masters—the First Sergeants and Sergeants Major—need to figure out the best way based on the rules in the drill manual. Then, once the drill masters develop the plan, multiple leaders work with different people who are serving roles within the military ceremony—making sure it all comes together.

So, why am I telling you this?

Well, I have ample experience taking complex things and teaching them in a way that "troops" can visualize their role within the bigger plan. And, in this way, I approach the Law of Moses. In each Phase, I point each person to his exact position—showing *exactly* how things must be built, and placed, and how each person is to perform his role for the various festivals, sacrifices and offerings.

As you progress within these pages, you mind will be drawn to the immense bulwark of the Law: You will begin to see the amazing, overwhelming nature of the Law—much as you would have stood in awe of one of my military ceremonies. And, just as each person cannot do everything on his own, so also my treatment of the Law demonstrates leadership. I will guide you to understand and find your place in the big picture—just as the First Sergeant guides and directs his troops.

Here I unveil to you the "drill master's presentation" of the Law. But be warned: As you progress, this Law proclaimed will become heavier and heavier. I will place the full weight of the Law *entirety* upon your shoulders—and I will challenge you to *keep it if you can.*

And, as I place challenges upon you—brick by brick—I will show you, o man, why you need a Savior. Truly, it is my greatest honor to serve you in this way. For this journey I will serve as your drill master. I will tell you exactly where to step, and exactly what to do in order to keep the perfect Law delivered by God. And, as we move forward, you will sense the overwhelming nature of what is presented—seeing the Law *as it is*—the great equalizer, levelling all humanity at the foot of the cross.

Therefore, I challenge you to step onto my field!

I challenge you to discipline yourself by the Law as I present it. Strip away all that hinders you. Prove yourself by examining all the Law's requirements. And, like me, you will find yourself *most unworthy*.
This is the whole point—to bring us all to speechless awe before God (Rom. 3:19-20).

Are you prepared for such a journey? If so, discipline yourself as you commit to the course ahead. Set your mind on understanding. I will teach you, dear friend.

Christians & The Law

Don't take shortcuts.

God delivered the Law to Moses as the revelation of the Heavenly pattern (Exo. 25:40). And at the end of this age, the ark will reappear—as it tells us in the book of Revelation. The festivals will be reestablished and the Law will continue throughout eternity (Isa. 4:5; 66:18-23; Ezek. 37:26-28; Amos 9:11; Zech. 14:16-21).

So, although the Law has its limits, it is incredibly significant—and will continue to be significant forevermore. Therefore, avoid hasty criticisms or dismissals of the Law.

If you want to discuss the Law, discipline yourself. Become a master within it. Learn what it actually says. Interact with the Law itself based on the knowledge you have gained through diligent study.

Since God delivered the Law to Moses . . . and if the God of the Bible is your God, then commit yourself to understanding the precepts of your God.

Don't dismiss the Law.

Many push the Law aside—as if it were completely nullified by the New Testament. However, as I stated, the ark will reappear, and the festivals will be kept in eternity, and the tabernacle itself is a reflection of the Heavenly dwelling, so all things within the Law will evermore remain significant.

The Lord Jesus said that not one jot will pass from the Law, yet many people who worship God give no attention to His Law. And, for that, their faith suffers—most grievously.

Therefore, I challenge you to learn the Law masterfully. Learn for yourself what it says. And, in this process, allow yourself to see the Heavenly pattern contained within it. Give your reverence to God's Law and it will impart to you a blessing of understanding.

I will leave you with this thought . . .

If the God of the Law, is your God, and if the Law fails to keep your interest, this is not a problem with the Law itself.

In order to be prepared for his mission, Moses needed to be disciplined by the wilderness—being stripped away from everything which would pull his interest from God's commands. Only then was Moses capable of listening and heeding.

Yet, is it no wonder, when the life of the 21st Century man is overwhelmed with attractions which keep his mind in a constant state of alert that he is incapable of sensing the gentle whispers of mountain-top wisdom. I fear the 21st Century man is tossed about so strongly by poor diet, social inputs and electronics that he would be altogether incapable of sensing any spiritual stirring.

So, if you find yourself distracted and incapable of focus, let me invite you into the *wilderness*. Step away from those things which entrench your mind. And by removing those things which afflict you with constant excitement, your mind can level over several weeks.

Then, re-approach the Law. You will find in your boredom that the Law gains vibrancy and your mind will be drawn to it.

Don't attempt to shortcut this personal process. Do this for yourself and your own faith. Discipline your mind so you can understand. Then move forward through this book.

An Explanation of LXX Notes

Throughout this book I include notes from the LXX.

So, what is the LXX?

"LXX" means "seventy," and is an abbreviation for the Greek Septuagint translation of the Old Testament.

Why do I include notes from the LXX?

English translations of the Old Testament use the Masoretic text, but interestingly, when New Testament authors quote the Old Testament, they are quoting from the LXX.

Perhaps you are not interested in this topic, so a short answer would be to say the LXX offers helpful elucidations in some cases where it is not offered in the Masoretic. So, in the preparation of this book, I carefully examined both texts. And, rather than mixing them with one another, I carefully differentiated between the two—noting when the LXX differs from the Masoretic.

If you are interested in this topic, I invite you to research the Septuagint and the Masoretic texts to arrive at your own conclusions.

Capitalizing, Italicizing & Underlining

Throughout this book, I choose to capitalize certain words—particularly those dealing with the tabernacle articles and priesthood. At times I capitalize a word, yet leave it uncapitalized in other areas. Although it violates normal rules of English, I do this for the purpose of *emphasis*—especially at times to help the reader to focus on certain things.

My goal in this book is to present topics and concepts so they are easy to understand. Therefore, I have chosen to defy normal rules of English in some cases where it contributes to better readability.

Definition of "Tabernacle" & "Temple"

Before diving into this book, it is important to elucidate a couple terms. Specifically, I need to explain the "tabernacle" and the "temple."

Concerning the "*tabernacle*" . . .

In the Old Testament Law of Moses, it discusses the establishment of the "tabernacle" as the place of worship. Simply stated, the tabernacle was a tent—capable of being moved from one location to another. Thus, the tabernacle was the worship location for God's people as they moved throughout the wilderness over the many years following their exodus from Egypt. Whenever God called the community to move, the priests and Levites (who were workers at the tabernacle) would simply pack up the tabernacle and all its items. Then they would travel to the next location where they would un-pack and reassemble the tabernacle tent.

Concerning the "*temple*" . . .

The "temple" is the permanent version of the tabernacle. Whereas the "tabernacle" was *temporary* and capable of being re-located; the "temple" was designed to be a *permanent* location.

In theory, the temple is indistinguishable from the tabernacle in function. All of the sacrifices and operations carried out in the tabernacle were carried out in the "temple." So, in this we see the only difference is that the temple was designed to be a *permanent* version of the tabernacle. In other words, when the temple was established, it "replaced" the tabernacle as the *one* place of special worship.

So, why did God's people replace the tabernacle with the temple?

Good question.

Originally, the Law of Moses was designed to be carried out through the use of the movable tabernacle tent.

So, what changed?

Well, during the reign of King David, God put it in his heart to desire to build a permanent temple in Jerusalem. Although David did not build the temple, he did transport articles from the house of the Lord to Jerusalem in preparation for the building of the temple (2 Sam 6). Most notably, David moved the ark of God to Jerusalem.

Then, during David's reign, the Lord's house remained capable of being moved to different locations. For example, when David fled Jerusalem during Absalom's rebellion, he took the ark with him (2 Sam. 15:24). And, since David took the ark, it is possible the priests and Levites also brought a tent to house the ark.

Many years later, during the reign of King Solomon, David's son, God called Solomon to build the "temple." And, at that moment, the tabernacle ceased being a movable structure. The location of the temple was fixed firmly within Jerusalem. (Even after it was destroyed, God once again called the people to re-build the temple in the same *permanent* location, as seen in the book of Haggai and Ezra 1-6.)

Of course, we are left to reflect on the purpose of transforming the tabernacle into the temple.

Was it the best *practical* choice?

In a frank assessment, we would be tempted to say that the tabernacle was vastly superior to the temple. Yes, the temple was magnificent in appearance—being adorned with costly stones and precious metals. But what was gained in appearance was lost in mobility. And, as it turns out, *mobility* was one of the most important aspects of God's house—being capable of being instantly packed up and moved wherever God directed.

Therefore, the *fixed* location of the temple made it entirely vulnerable. History shows us how the temple was desolated—<u>*seven times*</u> in fact (1 Kings 14:26; 2 Kings 12:18; 14:14; 16:8; 18:14-16; 24:13; 25:8-17).

Going one step further, we could wonder at what *may have happened* if God's people kept the tabernacle rather than the temple. We could be so bold to claim that the tabernacle *would* still be in operation today—having been capable of being moved every time a military threat arose, thereby making it immune to capture and destruction.

It is an interesting thought, right?

Well, in this perhaps we see the larger design: In commanding the transformation of the tabernacle into the temple, God moved to intentionally open it up to attack. By making the moveable tabernacle into a fixed temple, God made it possible for His people to be dispersed and scattered through its destruction. In other words, similar to the betrayal of Christ, when the temple was struck, the people scattered. I invite you to arrive at your own conclusions.

So, there you have it . . . The difference between the tabernacle and the temple is that one is a *moveable tent* and the other is a *permanent building*.

Throughout this book, be mindful of the differences between each. Specifically, remember the paradoxical strength of the tabernacle was its ability to be re-located—thereby making it immune to military threat. Also, be mindful that the Law of Moses *does not* command the building of a "temple." Rather, the Law of Moses requires *only* the tabernacle.

And, in remembering the Law of Moses <u>*only*</u> requires a tabernacle tent, perhaps we get one of the most foundational glimpses of true worship: God's people are not called to be *permanent* fixtures in this fallen world. Rather, God's people are called to live as strangers and pilgrims in this world, looking forward to the Heavenly country. Therefore, the tabernacle is vastly superior to the temple in preparing the hearts of the faithful.

So, I leave you with this thought . . .

Let go of your desire for permanence in this world. Live faithfully day-by-day, being capable of rising up and setting out wherever the Lord's Spirit leads you. And, by doing so, you can follow in the heavenly pattern of the tabernacle.

How Worship was Established in the 15ᵗʰ Century B.C. & Re-Established in 538 B.C.

Currently in the 21ˢᵗ Century, the temple is no longer present. Yet the tabernacle/temple is *absolutely required* if one desires to keep the Law of Moses.

Of course, there may be buildings which are called "temples" or "tabernacles," but I am not speaking about these. In order for a person to keep the Law, they must have *THE* tabernacle established. Only then can an individual be capable of properly offering sacrifices and observing specific requirements of the Law of Moses.

Frankly, without the temple/tabernacle, it is absolutely impossible to keep the Old Testament Law.

Period.

Keeping the Law requires sacrifices. And sacrifices require the tabernacle.

Therefore, if we have a heartfelt desire to keep the Old Testament Law, then we must *first* "re-establish" God's tabernacle/temple.

So, throughout this book I will explain exactly how God's people *could* accomplish this. This will leave you with an interesting perspective on the Law—perhaps a perspective which has not been considered for many centuries.

How could the Law of Moses be re-established?

In the Bible there were *two* specific times where God's people "established" the tabernacle/temple. . . .

First, in the 15ᵗʰ Century B.C., God called Moses to establish the tabernacle. This is discussed in the book of Exodus.

Second, after nearly seventy years in exile, God called Cyrus, king of Persia, to direct the re-building of the temple. This is discussed in Ezra chapters 1-6.

Thus, these two events provide us a template—showing us how God's people have established the proper worship of the Lord. And, by learning from them, God's people today can understand how they may properly re-establish Old Testament practices.

It is an interesting thought—isn't it? . . . The idea of re-establishing the Law of Moses.

Yet, contrary to what you have been told, re-establishing the Law of Moses *would not* require a temple. This is important to remember. Often, whenever this topic is discussed people immediately object on the grounds that it is impossible to re-build the temple on its old foundation—because it is currently occupied. However, as I said earlier, the Law of Moses *does not require a temple*. Instead, the Law of Moses *requires the tabernacle*. And, since the Law of Moses only requires the tabernacle, this means the tabernacle could be constructed <u>*anywhere—and transported anywhere*</u>. In other words, the tabernacle does not require a specific location.

What does this mean?

This means any objection raised on the grounds of the temple location being occupied is an irrelevant objection. The Law of Moses requires only the tabernacle. And, on Earth, there is absolutely nothing which would stop it from being constructed. Therefore, when people object to reestablishing the Law of Moses, they do so on the basis of artificial arguments foreign to Moses' teaching.

As you read this book, you will see this clearly. I will show you exactly how the Law of Moses could be reestablished—and the process could be started today.

So, as you prepare to read Phase #1, I hope you are encouraged by this unique perspective on the Law. I hope your mind is opened to consider new things. And I hope the Law comes alive within your mind.

Most of all, we need to let go of the artificial hang-ups people have attached to the Law over the centuries. Only then can we see the Law exactly as the Lord delivered it to Moses.

Therefore, I invite you to set aside what people have *taught about* the Law. Join me as we examine for ourselves *exactly* what the Law *itself* requires.

How to Keep the Law

Phase 1

The God-Appointed Leader

In order to "keep" the Old Testament Law, you first need a tabernacle (a place to worship). But before you can have a tabernacle, you first need craftsmen to build it and a group of priests to set it up and administer it.

But *even before* you can hire craftsmen or appoint priests, you first need a "Moses-type" leader to set all things in motion.

Therefore, in order to "keep the Old Testament Law," you first need a "Moses."

As we see in the book of Exodus, God began by calling Moses. Thus, this is the foundational step—*the very first step*—in keeping the Law. The "God-appointed leader" must be called to lead God's people. Before craftsmen are hired, before the tabernacle is constructed and before priests are appointed, a "Moses-type" leader must be called by God.

"Keeping the Law" is not an *individual* effort. An individual cannot keep the Law for himself. Rather, "keeping the law" requires God-appointed leadership.

God did not intend for individuals to worship Him in isolation. Rather, we see in the Law that worship is a corporate activity—as the *entire community* of God's people come together under God's appointed leadership to offer sacrifices at *one* tabernacle.

In other words, in order for individuals to be in right standing with God according to the Law, they *must* be under the leadership of the God-appointed leader (Deu. 18:18). Frankly, it was not enough to simply worship according to the pattern of the Law. Indeed, there were false leaders during the time of Moses who attempted to lead the people astray. Although these false leaders performed similar acts of worship to Moses and Aaron, they were rejected (Num. 16:1-17:10). Moreover, Moses warns God's people from following other false leaders who would rise up after his time (Deu. 18:20-22).

So, in order for one to "keep the Law of Moses," they *must* be under the authority of the God-appointed leader. This is the foundational characteristic of one who "keeps the Law of Moses."

Thus, if you intend to "keep the Law of Moses," the process *must* begin with your choice to follow the God-appointed leader. And, as others attempt to dissuade you from following the proper leader, you must remain true—eluding the false teachings of others who would lead you astray. This is the foundational factor which determines whether or not an individual is in the community of faith. Either you follow the God-appointed leader, or you do not (Deu. 18:18-19; 1 John 5:12).

Moving on . . .

So, what was the *role* of Moses?

In the establishment of the Old Testament Law, Moses was called by God to unite His people. Once God's people were delivered from Egypt, Moses served as their mediator before God. He received the commands from God and spoke to Him *face to face* (Exo. 33:11; Num. 12:8; Deu. 34:10).

And, as explained above, without a "Moses" the tabernacle cannot be built or administered—which is absolutely necessary for anyone venturing to keep the Old Testament Law.

As a result, we see that God-appointed leadership is necessary for anyone who intends on keeping the Law. By God-appointed leadership, I do not mean a pastor or a religious teacher who has been ordained *by people*. Rather, the God-appointed leader is one who is called *by God Himself*—just as Moses was.

This is further illustrated in the Bible . . .

When God desired to establish the tabernacle within Jerusalem, He called David, king of Judah and Israel (2 Sam. 7:2-13). Then, similar to Moses, David oversaw the movement of tabernacle articles and the administration of worship in God's house (2 Sam 6; 1 Chr. 16:1-7).

In the following generation, God called Solomon to transition the temporary tabernacle into a permanent temple within Jerusalem. And, similar to David and Moses before him, Solomon served to oversee the administration of the house of the Lord.

Much later in the Bible, we see in the books of Jeremiah and Lamentations that the Jerusalem temple was captured by the Babylonians. About 70 years later, in order for God to reestablish His place of worship, He calls Cyrus, the king of Persia, to allow exiles to return in 538 B.C. Cyrus sends nearly 50,000 exiles under the leadership of Sheshbazzar, governor of Judah, and Joshua, the high priest. Many years later, the temple was completed in 516 B.C., under the leadership of Zerubbabel, Haggai, Joshua and Zechariah (Ez. 1-6; Hag. 1-2; Zech. 1-14). Just as God instituted the Law through Moses, later God re-instituted the Law through these leaders.

So, we see clearly "keeping the Law" requires "start-up leadership." Keeping the Law is not a solo venture. Rather, it is a corporate venture—as the people of God are led in unity in the establishment of the Lord's house.

Therefore, if you venture to "keep" the Law of Moses, your journey *must begin* with your choice to follow the right leader—who has been appointed directly by God, in the same way as Moses, David, Solomon and Cyrus.

Get it?

Historically we see God provides a cadre of trusted advisors and supporters to complete the necessary work. When God called Moses, David, Solomon and Joshua to lead His people, God placed around these leaders gifted individuals to support them. Moses was supported by Aaron, Miriam, Reuel and Joshua, the military general. David was supported by his court and a number of prophets. Additionally, Solomon had a court appointed to see to the accomplishment of his will. Last, in the case of Joshua, the high priest, we see his calling was supported by the skilled craftsmanship of Zerubbabel and the prophesies of Haggai and Zechariah (Ezra 1-6).

So, what happened to those who rejected God-appointed leadership?

If one ventures to worship God, he must follow God's guidance. And, this creates a "black and white" scenario—where either a person is following God or they are not. There is no middle ground. In fact, this principle remains true in the entire Bible—to the ultimate extent of saying that those who have Christ have life but those who do not have Christ do not have life (1 John 5:12).

In the Law, Moses concludes by promising the people that the Lord would send another prophet like him (Deu. 18:18). Here Moses warns the people that they must listen to everything the prophet says, or they would be cut off from among God's people.

Seems harsh, right?

Well, remember what is at stake: Either things are done properly or they are not. There is no middle ground. In fact, in the construction of the tabernacle, everything had to be made according to the Heavenly pattern shown to Moses on the mount (Exo. 25:40; Heb. 8:5). Thus, in "keeping the Law" there is no such thing as "*kinda*" or "*good enough*." Either things were *completely correct* or they were *dead wrong*.

In the Deu. 18:18 prophecy—where Moses tells the people to expect another prophet like him—we see a glimpse of Christ. This prophecy was completely fulfilled in Christ Himself as the Prophet to whom God's people owed their allegiance. And this is plain in Scripture: Those who reject Christ are rejected by God (John 3:36).

But along the way through history, on its way to ultimate fulfillment in Christ, Moses' Deuteronomy 18:18 prophecy was partially-fulfilled many times. Truly, there were many critical points at which the Lord's prophets spoke messages which were absolutely critical for the people. And, when God's people chose to follow the teaching of the *God-appointed prophet*, they were blessed. But when some chose to reject the teaching of the God-appointed prophet, they suffered and in some cases were even "cut off" from their possession—just as Moses warned in Deuteronomy 18:18-19.

Perhaps the most notable example is the prophet Jeremiah. When God's people failed to heed the prophecies of this God-appointed leader, they were shaken from the Promised Land and sent into exile. Those who did not heed the prophet were "cut off" from among God's people.

Interestingly, we see Moses' Deuteronomy 18:18-19 prophecy applies to other God-appointed leaders following the 516 B.C. "re-establishment" of the temple. When commanding God's people to cease their practices of usury, Nehemiah warned them that God would shake them out of their possessions if they did not keep their oaths (Neh. 5:13). Moreover, Ezra led efforts to demand the people to cease their defiling practices in the re-established land—warning them that dissent would result in confiscation of their property in the Promised Land (Ezra 10:5-8). So, after the establishment of the temple worship, we see *God-appointed leaders* required absolute unwavering obedience to their commands. Those who risked dissent would lose their place among God's people—actually having their inheritance in the Promised Land confiscated. These are partial fulfillments of Deu. 18:19—foreshadowing the complete obedience which the Christ, in ultimate fulfillment, requires from those who follow Him.

Importance of the God-Appointed Leader

In the above discussion we explored the vital importance of following the *right leader*. And, beyond the reasons stated in this Phase, we find additional reasons which support the need for a God-appointed prophetic leader.

Now, as it is currently in the 21st Century, people discuss the rebuilding of the *temple* in Jerusalem. However, this creates problems—as the temple mount is currently occupied by other buildings. Moreover, according to tradition, in order to re-set the temple altar, one must know the *exact* location of the previous altar placed by Solomon. And, even more impossible, in order to reestablish the traditional temple priesthood, it would require a pre-established priesthood—which is not in existence.

In other words, to consecrate priests, you would first need priests . . . but to get priests you need to consecrate priests.

Seem confusing?

Well, it is.

However, fortunately for you, I am here to clarify the process for you . . .

According to the Law of Moses, found in the books of Exodus, Leviticus, Numbers and Deuteronomy, a "temple" is not required. In fact, during the time of Moses, there was no temple! Rather, the people had the "tabernacle."

This distinction is important because, in order to reestablish Old Testament faith, you do not need to rebuild the *temple*. Instead you need to rebuild the *tabernacle*.

And, in this distinction, there is a work-around for all the above problems with the temple I mentioned—location unavailability, exact location of altar, etc.

Truly, *all* of the "temple" problems can be solved with the "tabernacle."

How?

Well, as I stated above, first you start with *the God-appointed leader*. Then the God-appointed leader sets up a temporary "tent of meeting" outside the camp—where he meets with God face-to-face, just as Moses did (Exo. 33:11; Num. 12:8; Deu. 34:10). And this "tent of meeting" serves as the temporary headquarters to plan the building of the tabernacle, the courtyard and all the articles.

Then, the God-appointed leader is responsible for consecrating the first group of priests at the new "tent of meeting"—because he is granted authority from God to do so . . . similar to Moses.

And, during the Consecration Ceremony of the high priest, the tabernacle officially becomes the new "tent of meeting"—while the old "tent of meeting" is no longer used (see page 17).

Therefore, we see clearly that unlike the "temple," *reestablishment of the "tabernacle" poses no problems whatsoever*. The God-appointed leader could begin the process today—in fact. All the God-appointed leader needs to begin the process is a temporary "tent of meeting."

Period.

Therefore, there is no legitimate excuse why the tabernacle should not be rebuilt by those who desire to keep the Law of Moses. The tabernacle does not need to be placed in a specific location. So, it doesn't matter if there are other buildings on the "temple location" in Jerusalem. The God-appointed leader could build the tabernacle *now* in *any location* where God calls him to do so.

If the Law of Moses is to be followed, then all is needed is the God-appointed leader and a tent. Nothing else is required beyond this to initiate the process. Then, the God-appointed leader carefully reestablishes the priesthood, the tabernacle and all its articles through the authority God has placed upon him.

So, if you desire to follow the Law of Moses, realize you *must* have the tabernacle. Abandon thoughts of reestablishing the "temple"—as it is unnecessary and foreign to the Law of Moses. Only the *tabernacle* is required. And to get that, you must simply start with the God-appointed leader and a tent. Nothing more.

Therefore, if you venture to keep the Law, may God provide you with the necessary leadership to see His will accomplished. May God raise up trusted advisers to assist the one called in the accomplishment of his assigned mission. As God has always been faithful in the past, so He will ever remain faithful to those He calls. His Word will never return void, but will accomplish His will (Isa. 55:11).

In conclusion, to "keep the Law," you need *God-appointed leadership*. You must follow the right leader while avoiding false teachings which attempt to dissuade you. Only then does one find the proper footing upon which to build true worship. To keep the Law, you must begin by submitting to the authority of God's appointed leader among the community of faith.

In the Law of Moses, there is no such thing as a *solo* worshipper. You need God-appointed leadership and you need the community of faith.

How to Keep the Law
Phase 2
Tabernacle Construction

How to Reestablish the Tabernacle from Nothing

Of course, an immediate objection to the reestablishment of the tabernacle may be . . .

"We don't have the original ark, altar or any of the articles."

However, this objection is quickly defeated by a reference to the 538-516 B.C. reestablishment of the faith. In the book of Ezra, we see these people, despite only having *some* of the original pieces (Ezra 1:7-11), completely reestablished temple worship. Interestingly, Ezra 1:7-11 says nothing about the holy furniture of the tabernacle (ark, bread table, lampstand, incense altar, wash basin, altar table, etc.) It only mentions the return of unessential bowls, dishes and pans.

Yet, with only "bowls, dishes and pans," God's people had everything they needed to reestablish their faith. In fact, they reestablished prescribed offerings and celebrated the Festival of Tabernacles when *only the foundation of the temple* was laid (Ezra 3:3-6).

Therefore, we can conclude that the reestablishment of the Law of Moses would not require the *original* ark or tabernacle articles and components. Anyone who says they are intent on following the Law of Moses—yet uses "original items" as an excuse—is merely stalling.

Original items do not matter and they can be reconstructed. You don't need the *original* ark to reestablish the tabernacle.

Fundraising

So, once an individual completes Phase #1 of this book, it is time for Phase #2: Tabernacle Construction. In this phase, the individual joins with God's people to *raise funds* for the tabernacle's construction.

As was stated earlier, "keeping the Law" requires the tabernacle. It is absolutely impossible to keep the Law of Moses apart from the tabernacle/temple. So, for the person intent on following the Law, it is necessary to see God's tabernacle established. We see this clearly in the book of Haggai. . . .

In 538 B.C., nearly seventy years after Judah's exile to Babylon, the Persian king, Cyrus, finally allowed God's people to return to Jerusalem to rebuild the temple. However, God's people became discouraged and abandoned construction of the temple.

Then, at around 520 B.C., the prophet Haggai challenged God's people. While the people worked diligently to provide homes for themselves, they allowed the temple to remain in ruins (Hagg. 1:4). Haggai directed them to re-build the temple. His leadership was successful. Ultimately the temple was completed in 516 B.C.

In the book of Haggai, we see clearly it is not enough for one to simply "try their best" to keep the Law of Moses. For Haggai the temple was an absolute necessity—and he encouraged the people to reestablish it as the central location to exercise their faith in God.

Likewise, for the person who ventures to keep the Law of Moses today, the reestablishment of the tabernacle/temple is an *absolute necessity*. God does not wink at partial efforts or award prizes for a person doing "good enough." Everything in the Law of Moses is made after the Heavenly pattern, and it must be kept in its *fulness*. There is no such thing as tip-toeing through the Law. The tabernacle *must* be in operation.

But at this point you should not despair, my friend. As we move further throughout this book, I will explain to you *exactly* how the tabernacle and the Law are to be set up.

Now that we are convinced, just as Haggai, that the tabernacle/temple *must* be built, all that is left to do is the work itself. And this leads us to our present discussion in this current phase. In order to construct the tabernacle and its articles, we must have the funds and materials to do so.

As is the case with all construction projects, the planners must carefully consider the costs (Luke 14:28-30). So, before the tabernacle can be constructed, God's people must make determinations concerning the funding required to complete the project.

So, how did Moses support the construction of the tabernacle?

Freewill offerings from God's people.

During the leadership of Moses, God's people brought freewill offerings to provide materials for the construction/crafting of the tabernacle and its articles (Exo. 25:1-8; 35:4-29; 36:3-6). In the book of Ezra, we see freewill offerings were also received from God's people to fund temple construction (Ezra 2:68).

Therefore, in the re-construction of the tabernacle, it would be necessary to ask for *freewill offerings* from God's people. It makes sense. Because God desires His tabernacle to be established, we can trust He will put the desire to support it within the hearts of His people through the Holy Spirit.

What were other sources of funds for tabernacle construction?

Well, we see clearly that God Himself supported tabernacle construction. In the book of Exodus, we read God influenced the hearts of Egyptians to give gold and silver and clothing to God's people (Exo. 12:35-36). Doubtlessly, many of these materials found their way into the tabernacle through later freewill offerings.

Later, in the re-construction of the temple, we see *royal decree from the king* provided funding. Similar to the Exodus account, in the Ezra account we read the Persians provided God's people with gold, silver, goods, livestock and freewill offerings to support the re-establishment of God's temple (Ez. 1:4).
Moreover, King Cyrus orders the return of some of the previously plundered tabernacle articles—thereby removing the requirement for God's people to re-craft them (Ez. 1:7-11).

Finally, King Darius orders temple re-construction to be paid through funds from the royal treasury (Ez. 6:8-9).

Additionally, he rules temple employees to be tax-exempt, thereby allowing priests and Levites to devote themselves fully to their work within the temple (Ez. 7:24).

So, as God's people venture to re-establish the tabernacle, perhaps we could seek out similar means of funding. We can trust God will put it within people's hearts to give freewill offerings. And, God's people could also expect royal/government decree to assist in the process in some way—similar to how royal decrees assisted with re-construction in the past.

Appointing the Chief Craftsman

Once funding is gathered (or is at least projected to reach necessary goals), then construction crews and craftsmen can be hired.

At this stage it is necessary to appoint a chief craftsman to make plans and provide the God-appointed leader with requirements.

For example, during the time of Moses, he appointed two chief craftsmen, named Bezalel and Oholiab. (Or to be more accurate, God Himself selected these craftsmen by empowering them with His Spirit as explained in Exo. 31:1-11). Then these chief craftsmen oversaw the construction of the tabernacle and its articles (Exo. 37:1-39:31).

Likewise, in the book of Ezra, we see the crucial role of Zerubbabel in overseeing the re-construction of the temple.

To follow this pattern, it is necessary for God's people under the authority of the God-appointed leader to appoint a chief craftsman.

Gathering Materials & Special Considerations

Wood

Wood is used in the construction of many tabernacle articles, including the various tables, altars, poles, and the frames and crossbars of the tabernacle itself. Therefore, it is important to know what wood should be used.

In some translations of the Bible, it states "acacia" wood is to be used for these articles. However, in the LXX translation, it states "incorruptible wood" should be used. This is an interesting expounding of the concept behind the wood choice. Thus, we see the purpose in the use of acacia wood—as an "incorruptible" type of wood present in that region.

The main idea here is that the articles of the tabernacle should be made from wood which will stand the test of time. In other words, the tabernacle articles should not be made from gnarled wood which will warp and rot.

Precious Stones

The translation of some of the precious stones is obscured in the Law of Moses—with some of the types discussed being difficult to fully articulate. This results in disparity between various translations.

For example, whereas the precious stones listed for the ephod in order are carnelian, chrysolite, beryl, turquoise, lapis lazuli, emerald, jacinth, agate, amethyst, topaz, onyx and jasper; in the LXX, these same precious stones are different. The LXX lists, in order: sardius, topaz, emerald, carbuncle, sapphire, jasper, ligure, agate, amethyst, chrysolite, beryl and onyx.

Moreover, whereas some translations state that *onyx* stones were placed in the ephod shoulder piece, in the LXX it states *emeralds* were used.

So, clearly the *exact* identification of the precious stones needs to be articulated. This is another reason why "the God-appointed leader" is necessary for the reestablishment of the Law of Moses. Whereas people today are confused about the exact type of precious stones, the God-appointed leader after the order of Moses, could render a decision in these matters (Deu. 18:18).

Cubit

As seen below for each tabernacle article, the "cubit" is often used as the measurement standard.

So, what's a "cubit?"

A "cubit" is a unit of measurement, roughly 18 inches—covering the span from a man's elbow to the tips of his fingers. Of course, this would lead to variances—because not every man's cubit is the same length. To remedy this potential inconsistency in measurement, in Ezekiel 40:5, it mentions the use of standard measuring rods to ensure the cubit measurement was consistent.

So, how was the exact cubit length determined for use in the construction of the tabernacle and its articles?

This is an interesting point of discussion. Remember, in Exo. 25:40, the Lord told Moses to make sure everything was made according to the Heavenly pattern. And, we know Moses met with the Lord Himself—face to face, as a man speaks with his friend (Exo. 33:11; Num. 12:8; Deu. 34:10).

So, whose "cubit" was used in the construction of the tabernacle and its articles?

The Lord's cubit . . . The measurement of the Lord's own forearm to the tips of His fingers.

And it is likely Moses used a rod to capture the exact length. Then, that length was used in the construction of all the articles and the tabernacle.

After all, the standard of measurement would not have been made after the pattern of the world. Nor, would the standard of the cubit be made after the pattern of Moses himself. Rather, God—in all things—called Moses to ensure everything was constructed after the pattern of Him who called him.

Cool, huh?

This might lead to further problems, however, if one ventures to reestablish the Law of Moses and the tabernacle. After all, your measurement of the "cubit" should not be determined by you measuring *your own* forearm to the tips of your own fingers. The tabernacle was not to be made according to *our* patterns. Rather, the tabernacle is in all things reflective of the pattern of Christ and the cubit of His own body.

If you are interested in this topic, I invite you to research "theophanies," "Christophanies," and Old Testament appearances of Christ. Develop your own thoughts on this topic and see if you agree. My own perspective is that the cubit used was based on the bodily form of the preincarnate Christ who appeared to Moses and spoke to him face to face. This is the best possible solution to allow the tabernacle to be constructed based on the Heavenly pattern (Exo. 25:40; Heb. 8:5).

So, before you begin reconstruction of the tabernacle or its articles, be mindful to base your measurements on the standard of Christ Himself, rather than your own measurement of the "cubit."

The Location of Crafting

Although the Bible does not say *exactly* where the tabernacle articles were crafted, it is key to remember that the articles were *treated with reverence*—even when being constructed. In other words, the craftsmen would not be crafting the ark in a location where the people could *view it being crafted*.

So, where were the articles crafted?

Surely, they were crafted in a discrete location where they were shielded from on-lookers. Thus, it might be best to assume the items of the tabernacle and the garments were crafted in either the temporary tent of meeting, or in a similar location outside the camp.

Tabernacle Construction

Once funding is gathered and the chief craftsman is appointed, then the chief craftsman follows the example set by Bezalel, Oholiab and Zerubbabel—drawing up construction plans and supervising efforts to ensure completion.

So, would it be overwhelming to plan such a large construction project?

Perhaps.

But don't worry. I will provide below a *minimum* list of required articles which must be crafted for the tabernacle. Remember, simplicity is a good thing. The goal should be to re-establish the tabernacle in the simplicity of its original construction.

The chief craftsman should avoid all temptations to "add" extra things to the tabernacle (Deu. 4:2). Simply craft the *minimum* required articles and allow the tabernacle to be *exactly* how it was originally designed—after the Heavenly pattern.

Do not make anything extra (Deu. 4:2).

So, what are the *minimum required articles*? Just these . . .

Temporary - <u>Tent of meeting</u> (Exo. 33:7-9; Deu. 31:14-15)

#1 - <u>Courtyard</u> (Exo. 27:9-19; 38:9-20)
#2 - <u>Altar</u> (Exo. 20:24-26; 24:4; 27:1-8; 38:1-7)
#3 - <u>Bronze Utensils for Altar</u> (Exo. 27:3; 38:3)
#4 - <u>Wash Basin</u> (Exo. 30:17-21; 38:8)
#5 - <u>Tabernacle</u> (Exo. 26:1-37; 36:8-20; 40:1-33)
#6 - <u>Ark</u> (Exo. 25:10-22; 37:1-9; Num. 10:33)
#7 - <u>Bread Table</u> (Exo. 25:23-30; 37:10-16; Lev. 24:5-9)
#8 - <u>Lampstand</u> (Exo. 25:31-40; 27:20-21; 37:17-24; Lev. 24:1-4; Num. 8:1-4)
#9 - <u>Incense Altar</u> (Exo. 30:1-10; 30:34-38; 37:25-29; Lev. 10:1-2)
#10 - <u>Trumpets</u> (Num. 10:1-10)
#11 - <u>Garments of High Priest and Priests</u> (Exo. 28:1-8; 39:2-31)

Transportation - <u>Carts</u> (Num. 7:3-9)

This is a bare-minimum list of the items. To view the various components of each of the listed items, you will need to keep reading. For example, the tabernacle consists of various components—curtains, posts, bases, etc. So, to learn about all the components of each item, simply keep reading through this Phase. (It is all here for you in detail!)

My goal with the above list is to present readers with a minimum list of what would need to be within the tabernacle area. And the above list accomplishes that purpose. I want to make this easier for you, not harder.

Why did I order the items like this (from #1-#11)?

Practicality: I listed the above items in the order in which they would likely be placed in a new location following transportation. This is why "courtyard" is listed first (because you need the courtyard set—or at least marked out—before you place items within it). And this is why the various components which are placed within the tabernacle are after the tabernacle itself (because the tent must be set up before the items can be placed within it).

In other words, the above list could be used as a functional guide to help in setting up the tabernacle area. Furthermore, when the tabernacle is to be relocated, the list could simply be reversed—where the last items on the list are packed first. This is certainly what is presented in Num. 10:21, where it states the Kohathites were to remove the most holy items first from the interior of the tabernacle, then the tabernacle would be speedily disassembled and then reassembled at the new location. That way the Kohathites could move the most holy items directly back into their places at the new location. (If you are interested in this topic, I provide a detailed guide for tabernacle disassembly-transport-reassembly on pages 57-61.)

Easy peasy, right?

In the previous list, I placed the respective Bible passages next to each item. Please feel free to look up those passages as you reflect on each item.

So, let's get started! I will begin with an orientation diagram—helping you to visualize the relative placement of items within the tabernacle courtyard . . .

How to Set-up Tabernacle Area (Exo. 40:1-8)

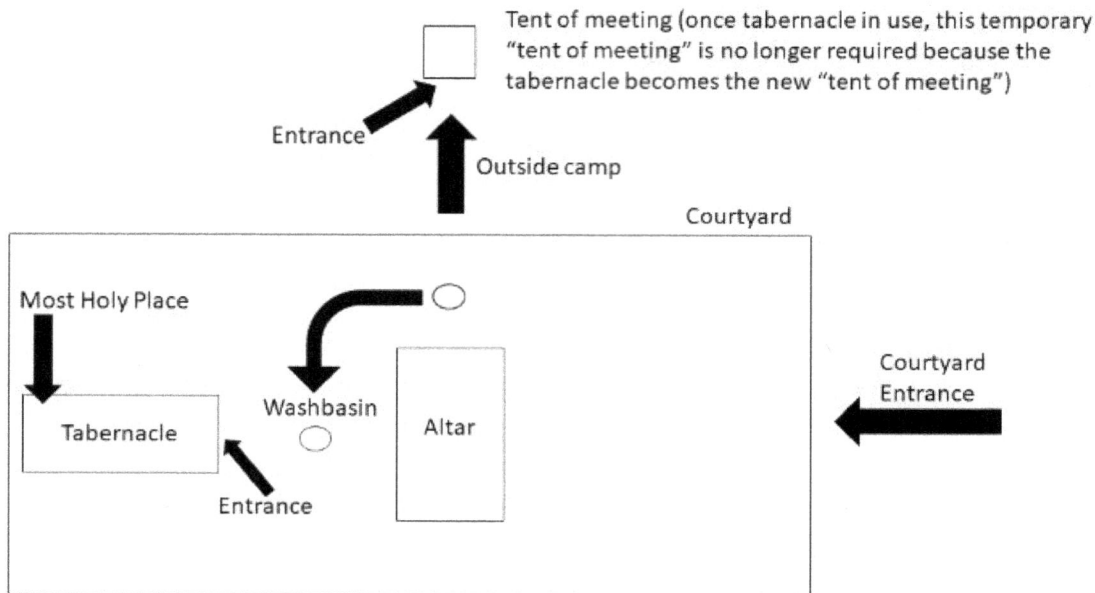

Tent of meeting (once tabernacle in use, this temporary "tent of meeting" is no longer required because the tabernacle becomes the new "tent of meeting")

Entrance

Outside camp

Courtyard

Most Holy Place

Courtyard Entrance

Washbasin

Tabernacle

Altar

Entrance

Now that you have seen how the tabernacle courtyard area is set up, let's discuss the specifics of each item within the tabernacle courtyard. To do this, I will provide information on each item in the order they should be transported into a new location and set up. This will make things as simple as possible . . .

In order to begin tabernacle construction, we must remember the process begins with a "Moses"—as "the God-appointed leader" directed to oversee construction. And, in order to start the process with the God-appointed leader, this leader needs a place where he can meet with God (since before the tabernacle is constructed, the God-appointed leader still needs to meet with God).

Make sense?

Therefore, in order to provide a holy place for the God-appointed leader to meet with God, a _temporary tent_ must be established. In the Law of Moses, the temporary tent which precedes the building of the tabernacle is called the "tent of meeting."

But we must remember the initial "tent of meeting" is temporary—only being used until the tabernacle is constructed and operational. And, once the tabernacle is operational, the tabernacle becomes the new "tent of meeting."

Thus, in my presentation of the tabernacle itself, we must begin by acknowledging the vital importance of the temporary "tent of meeting" which precedes tabernacle construction. So, here is information on the temporary "tent of meeting" . . .

Temporary - <u>Tent of meeting</u>
(Exo. 33:7-9; 40:32; Deu. 31:14-15)

- The "tent of meeting" is a *temporary* tent used prior to the completion and consecration of the tabernacle. Once the tabernacle is constructed and consecrated, the tabernacle becomes the new "tent of meeting."
- Location: Outside the camp while tabernacle is being constructed
- Those desiring to inquire of the Lord go to the tent of meeting
- Washing at wash basin required for all who visit it—so while the first "tent of meeting" is established, the wash basin (once crafted) is placed between the altar and that location. But once the tabernacle is constructed and consecrated, the wash basin is moved between the altar and the tabernacle (as the new "tent of meeting"). For help visualizing this, see the above illustration on page 16.
- The Lord met with Moses at both the temporary tent of meeting and the tabernacle—as the new tent of meeting.

Now, we will discuss the various items and articles within the tabernacle courtyard area. Remember, these items will be presented in the general order in which they will arrive in a new location.

In the Law of Moses, the tabernacle was designed to move to new locations whenever the Lord directed the people to do so. Therefore, I will present these tabernacle components in the precise order in which they would arrive and be placed in a new location . . .

#1 - __Courtyard__ (Exo. 27:9-19; 38:9-20)

- Courtyard dimensions:
  South 100 cubits wide, 20 posts,
  > 5 curtains (20x5 cubits each)
  North 100 cubits wide, 20 posts,
  > 5 curtains (20x5 cubits each)
  West 50 cubits wide, 10 posts,
  > Curtains mirror those from East side
  East 50 cubits wide, 10 posts,
  > 1 curtain for entrance (20x5 cubits),
  > 2 curtains flanking (15x5 cubits each)

- Curtains
  Made of blue, purple and scarlet twisted linen
  16 total curtains . . .
  (14) 20 cubits wide x 5 cubits high
  (2) 15 cubits wide x 5 cubits high for East & West

- Posts
  60 total posts
  Made with bronze bases
  Silver hooks and bands
  Tops overlaid with silver

- <u>Tent pegs</u> (bronze)

- <u>Entrance</u>:
  On East side
  Entrance has (1) 20-cubit wide curtain & 4 posts
  Flanked with (2) 15-cubit curtains, 3 posts each

Next, we will discuss the altar. Note the simplicity of the altar itself. God designed this special place of worship to be natural in appearance. The people were not permitted to use tools to alter the altar area. Rather, the stones used were kept in their natural appearance. At every new location, the priests would need to seek out and move twelve new stone pillars—lugging them to the altar site.

Why is this significant?

Well, since the stones represent the tribes of God's people, they are kept rugged—demonstrating that the Lord interacts with His people, warts and all. In other words, God isn't fooled by mere appearances. We cannot dress ourselves with tools to pretend like we are something different.

Moreover, the priests and Levites were required to move the stones (although it doesn't specify how they did this)—feeling for themselves the extreme burden it is to carry the people. Thus, God's established religious leaders were to carry within themselves an empathy for God—recognizing the great burdens endured by the Lord as He provides for the needs of all people. At every new location, the religious leaders would be reminded of the burden constantly maintained by their God.

So, when you see the altar, take note of the stones. If you had to lug these boulders, I guarantee you wouldn't be able to forget them! To be a faithful priest or Levite, one had to be willing to endure the struggle and the bruises they gained from striving to bring their people to atonement.

Do you have such love for your people—that you are willing to strive and endure personal pain to get them to the altar of atonement?

The Law of Moses demands this personal empathy from its religious leaders—and it uses boulders to discipline them to develop heartfelt empathy.

The entire job of the religious leader is little more than moving stones. Once the altar stones are in place, they merely shift their attention to other stones—working with equal fervor on the stone hearts of the people for whom they have been appointed.

#2 - <u>Altar</u> (Exo. 20:24-26; 24:4; 27:1-8; 38:1-7)

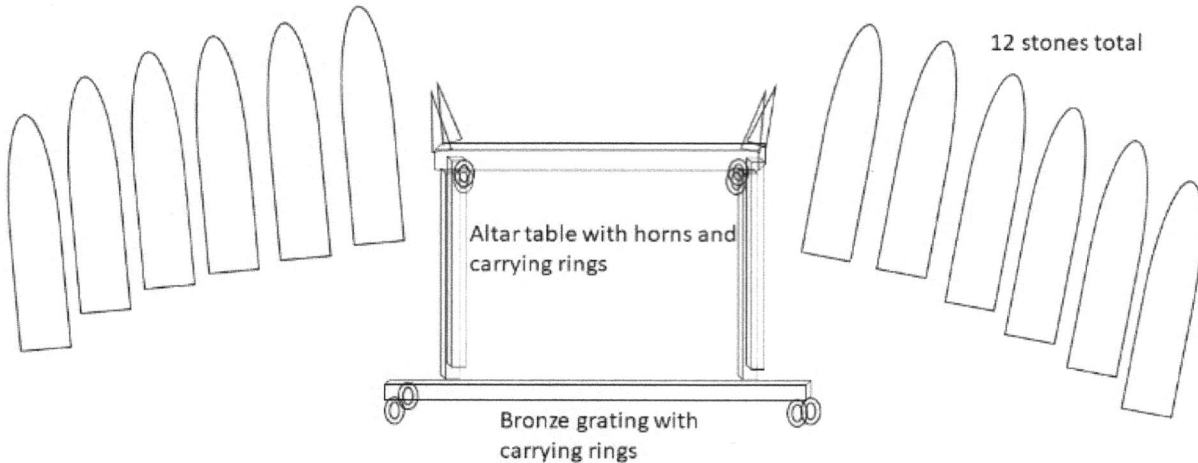

12 stones total

Altar table with horns and carrying rings

Bronze grating with carrying rings

- <u>Location</u>
  -Made of earth or stone on site
  -No tool can be used in set-up
  -No steps
  -Twelve stone pillars representing the 12 tribes

- <u>Altar table</u>
  -Made of incorruptible/acacia wood boards
  -Hollow center
  -Dimensions: 3 cubits tall, table top 5 cubits square
  -Horns placed on each of the four corners
  -Table and horns overlaid with bronze
  -Bronze carrying rings
  -Altar table must have a rim, capable of holding all bronze utensils on tabletop during transport (Num. 4:13-14).

- <u>Carrying poles</u>
  -Four poles of incorruptible/acacia wood overlaid with bronze
  -Poles inserted under altar table and grating
  -Table and grating carried by shoulder separately

- <u>Grating</u>
  -Made of bronze network
  -Bronze carrying rings on four corners
  -Placed below altar table

- <u>Fire & Ashes</u>
  -Burnt offerings are left burning overnight (Lev. 6:9)
  -Fire always remains burning on the altar table (except when tabernacle being relocated) (Lev. 6:12). Wood is added and arranged upon the fire (Lev. 1:7).
  -Every morning: Firewood added and smoldering pieces from the previous day are rearranged, ensuring the fire never goes out (Lev. 6:12). This should be done around the time of the "morning offering"—when the bread table, incense altar and lampstand are also tended. And, by implication, the altar table fire should also be tended around the time of the "evening offering" as well. (For more information on the "morning offering" and "evening offering," see pages 163-164.
  -Ashes: placed in pile east of the altar table (Lev. 1:16). To dispose of the ash pile: (1) the priest changes his clothes—leaving behind his normal priestly clothes, (2) he relocates the ashes to a ceremonially clean place outside the camp, and (3) upon his return to the tabernacle area, the priest changes his clothes, clothing himself again with his normal priestly clothes (Lev. 6:10-11) (for an illustration of the priests' clothing, see page 50).

Now, some of my "artistic renderings" of these various items may look funny, but this is by design. I want all these items to look as "simple" as possible. People tend to overcomplicate things. I do not want to overcomplicate the Law, so I have made my drawings as simple as possible.

Get it?

I am showing you how these Bible passages can be simply kept by removing all the fluff people tend to <u>add to</u> religion (Deu. 4:2). In some cases, people add fluff to intentionally put things beyond the reach of others. However, I am putting everything here within <u>arm's reach for you</u>. Hopefully my simple drawings click for you and help you to grasp how the big picture works.

Horns & Their Purpose

When reading about these tabernacle articles, you will notice the presence of "horns" on the four corners of both the altar table (described above) and on the incense altar (described on page 44).

What are these "horns?"

Well, the Law of Moses doesn't specify what type of horns. But we do know horns represent the strength of an animal. So, in these two special places of atonement—where blood is placed on the altar table and incense altar—perhaps the Lord grants us a constant reminder: "that our salvation in the Lord is our strength." And, that is a powerful thought.

When considering what takes place on the incense altar, we can apply this thought even further. We see in Revelation 5:8 & 8:4 incense represents the prayers of the saints. In other words, our prayers are the most "powerful" means we have during our earthly lives. Prayers are our strength.

So, what is the *purpose* of the horns?

I have heard it (incorrectly) said that the horns on the altar were used to tie down ropes to fix animal sacrifices in place on the altar.

This is ridiculous for several reasons . . .

First, the Law of Moses does not require animal sacrifices to be *bound by ropes*. Of course, it does not say the high priest couldn't use ropes, but neither does it require him to do so.

Second, many of the ceremonies and offerings described on pages 205-238, require the animals to be slaughtered *at the tabernacle entrance*, and in some cases *north of the altar table*. This would preclude the idea of having to tie down an animal on the altar table itself.

Third, as discussed above, in Lev. 6:12, it states the wood fire on the altar table *must never go out*—and the only time it could would be when it was being transported (as shown on pages 57-61). So, the idea of somehow tying an animal onto a table by using its four corners—*while a wood fire is burning* underneath it—is absurd.

Fourth, it is wrong to assume the horns were on the altar table to tie down what was placed upon it, because this logic is defeated by the presence of horns on the "incense altar." In other words, if one thinks the horns are on the altar table to tie down *animals*, then they must also assume the horns on the "incense altar" are there to "tie down" the *incense*. This is ridiculous.

Therefore, when considering the horns, remain mindful of their *stated* purpose. They simply represent strength. And, in the Law of Moses they are special locations where blood is applied by the finger of the high priest and priest. Thus, the purpose of the horns is to signify atonement, not to tie things down.

Make sense?

Now let's discuss the next component. Where you have an altar for sacrifices, you will need utensils and vessels to perform your services . . .

#3 - <u>Bronze utensils</u>—pots, shovels, bowls, meat forks, firepans for altar (Exo. 27:3; 38:3)

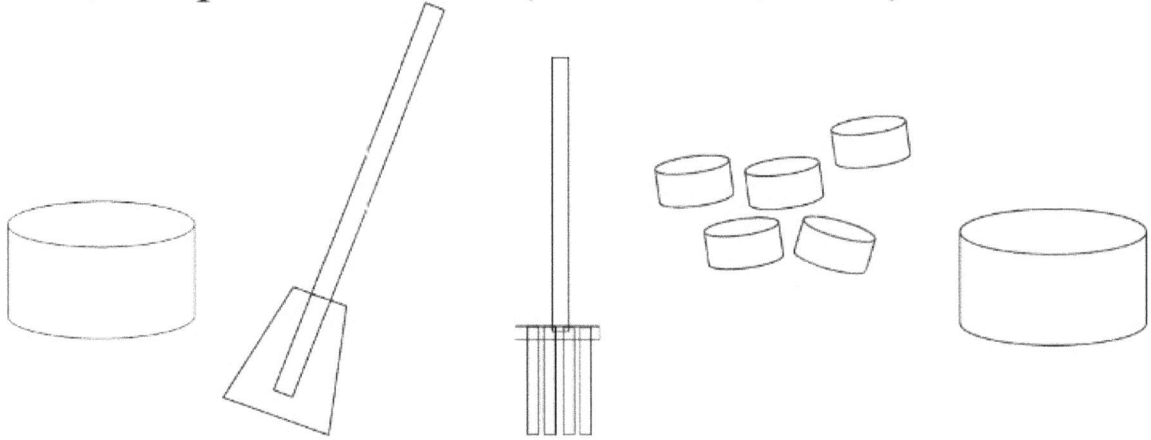

- Utensils made of bronze (pots, shovels, bowls, meat forks and firepans)
- Used in altar services

And, whenever messy sacrifices are performed, you will need a place for priests to wash themselves . .

#4 - <u>Wash basin</u> (Exo. 30:17-21; 38:8)

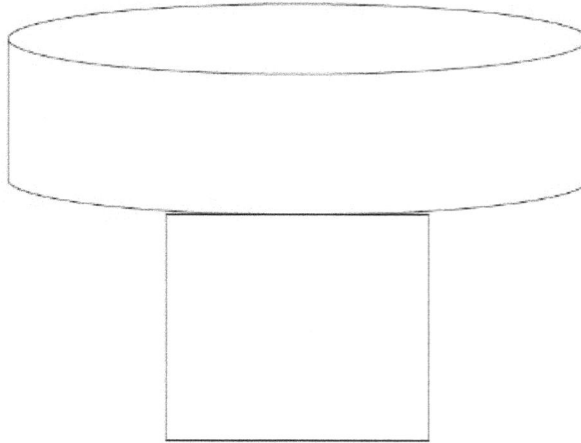

- Made of bronze
- Bronze base
- Placed between the altar and tent of meeting
- Filled with water
- Washing at wash basin required for all who visit the tent of meeting, altar or tabernacle—so while the first "tent of meeting" is established, the wash basin is placed between the altar and that location. But once the tabernacle is constructed and consecrated, the wash basin is moved between the altar and the tabernacle (as the new "tent of meeting").

- <u>Coverings Used for Transportation (Num. 4:14)</u>
  -First, according to the LXX, the wash basin is covered with a purple cloth.
  -Then the wash basin and its base are placed within a covering of blue durable leather (LXX).
  -Last the wash basin and its base are placed upon carrying bars
  (LXX).

So, to re-cap, look again at the depiction below—finding in the illustration the locations of the courtyard, altar and wash basin.

How to Set-up Tabernacle Area (Exo. 40:1-8)

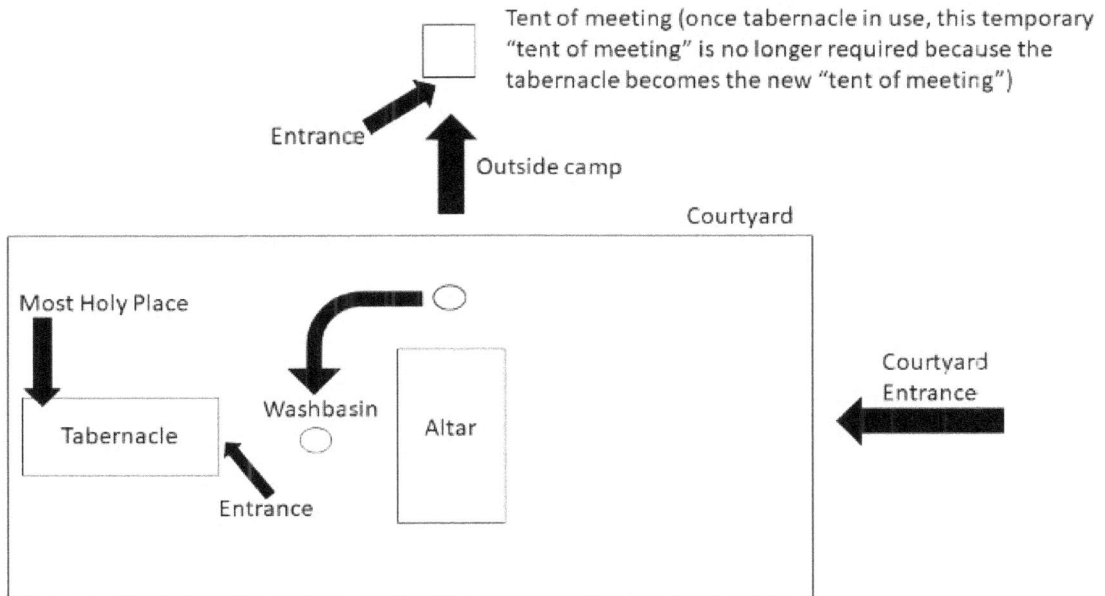

Tent of meeting (once tabernacle in use, this temporary "tent of meeting" is no longer required because the tabernacle becomes the new "tent of meeting")

Entrance

Outside camp

Courtyard

Most Holy Place

Courtyard Entrance

Washbasin

Altar

Tabernacle

Entrance

Did you find them?

Put your finger on the courtyard...

now the altar...

now the wash basin.

I don't want to confuse you, so make sure you get it before reading further.

. . . Now that the courtyard, altar and wash basin are set, the tabernacle can be placed within the courtyard.

Put your finger on the tabernacle in the above illustration. Then once you find it, keep reading . . .

The tabernacle is the most complex item within the courtyard, so it will help if you already understand some of the more straightforward items—like the courtyard, altar and wash basin. And since you can now "see" those items for yourself, you have already made a great deal of progress.

To simplify the tabernacle, I will present it to you in layers. To help yourself understand, think of how you would build a big cake—for a birthday or a wedding. A large cake has layers and has to be put together in steps.

Likewise, the tabernacle, as a tent, has multiple layers—which must each be placed in order. So, I will begin by presenting the lowest layer, then I will explain what goes on top of each layer.

So, let's begin with the dimensions of the tabernacle. To begin setting up the tabernacle, you must find a location which is the proper size . . .

#5 - <u>Tabernacle</u> (Exo. 26:1-37; 36:8-20; 40:1-33)

- <u>Tabernacle dimensions</u>:
  - 10 cubits high (height of frames)
  - 20 cubits long, 8 cubits wide

First, set the frames and crossbars . . .

Tabernacle Frames (58) and Crossbars (5 from south-north) (5 from west)
Dimensions: 10 cubits tall, 20 cubits long, 8 cubits wide

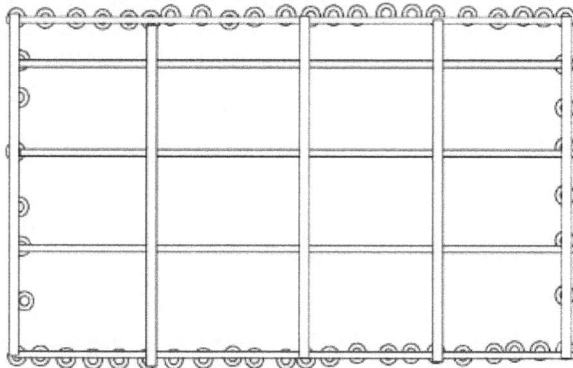

- <u>Frames</u>
  - Made of incorruptible/acacia wood
  - Dimensions: 10 cubits long and 1.5 cubits wide
  - Each has projections set parallel to one another. LXX interprets this as each post having two joints answering to one another.
  - Each frame has two silver bases
  - Each frame has a gold ring to insert crossbar
  - 58 total frames . . .
  - South side of tabernacle has 20 frames
  - North side of tabernacle has 20 frames
  - West side of tabernacle has 8 frames—with 2 of them in the corners

- <u>Crossbars</u>
  - Made of incorruptible/acacia wood overlaid with gold
  - Five located on the north side of the tabernacle, five on the south side, and five on the west side

<u>Different ideas for the frames and crossbars</u> . . .
Although we cannot know for sure how the original frames and crossbars were configured, we can use the dimensions provided in the Torah to develop some good ideas that would provide a stable structure for the tabernacle.

This is what I think . . .
The Torah says each frame is 10 cubits high and 1.5 cubits wide. And, when considering the tabernacle interior is about 8 x 20 cubits and there are 58 total frames, this means the vertical frames would be overlapping one another (because their bases would only be one cubit apart from one another). So, how would this look? I think the side view would look something like this . . .

So, the interior of the tabernacle would appear like a row of wood paneling, with each vertical post and its two silver bases pressing against the frame and bases next to it. Thus the bases underneath could be similar to blocks with creases where the posts could slide into. And, the two projections at the bottom of the posts could move outward at 90-degree angles, forming a "cross" pattern on the bases when they were pushed together. In this way, the bases would be pushed together on the posts, wedging it between.

And, interestingly, if this is the case, then the Linen Curtains with the cherubim pattern, which formed the bottom layer of the covering, were *completely* concealed—by the posts underneath and the Goat Hair Curtains above. This would certainly fit with the theme of the tabernacle itself—which was crafted to conceal from within. First the ark conceals the tables of the Law. Then the curtain of the Most Holy Place concealed the ark. Thus, it would make sense if the bottom layer of covering, the most ornate Linen Curtains with the cherubim pattern was even more concealed—shielded from the eyes of onlookers.

Stability

When reflecting on the placement of the tabernacle frames, posts and bases, remember their purpose . . . to provide stability to the structure.

Within the Levites, the Merarites were tasked with carrying, setting up and disassembling all these structures of the tabernacle and the courtyard. In addition to these components, they also used rope and tent pegs.

So, here's the question . . .

On an especially windy day, do you think the Merarites would have set additional rope and pegs to grant further support to the tabernacle and the courtyard?

Of course they would.

Or, if God directed the tabernacle to be placed in a location where there was a strong prevailing wind—like on the coast of a body of water or near a large open field—would the Merarites anticipate how the prevailing wind would cause the tabernacle and courtyard to shift?

Of course they would.

Therefore, when reflecting on the placement of the bases, posts, crossbars, rope and tent pegs, keep in mind the Merarites may have shifted them depending on prevailing winds and other factors to ensure the structures had the most stability. For this reason, do not get too bogged down with thoughts of *exactly* how to place them. The Merarites, under the direction of Ithamar the priest, were tasked with the decisions of how to best set up the tabernacle and the courtyard structures. And the exact set-up at various locations may have needed to take into account factors like prevailing winds, inclement weather, etc.

Back to assembling the tabernacle . . .

Now that the first layer of the wooden frames is set, let's start laying the curtains on top . . .

Second, stack the four layers of curtains (linen, goat hair, ram skins dyed red, durable leather) . . .

On the bottom are the Linen Curtains—(2) Sets of 5 Curtains, joined by 50 clasps in center rings

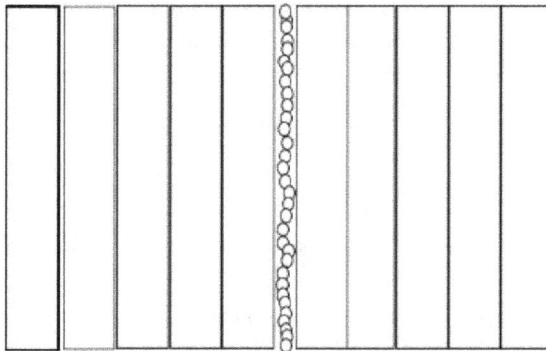

- Linen Curtains
  -Made of blue, purple and scarlet yarn
  -Each curtain with a cherubim design woven into the pattern
  -10 total curtains . . .
  -Each 28 cubits long x 4 cubits wide, with 50 blue yarn loops on the end curtain for each set
  -Arrange the curtains by making them into 2 sets of 5 curtains each, joined together
  -Each end curtain for each set has 50 blue yarn loops on its side so it can be attached to the other set

- Clasps for Linen Curtains
  -Made of gold
  -Used to join together the two sets of (5) 28-cubit long curtains detailed above
  -Gold clasps join together the blue yarn loops of the curtains

Third, on top of the Linen Curtains are the Goat Hair Curtains . . .
Goat Hair Curtains—(1) set of 5 curtains and (1) set of 6 curtains, joined in center with 50 rings
Make sure there are 2 cubits of Goat Hair Curtain overlap on both the east and west sides and
1-cubit overlap on both the south and north sides.

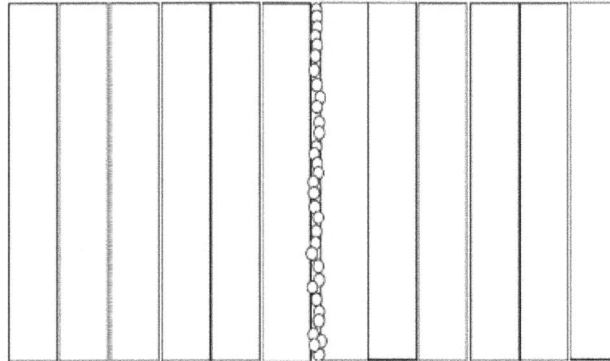

Last, stack on top of the Goat Hair Curtains, the layers of Ram Skins Dyed Red and
Durable Leather. Then stretch and lift all four layers of cloth onto the frames and
crossbars, team-lifting them altogether.

- <u>Goat Hair Curtains</u>
  -11 total curtains . . .
  -Each 30 cubits long x 4 cubits wide
  -Arrange the curtains by making them into 1 set of 5 curtains and 1 set of 6 curtains, joined together
  -Each end curtain for each set has 50 loops on its side so it can be attached to the other set
  -The (2) sets are joined together *offset*, so that the set with the 6th curtain leaves 2 extra cubits of goat hair curtain at the entrance of the tabernacle and then the 2 extra cubits of goat hair curtain lays on the ground at the other end of the tabernacle (see diagram)
  -Place goat hair curtains on top of the linen curtains, ensuring the goat hair overlaps by 2 cubits on the entrance side and overlaps by 2 cubits on the opposite side
  -Entrance: The goat hair curtain is to be folded over double (2 times) to form the tabernacle entrance (see diagram). When tabernacle will be used, the linen curtain layer underneath the goat hair curtain must be folded up along with it.
  -All extra overlapping goat hair curtain material lays on the ground on other sides (south, north, west)

- <u>Clasps for Goat Hair Curtains</u>
  -Made of bronze
  -Used to join together the two sets of long curtains detailed above
  -Bronze clasps join together the loops of the curtains

- <u>Covering of Ram Skins Dyed Red</u>
  -Placed on top of goat hair curtains

- <u>Covering of Durable Leather</u>
  -Placed on top of covering of ram skins
  -LXX says this layer of durable leather is blue

Now, you may be wondering why there are size differences between the bottom layer of Linen Curtains and the Goat Hair Curtains.

This is so the stitching is covered by the cloth of the higher layer. This makes it so that the stitching of the Linen Curtains does not "line-up" with the stitching of the Goat Hair Curtains. This is important because it better supports the structure as the wind blows on it. Moreover, it provides increased waterproofing in the case of rain.

Last, the layers of Ram Skins Dyed Red and Durable Leather provide a final practical layer to preserve the linen underneath from weathering effects.

Cool, huh?

Now that the tabernacle is set-up, all that is left is to place the required items within it. . . .

Tabernacle Interior

Set up the <u>Entrance</u> . . . Once the layers are on top of the frames and cross bars, all that remains is to set up the Entrance and interior. For the entrance, fold up the hanging Goat Hair Curtain two times, along with the Linen Curtain underneath to form the entrance opening. Then place the five entrance posts along the entrance and hang the special entrance curtain of blue, purple and scarlet yarn on the posts.

Last, set up the <u>Most Holy Place</u> . . .

Tabernacle Interior

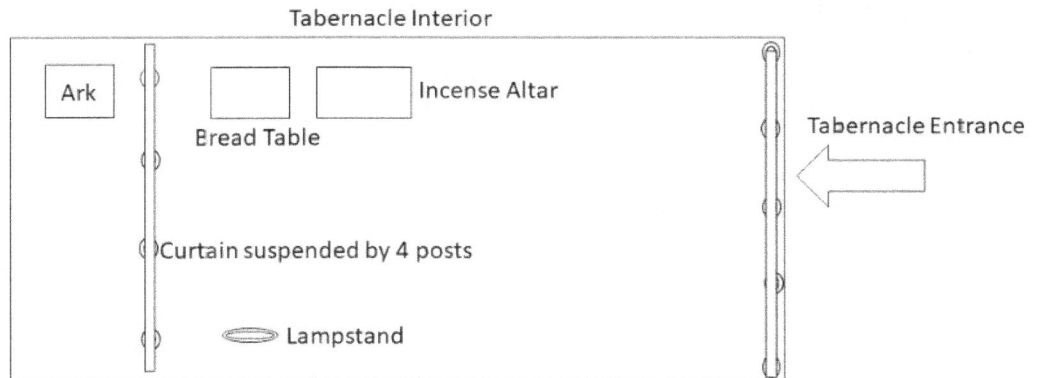

- <u>Most Holy Place</u>
   -Located at north side of tabernacle
   -Curtain made of blue, purple and scarlet yarn with cherubim design woven into fabric
   -Suspend curtain with gold rings attached to (4) incorruptible/acacia wood posts overlaid with gold seated in silver bases
   -Ark placed behind curtain
   -Bread table placed in front of curtain
   -Lampstand placed on south side opposite the table
   -Incense altar is also placed on the opposite side of the shielding curtain from the ark (For more information on the placement of the incense altar, see my discussion of Heb. 9:4 on page 45.)

- <u>Entrance</u>
   -The goat hair curtain set with the 6th curtain, causing the half curtain extension, is to be folded over double to form the tabernacle entrance (see diagram)
   -Entrance curtain: made of blue, purple and scarlet yarn, suspended from gold hooks attached to five posts of incorruptible/acacia wood overlaid with gold seated in five bronze bases

Positioning of Tabernacle Articles

In my presentation of the tabernacle diagram, I place the articles only based on what the Law of Moses says about each one. So, what are some important things to consider when it comes to the placement of items in the tabernacle?

First, the tabernacle is not placed in a fixed location. Rather, it is designed to be moved from one location to another. This means the point is not to *perfectly* place the lampstand, bread table and incense altar. After all, the tabernacle will be moved—again and again.

Second, when being mindful of the first point above, we remove artificial ideas about the tabernacle articles. For example, in the *temple* the incense altar was placed between the bread table and the lampstand. But the Law of Moses does not require this positioning. It simply requires the incense altar to be placed on the other side of the shielding curtain from the ark (pg. 44). In other words, the Law only requires the incense altar to be placed in the same room as the bread table and lampstand—but not in a specific position.

Third, the tabernacle had specific dimensions which may have actually made it impractical to put the lampstand, incense altar and bread table too close to one another. Given the dimensions discussed on pages 28-31, the tabernacle interior would have only been about eight cubits wide. So, it might have actually been impractical to crowd the incense altar between the bread table and lampstand against the shielding curtain.

Fourth, when considering the lampstand and incense altar also had fire/smoke being produced upon them, it would have been necessary to give them some space away from the walls of the tabernacle. This presents another factor which necessitates the reasonable decision to spread out these articles in the tabernacle rather than crowding them together.

Fifth, placing the incense altar first—where a person encounters it before the lampstand and the bread table makes sense. The incense altar symbolizes the prayers of the saints, and also the presence of the Holy Spirit. And, it is prayer and the Holy Spirit which leads us into the very presence of God—where we are invited to eat with Him.

Get it?

Sixth, outside the tabernacle entrance was the altar table—which bore a horned similarity to the incense altar. So, the way they are positioned in my diagram makes sense, as if these two tables are contrasting one another from outside and inside the entrance of the tabernacle.

In conclusion, when considering the positioning of the tabernacle articles, avoid a dogmatic position which requires precision. After all, the Law of Moses does not demand precise placement of these articles, but just gives general instructions, i.e. place on the other side of the shielding curtain opposite the ark. Moreover, no matter how the tabernacle articles are placed—they will be moved again and again. In other words, they will never be placed in the same *exact* positions.

And, with that, you completed the set-up of the most complicated item—the tabernacle. You might need to re-read this section, however, to make sure it sank in. If you feel you have a good handle on the tabernacle, let's discuss each of the interior items in more detail . . .

#6 - <u>Ark</u> (Exo. 25:10-22; 37:1-9; Num. 10:33)

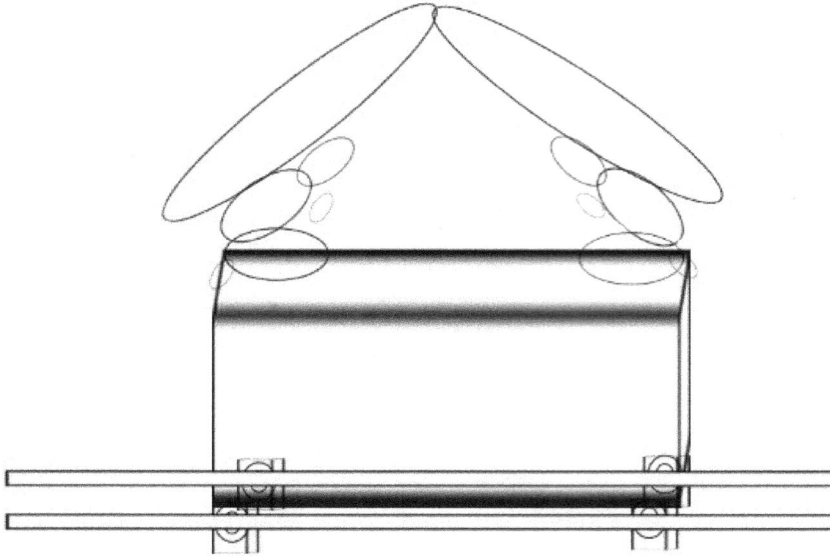

-Made of incorruptible/acacia wood
-Dimensions: 1.5 cubits tall, top 2.5 x 1.5 cubits
-Overlaid with gold and has gold molding
-Gold carrying rings fastened to four feet
-Tablets of covenant law placed within
-Placed behind curtain of the Most Holy Place in the north side
-Ark is the location where Moses would meet with the Lord in the Most Holy Place

- <u>Atonement Cover</u>
   -Forms top of ark
   -Dimensions: 2.5 x 1.5 cubits
   -Two cherubs of hammered gold attached on ends of atonement cover
   -Cherubs have wings spread upward, overshadowing the cover, facing each other, looking at the cover

- <u>Carrying poles</u>
   -Two poles of incorruptible/acacia wood overlaid with gold
   -Poles left inserted in rings at all times
   -Ark carried by shoulder

- Coverings Used for Transportation (Num. 4:4-6)
  -The Most Holy curtain, also known as the "shielding curtain" is placed on ark.
  -Then a covering of blue.
  -Last a covering of durable leather (LXX says this is blue).
  -The carrying poles are never removed from the ark.

The Significance of the Shielding Curtain (Num. 4:5)

The curtain which separates the most holy place—where the ark is placed—from the rest of the tabernacle interior is called the "shielding curtain."

So, why is it called "shielding," rather than simply referring to it as a "curtain"—similar to all the others?

To answer that question, consider the illustration of the tabernacle interior found on page 33. Note how the shielding curtain is suspended from four posts.

Do you see it?

Okay, when considering the purpose of the curtain—to "shield"—we may gain insight concerning how the ark itself was transported. When the tabernacle needed to be relocated, the high priest and his sons could simply approach the other articles contained within the tabernacle, as explained on pages 57. In other words, the high priest could simply grab the cloths to cover the bread table or the incense altar and place the covering on them. No problem.

But the ark was different.

When the high priest needed to prepare the ark for transport, he would not simply walk up to it—like he would the other articles.

Get it?

The high priest would need to completely "shield" himself from the ark—taking great care to avoid carelessly looking upon it (Num. 4:5). Therefore, it is most likely the "shielding curtain" is called this as a perpetual reminder of its true function. Whenever the ark needed to be moved, the high priest would stand outside the most holy place in the tabernacle. Then he would disconnect the "shielding curtain" from the posts which suspended it. And, with the "shielding curtain" held in front of his entire body, he would slowly approach the north corner of the most holy place, until the shielding curtain touched the ark. Then he would cover the ark. So, the high priest would cover the ark while ensuring he never looked at it.

And, likewise, once the tabernacle reached its new location, the high priest would lift the covering off the ark and immediately hold it in front of his entire body and face. Then he would walk backward and to his right until he reached each of the four posts in turn—where he attached the "shielding curtain."

So, what does this mean?

Whenever the ark was prepared for transport—covered and uncovered—it was accomplished without being looked upon. The high priest shielded himself with the "shielding curtain" as he moved toward the ark and away from it.

As a side note—now that I have explained this—pay attention to artistic renditions of the ark. Often artists portray the ark as being hoisted up amid large groups of people—where you can see the cherubim upon the mercy seat. However, the ark was not carried in this way. The ark was "covered" when transported—and even in the tabernacle itself, the high priest took great care to "shield" himself from its holiness.

Even on the Day of Atonement, when the high priest entered the most holy place—he approached the ark while averting his eyes through a thick veil of incense smoke—two handfuls in fact, which were left smoldering in that small room while he prepared the blood to be brought within (see page 185). In other words, the Law of Moses goes to great lengths to ensure the ark never receives an idle gaze—even by the high priest.

#7 – **Bread Table**

(Exo. 25:23-30; 37:10-16; 40:22-23; Lev. 24:5-9)

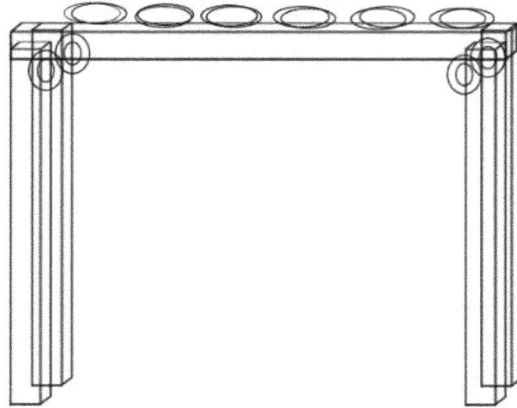

-Made of incorruptible/acacia wood
-Dimensions: 1.5 cubits tall, table top 2x1-cubits
-Table overlaid with gold
-Gold carrying rings on each corner
-Table has handbreadth-wide rim with gold molding on it. LXX translates this as a twisted wreath.
(This rim is important because in Num. 4:7 it says the table was transported with the dishes and bread remaining on it. So, the rim has a functional purpose in preventing the items from sliding off the table during transport. Therefore, the rim would need to be high enough to prevent the items from sliding off during transport.

- <u>Carrying poles</u>
  -Four poles of incorruptible/acacia wood overlaid with gold
  -Poles inserted under table
  -Table carried by shoulder

- Placed in north part of tabernacle in front of the Most Holy Place's curtain
- Gold plates, dishes, pitchers and bowls placed upon it for pouring out drink offerings

- <u>Bread</u>
  -Twelve loaves of fresh unleavened bread (two-tenths of an ephah each) are placed upon table daily. The loaves are set out in two rows of six each.
  -Unlit incense placed upon this table next to each of the bread rows. LXX states unlit sacred incense *and salt* are placed next to each of the bread rows.
  -Bread eaten by the priests in the sanctuary area

- <u>Coverings Used for Transportation (Num. 4:7-8)</u>
  -First a covering of blue is placed. (The LXX says this first layer is purple.)
  -Then a covering of scarlet.
  -Last a covering of durable leather (LXX says this is blue).
  -Finally, the carrying poles are inserted.

Why would the first covering layer be purple—as the LXX states?

Perhaps this is to identify the kinship between the Altar Table—where burnt offerings are presented, and the Bread Table. At both locations, food is said to be presented before the Lord. And in this similarity, it could be that the purple cloth, the color of royalty, would identify that the food of God is being presented at these specific locations (Lev. 21:6-22).

Cool, right?

Another question for consideration . . .

Did Moses ever break bread with the Lord in the tabernacle?

As it is stated, Moses met with the Lord face to face, speaking to Him as a man would speak to his friend (Exo. 33:11; Num. 12:8; Deu. 34:10). So, during these meetings within the tabernacle as the "tent of meeting," did Moses ever eat with the Lord?
　　It is interesting to ponder—especially when considering how these meetings may have foreshadowed the arrival of the Lord Jesus, with whom the disciples also interacted and broke bread.
　　What do you think?

#8 - <u>Lampstand</u> (Exo. 25:31-40; 27:20-21; 37:17-24; Lev. 24:1-4; Num. 8:1-4)

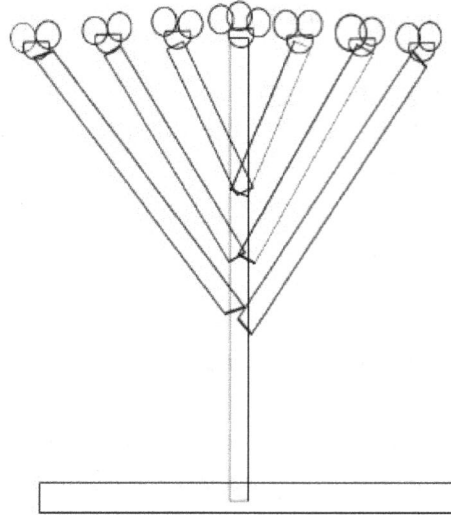

-Made of pure hammered gold, 1 talent in weight

-Has a base, shaft, and cups. LXX refers to the shaft as the "stem."

-Six branches extend from the sides of the lampstand shaft—three branches from each side

-Each branch has three flower cups with buds and blossoms (18 total flower cups on 6 total branches). LXX describes the flower cups as lilies.

-Top of lampstand shaft has four cups shaped like almond flowers with buds and blossoms. LXX states the four cups are shaped like almonds—not almond flowers.

-Designs on the shaft of the lampstand: Flower buds designs are located under each of the six branches on the shaft

-Seven total lights are to be placed on the entire lampstand—one light on the lampstand at the top of the shaft, and one light on top of each of the six branches

-Wick trimmers and trays are made of pure gold

-Clear oil of pressed olives are used for the lights

-Lamps remain lit from evening to morning—being tended by the priests

- <u>Coverings Used for Transportation (Num. 4:9-10)</u>
-First the Lampstand is covered with blue cloth.
-Then the Lampstand and its accessories are covered with durable leather (LXX says this is blue).
-Last, it is placed upon a carrying frame.

Configuration of Lampstand cups to project light forward . . .

Front view of center lamp on
the shaft/stem

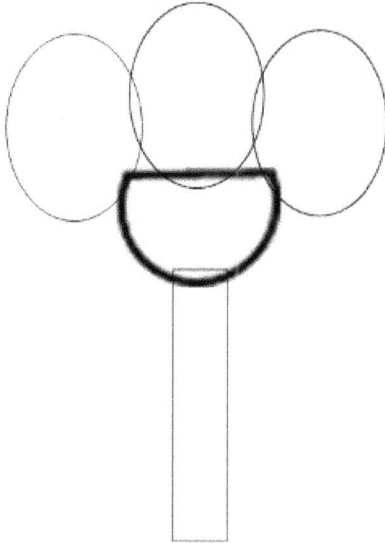

In Exo. 25:37 it states the light of the lampstand needs to illuminate the area in front of it. So, how was this done?

Think of a car's headlights. Reflective surfaces are placed around the source of light to magnify and direct it forward.

Likewise, with the lampstand, the multiple cups can be used to produce a similar effect. One cup could hold the light, while the other cups could be placed vertical behind the flame to project the light forward. This is one way the lampstand could be designed to achieve the requirement of Exo. 25:37—allowing it to focus light in front of the lampstand.

Next, let's discuss the incense altar . . .

#9 - <u>Incense altar</u> (Exo. 30:1-10; 30:34-38; 37:25-29; 40:5; Lev. 10:1-2)

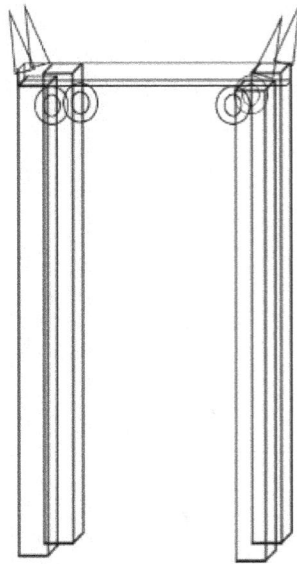

-Made of incorruptible/acacia wood
-Dimensions: 2 cubits tall, table top 1-cubit square
-Horns placed on each of the four corners
-Table and horns overlaid with gold
-Table has gold molding. LXX describes this molding as a "wreathing."
-Gold carrying rings below the gold molding

- <u>Carrying poles</u>
  -Four poles of incorruptible/acacia wood overlaid with gold
  -Poles inserted under incense altar
  -Table carried by shoulder

- <u>Requirements</u>
  -Placed in front of the Most Holy Place curtain in Tabernacle
  -Sacred incense continually burned upon it, placed in morning and at twilight when lamps tended. LXX translates this as fine, compound incense
  -No offering other than the prescribed sacred incense formula
  -Once a year the high priest or his replacement places blood atonement on its horns (see page 185)

- <u>Sacred Incense formula</u>
  -Equal amounts of gum resin, onycha, galbanum, frankincense. LXX states the sacred incense formula consists of sweetherb, stacte, onycha, sweet galbanum.

- <u>Coverings Used for Transportation (Num. 4:4-6)</u>
  -The Incense Altar is first covered with blue cloth.
  -Then it is covered with durable leather (LXX says this is blue).
  -Finally, the carrying poles are inserted.

<u>The Incense Altar & Hebrews 9:4</u>

In the above diagram, I use Exo. 40:5 to place the incense altar in its depicted position. It is located opposite the ark on the other side of the shielding curtain. And, if Exo. 40:5 is an indication in order of placement, then it is seen that the incense altar should be the closest to the tabernacle entrance curtain—since the other altar table is mentioned right after it. Make sense?

However, when reading Heb. 9:4, we see in some English translations it states the incense altar is placed *inside* the shielding curtain *next to the ark*. I believe the book of Hebrews is referring to a different golden censer in Heb. 9:4 and not the incense altar itself. Let me explain . . .

Simply put, every morning and every evening the high priest performed tasks at the incense altar (offering incense evening and morning), lampstand (tending evening and morning) and the bread table (placing and removing showbread). This being the case, the incense altar would need to be accessible on a daily basis. And, if the incense altar is placed on the opposite side of the shielding curtain, then the high priest would not have access to offer incense. Therefore, Heb. 9:4 must be referring to a different golden censer, or bowl, which was placed next to the ark.

So, what was this additional censer to which Hebrews 9:4 refers? What censer was left on the other side of the shielding curtain with the ark?

To answer this question, consider the Day of Atonement (see page 185). During the Day of Atonement, the high priest would take a censer, put coals from the altar upon it and two handfuls of incense—as seen in Step #8 in the Day of Atonement ceremony on page 185. Then when the high priest later re-enters the most holy place to place blood upon the ark, the most holy place would be filled with smoldering smoke from the burning incense.

For this reason, it is best to conclude the reference of Hebrews 9:4 is pointing to the special censer used on the Day of Atonement—which was left behind the shielding curtain.

What do you think?

So, to review all we have discussed, here is a depiction of how the tabernacle area is set-up . . .

How to Set-up Tabernacle Area (Exo. 40:1-8)

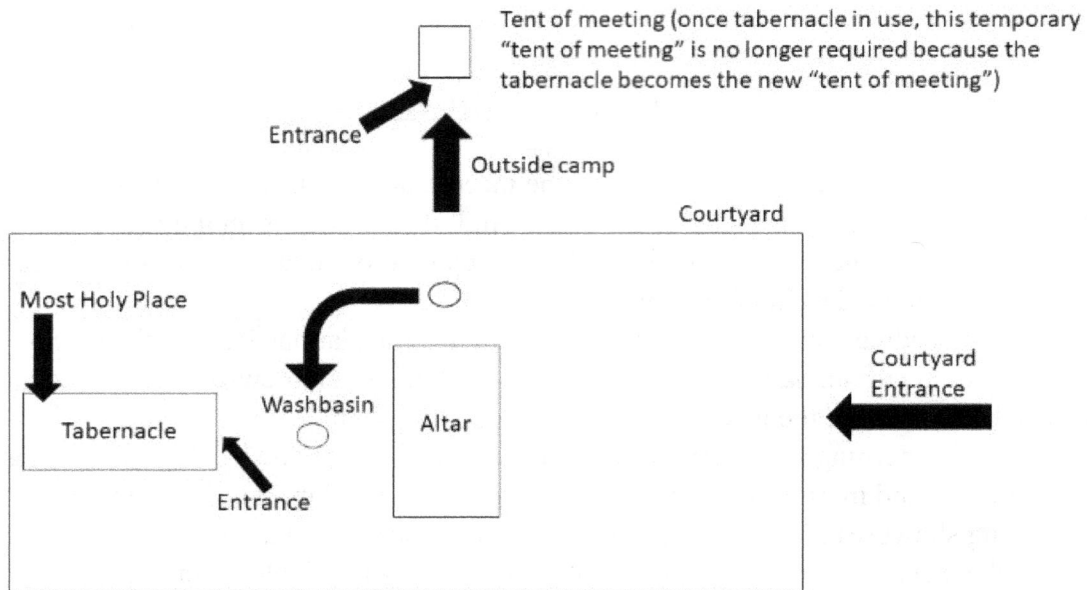

Tent of meeting (once tabernacle in use, this temporary "tent of meeting" is no longer required because the tabernacle becomes the new "tent of meeting")

Entrance

Outside camp

Courtyard

Most Holy Place

Courtyard Entrance

Tabernacle

Washbasin

Altar

Entrance

Alright, that does it for the items within the tabernacle courtyard area. Good job! Now, let's discuss some of the additional items which will need to be crafted to provide for the ministry of the priests. We will begin with the trumpets . . .

#10 - <u>Trumpets</u> (Num. 10:1-10)

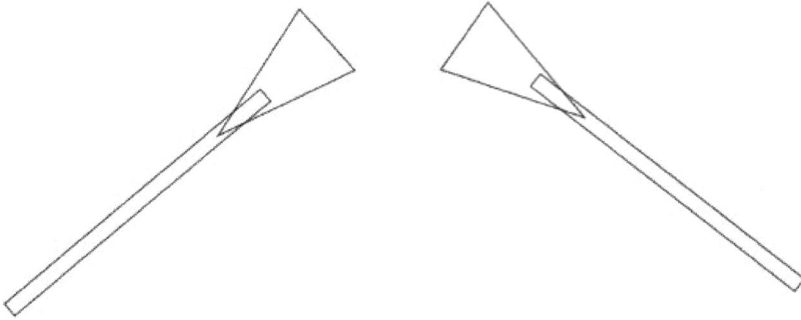

-Two trumpets
-Made of hammered silver

- Sounding
-<u>Gathering blasts</u>: When *one trumpet* is sounded, only the leaders gather before the tent of meeting. When *both trumpets* are sounded, all the people gather before the tent of meeting.
-<u>Setting out blasts</u>: When setting out, the *first blast* signals the tribes on the east to set out. Then, the *second blast* signals the tribes on the south to set out. LXX adds that the *third blast* signals the west to set out, and the *fourth blast* signals the north.
-<u>Battle blasts</u>: Both trumpets sounded when going into battle against an enemy in your own land.
-<u>Festival & New Moon blasts</u>: Both trumpets sounded signaling when burnt offerings and fellowship offerings are to be made during festivals.

- <u>Coverings Used for Transportation (Num. 4:12)</u>
-If not carried by the High Priest during Tabernacle relocation, the Trumpets could be transported along with all the other additional ministry items from the Tabernacle.
-If transported, the Trumpets would first be covered with blue cloth.
-Then they would be covered with durable leather (LXX says this is blue).
-Last, the Trumpets would be placed upon a carrying frame.

And, now we move on to our last section—discussing the clothing articles of the High Priest, and the clothing of the normal priests. (For simplicity, the sons of the high priest are referred to as "normal priests.")

When preparing this book, I was especially touched by all the symbols present within the High Priest's articles—particularly the ephod. As you read and examine my illustrations, I hope this section is equally as moving for you as well.

To begin this presentation on the priestly garments and articles, I will start by showing you my illustrations. Then, after considering the illustrations, carefully read through the descriptions of each article to gain a full picture of how it all works . . .

#11 - <u>Garments of High Priest and Priests</u>
(Exo. 28:1-5; 39:22-31)

<u>For the normal priests</u>, consisting of (1) standard undergarment, (2) standard tunic, (3) standard robe, (4) standard sash and (5) standard turbans
&
<u>For the High Priest</u>, consisting of (1) standard undergarment, (2) standard tunic, (3) special ephod articles, (4) special robe, (5) standard sash and (6) special turban.

First, let's discuss how the normal priests were dressed . . .

How to Dress a Normal Priest (in order) . . .

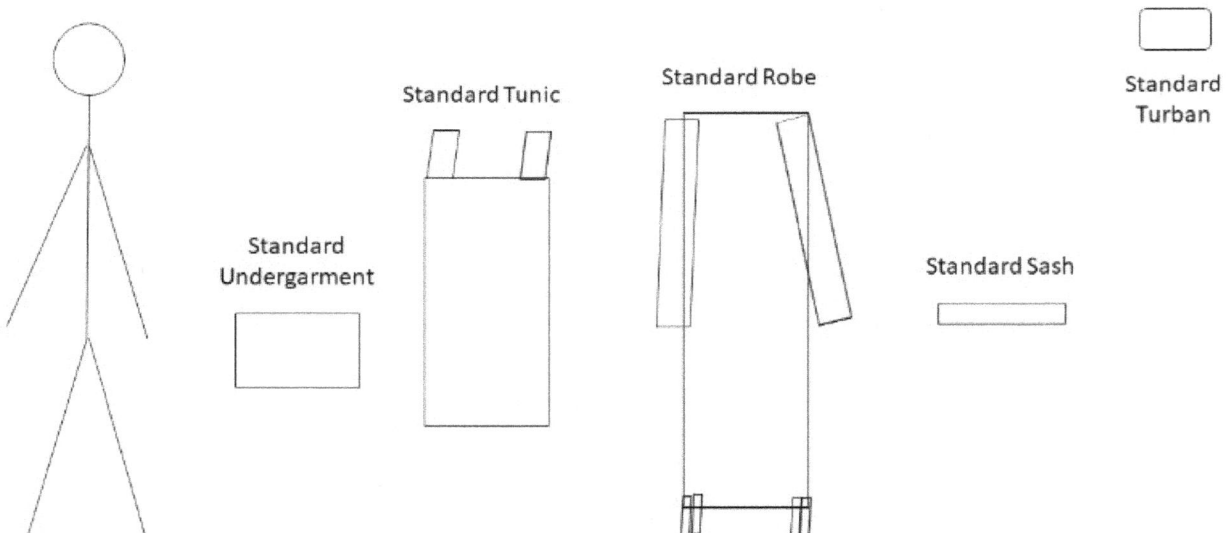

Standard Tunic

Standard Robe

Standard Turban

Standard Undergarment

Standard Sash

How to dress the High Priest (in order) . . .

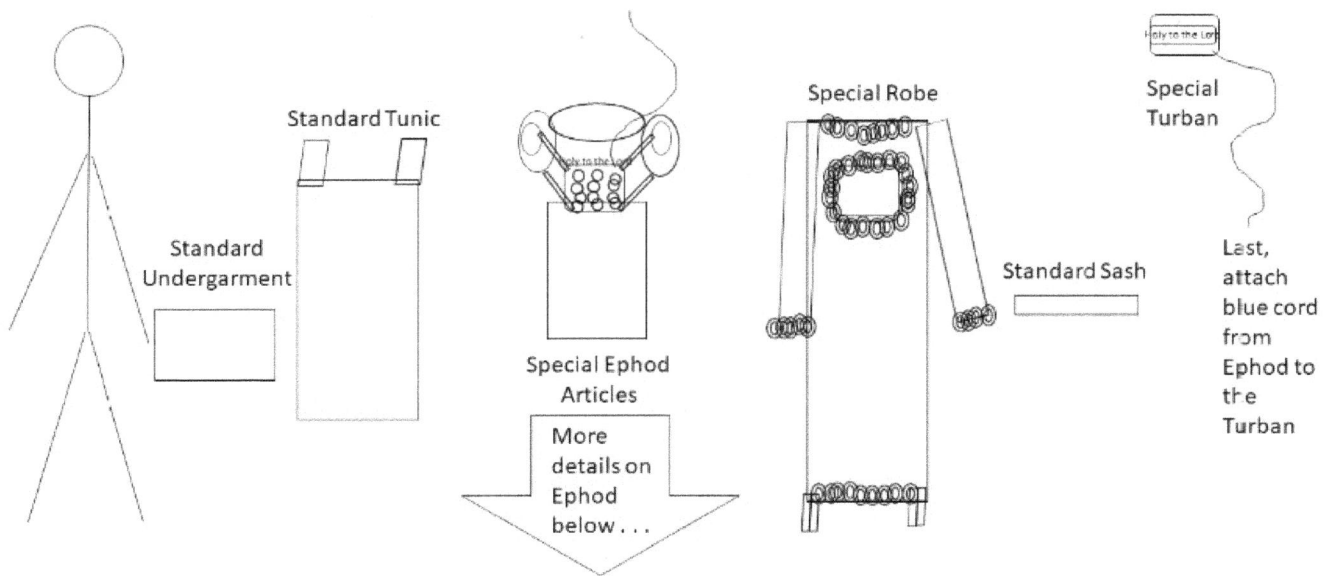

Standard Tunic

Special Robe

Special Turban

Standard Undergarment

Special Ephod Articles

More details on Ephod below . . .

Standard Sash

Last, attach blue cord from Ephod to the Turban

This is how the Ephod Articles are placed upon the High Priest . . .

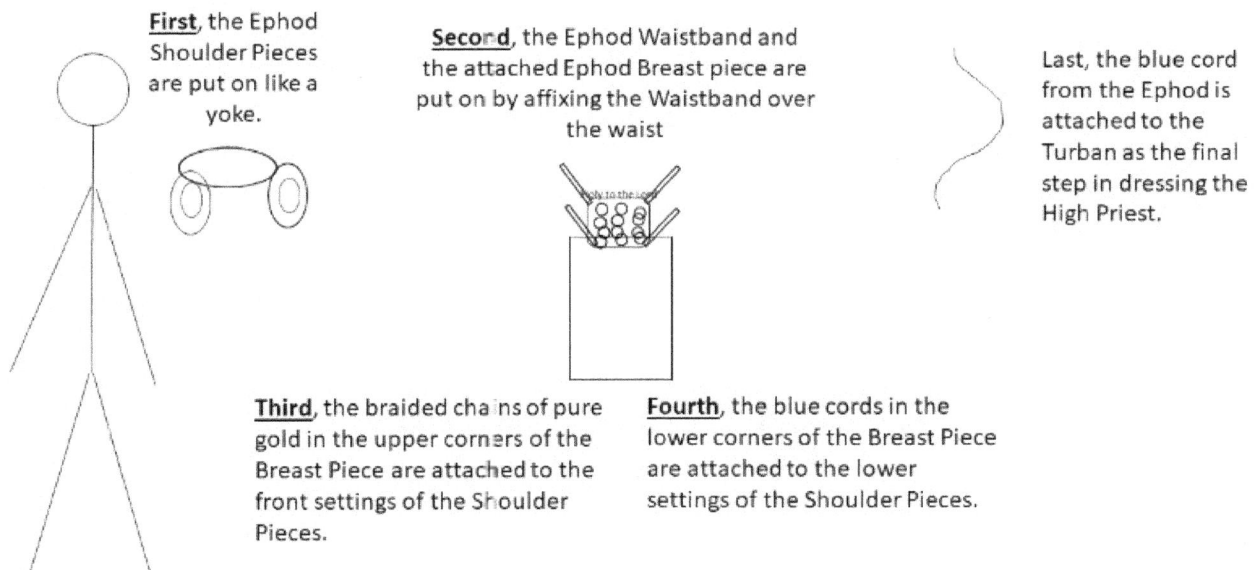

First, the Ephod Shoulder Pieces are put on like a yoke.

Second, the Ephod Waistband and the attached Ephod Breast piece are put on by affixing the Waistband over the waist

Last, the blue cord from the Ephod is attached to the Turban as the final step in dressing the High Priest.

Third, the braided chains of pure gold in the upper corners of the Breast Piece are attached to the front settings of the Shoulder Pieces.

Fourth, the blue cords in the lower corners of the Breast Piece are attached to the lower settings of the Shoulder Pieces.

51

- **Special Items for the High Priest**

-*Special Robe of the High Priest*:
  - -Made from weaved blue cloth (Exo. 39:22-26). LXX says this is a full-length robe.
  - -Center: In the center of the chest there is a collared, reinforced opening to reveal the ephod underneath.
  - -Hem: The hem of the high priest's robe is decorated with pomegranates of finely twisted linen and blue, purple and scarlet yarn, with pure gold bells attached on the hem alternating between all the pomegranates. (This is different from the robes of the other priests—which lacked the pomegranate and gold bell hem, and were simply made of blue, purple and scarlet yarn.)
  - -Blue cord tassels on corners of garment (Num. 15:38)

-*Ephod plate of the High Priest*:
  - -Plate made of pure gold (Exo. 39:30)
  - -The plate has gold filigree settings for twelve precious stones—mounted in four rows of three: carnelian, chrysolite and beryl; turquoise, lapis lazuli and emerald; jacinth, agate and amethyst; topaz, onyx and jasper. In the LXX, these same precious stones are different: The LXX lists, in order: sardius, topaz, emerald, carbuncle, sapphire, jasper, ligure, agate, amethyst, chrysolite, beryl and onyx.
  - -Inscriptions: Has an inscription similar to a seal, stating, "*Holy to the Lord*." Then above each precious stone is the name of each tribe in order.

-*Ephod breast piece of the High Priest*:
  - -Made from blue, purple and scarlet yarn and finely twisted linen, with strands of hammered thin sheets of gold weaved into the fabric
  - -LXX says ephod breast piece has weaved fringes, which is a chain-work of pure gold (Exo. 28:22).
  - -Dimensions of the breast piece: One span long and wide, folded double (Exo. 39:9)
  - -Four gold rings are attached to gold filigree settings in the corners of the breast piece (Exo. 39:16-21)
  - -Braided chains of pure gold, similar to a rope, are each attached to a gold ring in the upper corners of the breast piece on one end, and at the other end are connected to the front of the ephod shoulder piece
  - -Blue cord is used to connect the two rings in the lower corners of the ephod breast piece (on the ephod waist band) with the bottom of the ephod shoulder piece (Exo. 39:18-21).
  - -Contains a pouch, or some area upon it, to hold the Urim and Thummim (Exo. 28:30).

-*Urim and Thummim* (Exo. 28:30)
  - -These items, which are likely similar to lots which could be cast for decision making, were placed within the ephod breast piece.
  - -LXX says in Exo. 28:26 the Urim and Thummim are called "Manifestation and Truth"— which could be translated as "revelation" and "fulness," respectively. (For more information, see page 148.)

-*Ephod waistband of the High Priest*:
   -Attached to the ephod breast piece
   -Made from blue, purple and scarlet yarn and finely twisted linen, with strands of hammered thin sheets of gold weaved into the fabric

-*Ephod shoulder pieces of the High Priest*
   (Exo. 28:7-14; 39:4-7):
   -Attached to two corners of the ephod plate
   -Made from blue, purple and scarlet yarn and finely twisted linen, with strands of hammered thin sheets of gold weaved into the fabric to be like the ephod waistband
   -Two precious stones (onyx) are engraved with the names of the 12 sons of Israel—6 names on each stone in the order of their birth. Then the stones are mounted in gold filigree settings on the shoulder of the ephod shoulder piece.
   -Two braided chains of pure gold are attached to the gold filigree settings so they can be attached to the ephod breast piece below.

-*Ephod blue cord of the High Priest*:
   -Affixed to the ephod plate (Exo. 39:31)
   -After putting on the ephod, the high priest attaches the blue cord to his turban.

-Special Turban of the High Priest
-Made from blue, purple and scarlet yarn and finely twisted linen
-Has gold plate on front, inscribed with "Holy to the Lord"—according to LXX Exo. 28:32-33

- ### Standard Items for Normal Priests

-For simplicity, the *sons of the high priest* are referred to as "normal priests."

-Standard Robes (for normal priests)
-Made from blue, purple and scarlet yarn and finely twisted linen (Exo. 28:4-5). LXX says this is a full-length robe
-Blue cord tassels on corners of garment (Num. 15:38)

-Standard Turbans (for normal priests)
-Made from blue, purple and scarlet yarn and finely twisted linen

- ### Standard Items used by Both the High Priest and Normal Priests

-Standard Tunics (for priests and High Priest)
-Made from blue, purple and scarlet yarn and finely twisted linen

-Standard Sashes (for normal priests and High Priest)
-Made from blue, purple and scarlet yarn and finely twisted linen

-Standard Undergarments (for normal priests and High Priest)
-Made from blue, purple and scarlet yarn and finely twisted linen

At this point, please feel free to review all the illustrations. Perhaps it would be good for you to go back over the pictures I presented, giving yourself a mental quiz on each of the items.

Can you "see" it?

Do you understand?

If you have gained understanding, then the Law of Moses should no longer feel cryptic to you. You should be able to sense how the big picture worked. And I am blessed to have had the opportunity to share this precious information with you. I trust it will enhance your walk with Christ.

Easy, right?

The Order of Names on the Ephod Plate

In the above discussion of the ephod plate on page 52, I noted that the names of each tribe of Israel is inscribed above the stones—one name for each stone. However, in the Bible it does not specify the order of the names.

So, what is the order for the names on the ephod plate?

I think there are two ways to approach this—both of which might be valid.

First, in the crafting of the ephod plate it might be best to inscribe the names in the order of their birth—similar to the birth-order names which are inscribed on the ephod shoulder pieces.

Or, the names on the ephod plate could be inscribed in the order of march and camping—as detailed on page 52. If the names were inscribed in the order of march, it might serve to keep the high priest mindful of the prescribed order which the Lord established in the camps around the tabernacle.

What do you think? Do you think the inscribed names on the ephod plate should be in *birth-order* or in *marching-order*?

Back to our discussion of the tabernacle items . . .

The last point for me to discuss is how the various items were carried from one location to another. All of the items with poles were carried by shoulder. But the other items without poles were able to be carried by cart . . .

Transportation - <u>Carts</u> (Num. 7:3-9)

-    **<u>Tabernacle Caravan (consisting of six total carts and twelve oxen)</u>**

-According to Num. 7:3-9, the twelve tribes each present an ox and every pair of tribes present a cart. So, the tribes are "yoked" to one another in the presentation of the six carts and twelve oxen.

-<u>Kohathites</u> did not use carts because they carried all the holy things by shoulder (Num. 4:4-14). Of note, once the most holy items were placed within the interior of the tabernacle, the Kohathites were strictly forbidden from reentering the tabernacle to view the items (Num. 4:20). Moreover, the Kohathites were strictly forbidden from "touching" and of the items they carried—they could only touch the carrying poles or carrying frames (Num. 4:15). The Kohathites could only enter the tabernacle after the priest covered all the articles. Then, upon reaching a new location, the priests needed to ensure the Kohathites were out of the tabernacle before they began uncovering the tabernacle
articles.

-<u>Gershonites</u> used two carts and four oxen. In Num. 3:25-4:26, it states the Gershonites were responsible for carrying the Tabernacle curtains, in addition to the Courtyard curtains and rope.

-<u>Merarites</u> used four carts and eight oxen. In Num. 3:36, it states the Merarites were responsible for carrying the Tabernacle frames, crossbars and bases, in addition to the Courtyard frames, posts, bases, tent pegs and rope.

How to Relocate the Tabernacle in 11 Steps

So, how were the items carried?

How was the tabernacle relocated?

Simple. In a series of steps . . .

First, *the High Priest and his sons would place the Most Holy curtain (also called the "shielding curtain") on top of the <u>Ark</u>, followed by a curtain of durable leather and a curtain of blue cloth. Then they would adjust the poles so they could be grasped by the Kohathites (Num. 4:4-6). (Remember, the carrying poles are <u>never</u> removed from the Ark.)*

Second, *the High Priest and his sons spread a blue cloth on top of the <u>Bread Table</u>, followed by a scarlet cloth, and last a layer of durable leather (Num. 4:7-8). Then they insert the carrying poles into the Bread Table. (The LXX says the first layer of cloth on the Bread Table is purple, not blue.)*

Third, *the High Priest and his sons cover the <u>Lampstand</u> with a blue cloth. Then it is wrapped in a layer of durable leather, along with all its accessories. Last, it is placed on a carrying frame—so the Kohathites touch the carrying frame only (Num. 4:9-10).*

Fourth, *the High Priest and his sons cover the <u>Incense Altar</u> with a blue cloth, then a layer of durable leather. Then they insert the carrying poles (Num. 4:11).*

Fifth, *the High Priest and his sons wrap all <u>additional ministry articles</u> from the tabernacle in a blue cloth, then a layer of durable leather. Then they are placed on a carrying frame.*

Sixth, *the High Priest and his sons, remove the ashes from the <u>Altar</u> and spread a purple cloth on it (Num. 4:13-14). Then they place all the <u>Bronze Utensils</u> upon the purple cloth. Then on top of the Bronze Utensils and the Altar, they spread a covering of durable leather. Then they insert the carrying poles.*

Seventh, *(in the LXX) it says the High Priest and his sons cover the <u>Wash Basin</u> with a purple cloth. Then they place the Wash Basin and its base in a blue cloth (Num. 4:14). Then the covered Wash Basin and its base are placed upon bars for movement.*

Eighth, *the Kohathites lift and begin carrying all these items that were prepared by the High Priest and his sons. The Kohathites could only enter the tabernacle <u>after</u> the priest finished covering <u>all</u> the articles. (At this time, the priests station themselves with each of the travelling groups of Levites to serve as supervisors—as discussed further on page. This is important so that the priests could deal with any problem which might emerge on the road to the next location. See page 76.)*

Ninth, once the Kohathites remove the covered items from the tabernacle area, the Gershonites remove and pack all the curtain coverings from the <u>Tabernacle</u> and the <u>Courtyard</u>. The curtain coverings are packed in the two Gershonite carts.

Tenth, the Merarites remove and pack all the crossbars, frames, posts, bases, tent pegs and rope from both the <u>Tabernacle</u> and <u>Courtyard</u>. These items are packed in the four Merarite carts.

Last, as they travel to the new location, the order of march is reversed: with the Gershonites catching up on the road and passing the Kohathites. Then the Merarites pass both the Kohathites and the Gershonites on the road. Then at the direction of the God-appointed leader, the Merarites are the first to set up in the new location—beginning the placement of the Courtyard and Tabernacle frames, posts, bases, crossbars, tent pegs and rope. Then the Gershonites arrive—placing the curtains on the assembled wooden structures. Finally, the Kohathites arrive in the newly set-up Tabernacle Courtyard area—once it is fully assembled. The Kohathites walk into the completely set-up area, and place the shoulder-carried items in position—leaving all the coverings in place. And, as this process is completed, the High Priest and priests ensure the Kohathites are out of the Tabernacle before they begin removing coverings. Then they resume the service of the Tabernacle and Altar.

Make sense?

I hope you can visualize this process—the relocation of the Tabernacle in eleven steps. If you need help "seeing" it, here is a helpful illustration . . .

How to Relocate the Tabernacle in 11 Steps

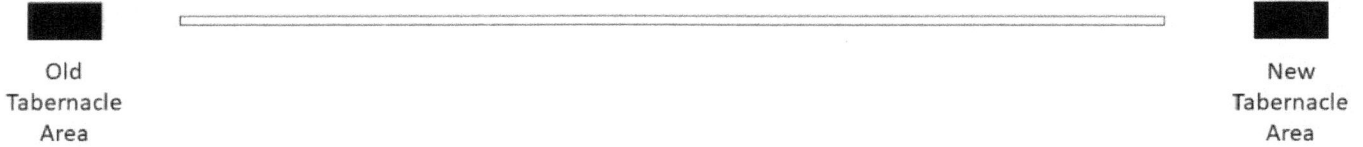

Old
Tabernacle
Area

New
Tabernacle
Area

Steps 1-7: High Priest and his sons prepare
the holy items for transport: the Ark,
Table, Lampstand, Incense Altar,
Additional Tabernacle Items, the Altar and
the Wash Basin.

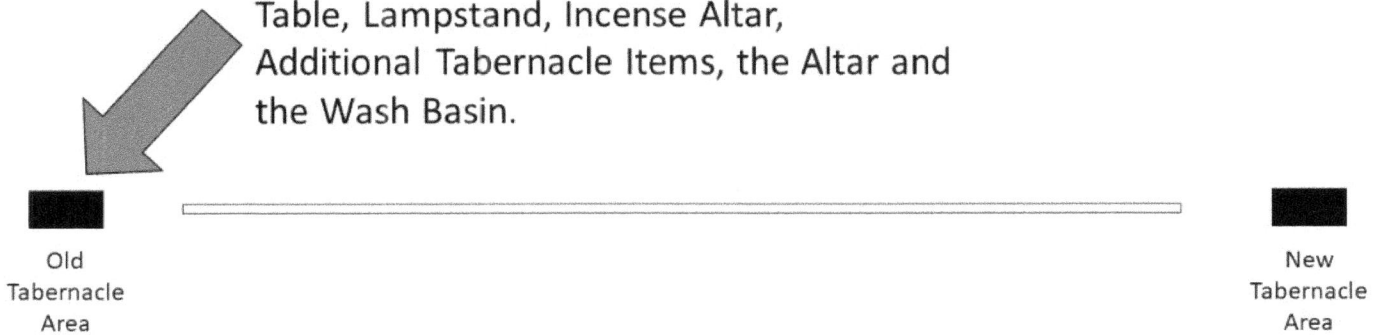

Old
Tabernacle
Area

New
Tabernacle
Area

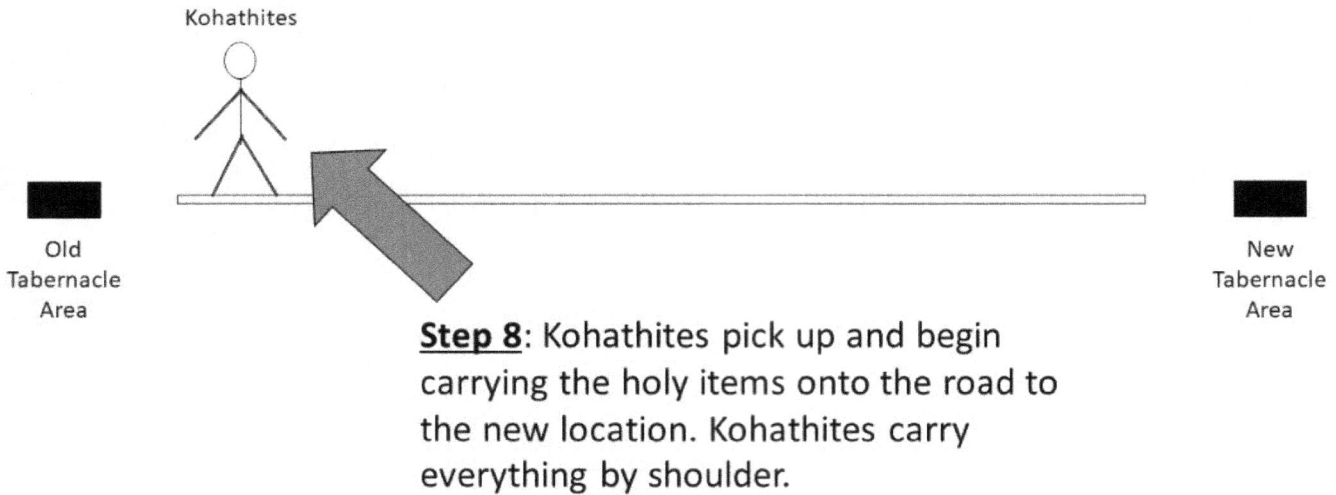

Step 8: Kohathites pick up and begin carrying the holy items onto the road to the new location. Kohathites carry everything by shoulder.

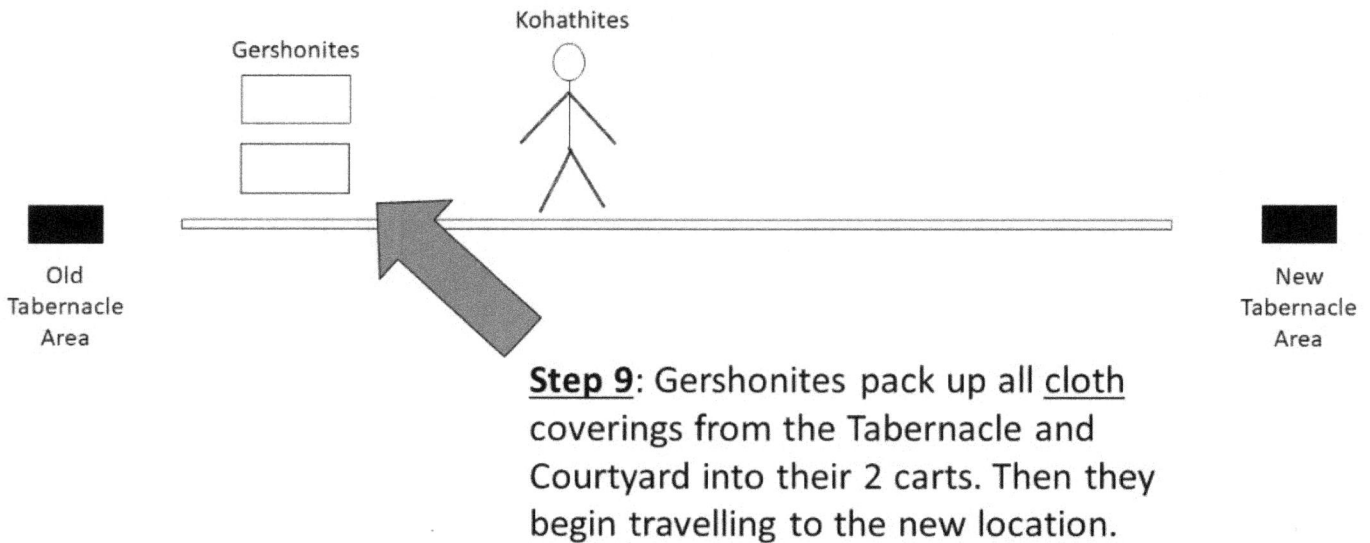

Step 9: Gershonites pack up all <u>cloth</u> coverings from the Tabernacle and Courtyard into their 2 carts. Then they begin travelling to the new location.

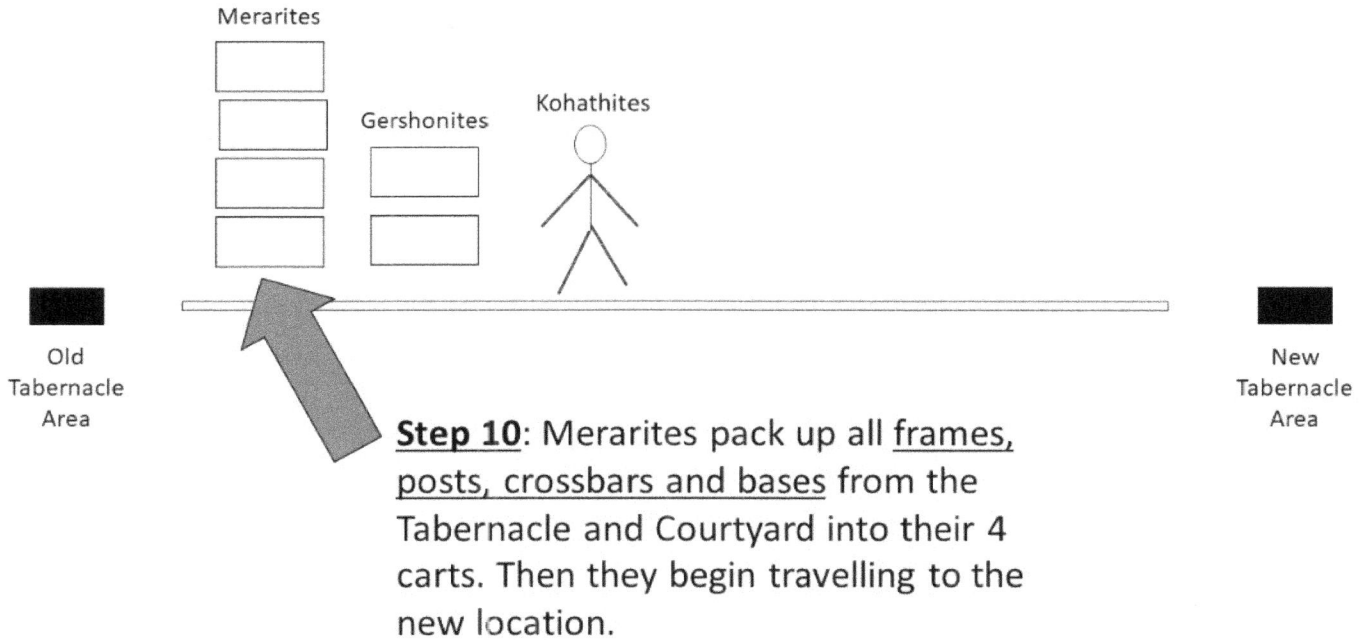

Step 10: Merarites pack up all <u>frames, posts, crossbars and bases</u> from the Tabernacle and Courtyard into their 4 carts. Then they begin travelling to the new location.

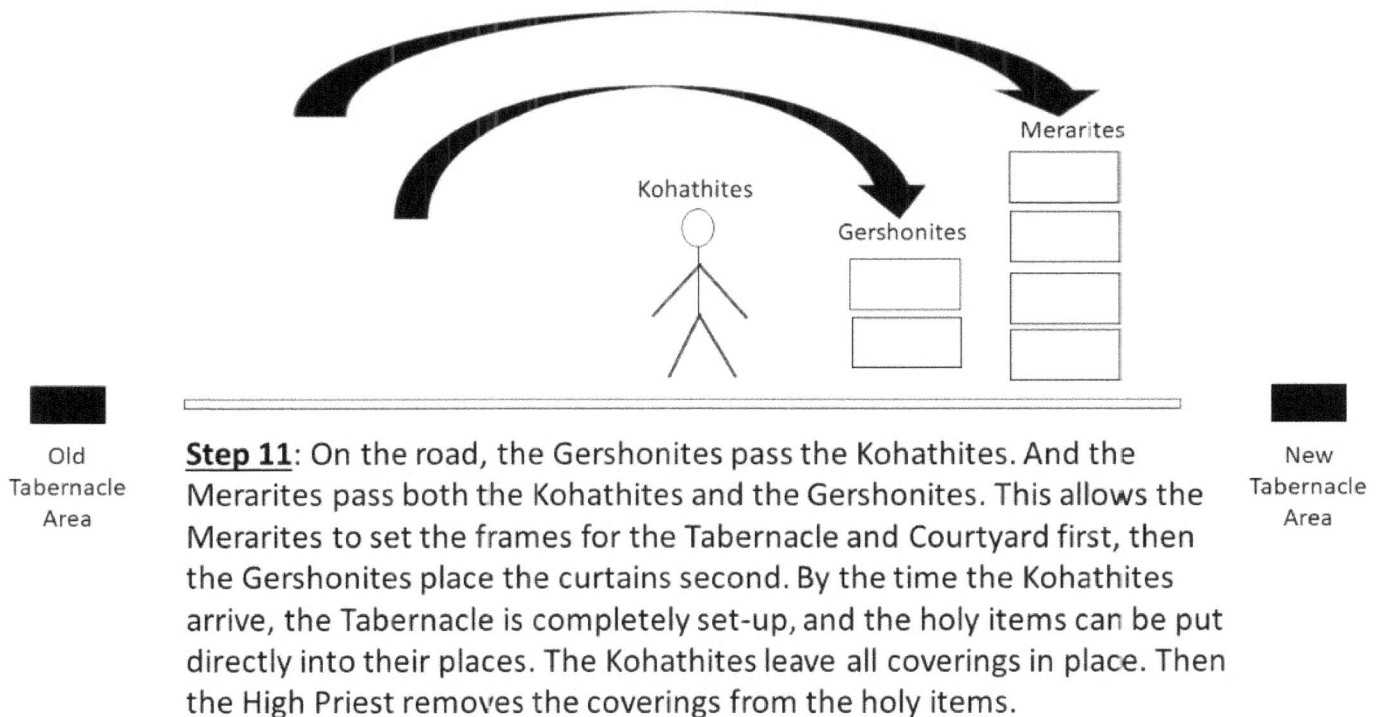

Step 11: On the road, the Gershonites pass the Kohathites. And the Merarites pass both the Kohathites and the Gershonites. This allows the Merarites to set the frames for the Tabernacle and Courtyard first, then the Gershonites place the curtains second. By the time the Kohathites arrive, the Tabernacle is completely set-up, and the holy items can be put directly into their places. The Kohathites leave all coverings in place. Then the High Priest removes the coverings from the holy items.

Additional Items

Question . . .

In our previous discussion on the tabernacle, I noted that "additional ministry items" from the Tabernacle were placed within a blue cloth and set atop a carrying frame (see page 57).

Now, if you have a knack for being thorough, you may wonder to yourself, "What <u>additional</u> items?" Or, you may ask yourself why there are additional items in the Tabernacle.

Answer: Remember the goal is simplicity. The whole point of the Tabernacle is that it would not have a bunch of unnecessary stuff. So, the additional items would be those things which might be useful in a pinch, or those items which would be needed for the continued services at the Altar Table.

For example, within these additional items, it is likely there may have been extra priestly garments—especially in the case that something happened to ruin a priest's clothing. This definitely appears to be the case when we consider the special clothes worn by the priests when transporting ashes, or the special clothes worn by the High Priest on the Day of Atonement (Lev. 16:23; and page 185).

Moreover, rather than needing to fire up a forge to make new bronze utensils, or scrambling to find a replacement tent peg, the additional items would have provided a general stock of replacement items to ensure losses were immediately covered.

And, the most obvious answer is that the Trumpets themselves and the gold and silver dishes (Num. 7:84-85) would be identified as "additional items" which needed to be covered with blue cloth and transported on a carrying frame—if they were not carried by the High Priest.

Got it?

Conclusion: Tabernacle Construction Planning

Of course, in the construction of the tabernacle and its articles, it would be necessary for the God-appointed leader and his cadre to go over the Law *extensively*—ensuring nothing is missed. Although the above list of required articles can be used as a basic guideline, the God-appointed leader should check and re-check his plans to ensure everything is made according to the established pattern. This is exactly what Moses did, when the Lord Himself reminded Moses to ensure everything was made according to the Heavenly pattern shown to him on the mount (Exo. 25:40; Heb. 8:5). This requires diligence and attention to detail. Hopefully my work here presents a good "starting point."

How to Keep the Law
Phase 3
Overseeing the Tabernacle

<u>Importance of the God-Appointed Leader</u>

In "Phase #1: The God-Appointed Leader," we discussed the vital importance of following the "right" leader. And, beyond the reasons stated in that phase, here we find additional reasons which support the need for the God-appointed prophetic leader.

To briefly re-cap, let's revisit what was said in Phase 1 . . .

As it is currently in the 21st Century, people discuss the rebuilding of the *temple* in Jerusalem. However, this creates problems—as the temple mount in currently occupied by buildings. Moreover, according to tradition, in order to re-set the temple altar, one must know the *exact* location of the previous altar placed by Solomon. And, even more impossible, in order to reestablish the traditional temple priesthood, it would require a pre-established priesthood—which is not in existence. In other words, to consecrate priests, you would first need priests, but to get priests you need to consecrate priests.

Seem confusing?

Well, it is.

However, fortunately for you, I am here to clarify the process for you . . .

According to the Law of Moses, found in the books of Exodus, Leviticus, Numbers and Deuteronomy, a "temple" is not required. In fact, during the time of Moses, the people had the "tabernacle."

This distinction is important because, in order to reestablish Old Testament faith, you do not need to rebuild the *temple*. Instead you need to rebuild the *tabernacle*.

And, in this distinction, there is a work-around for all the above problems with the temple. All of the problems can be solved with the tabernacle.

How?

Well, as I stated above, first you start with the God-appointed leader. Then the God-appointed leader sets up a temporary "tent of meeting" outside the camp—where he meets with God face-to-face, just as Moses did. And this "tent of meeting" serves as the temporary headquarters to plan the building of the tabernacle, the courtyard and all the articles.

Then, the God-appointed leader is responsible for consecrating the first group of priests and the tabernacle—because he is granted authority from God to do so . . . similar to Moses.

Last, once the tabernacle itself is consecrated, it becomes the new "tent of meeting" and the old "tent of meeting" is no longer used.

Therefore, we see clearly that unlike the "temple," reestablishment of the "tabernacle" poses no problems whatsoever. The God-appointed leader could begin the process today—in fact. All the God-appointed leader needs to begin the process is a "tent of meeting."

Period.

Therefore, there is no legitimate excuse why the tabernacle should not be rebuilt—especially if any group claims they are keeping the Law of Moses. The *tabernacle* does not need to be placed in a specific location; so, it doesn't matter if there are buildings on the *temple* location in Jerusalem.

If the Law of Moses is to be followed, then all is needed is the God-appointed leader and a tent. Nothing else is required beyond this to initiate the process. Then, the God-appointed leader carefully reestablishes the priesthood, the tabernacle and all its articles through the authority God has placed upon him.

So, if you desire to follow the Law of Moses, realize you must have the *tabernacle*. Abandon thoughts of reestablishing the *temple*—as it is unnecessary and foreign to the Law of Moses. Only the tabernacle is required. And to get that, you must simply start with the God-appointed leader and a tent. Nothing more.

You see, many people are confused by the Law of Moses because they think of it as a merely moral *set of rules*. However, the Law of Moses is first a *ceremonial guide*—directing God's people how to establish and maintain His special place of worship.

So, you *must* have the tabernacle/temple in order to "keep the Law of Moses." And, once you have the tabernacle, it won't run itself. It will need leadership and procedures to ensure things are done properly.

These thoughts bring us to the topic of this Phase—*How to administer and oversee tabernacle operations*.

Within any organization, especially one as nuanced as the tabernacle, constant oversight is required. So, if you have priests and Levites working at the tabernacle, you will need leadership to ensure they are performing their jobs properly (Lev. 10:16-20).

This oversight is the responsibility of the God-appointed leader—just as we discussed in Phase #1. And in this responsibility, the God-appointed leader is assisted by the High Priest and priests (Exo. 38:21; Num. 3:32; 4:16, 28, 33; 7:8).

Remember, in human organizations, things do not automatically go according to plan. Just because the God-appointed leader appoints priests, this does not mean that the priests will perform perfectly. So, the oversight provided by the God-appointed leader and the High Priest provide a constant check and balance process—whereby things are consistently monitored to ensure they stay true to the pattern commanded by God (Exo. 25:40; Lev. 10:16-20).

For example, the reestablishment of the temple in 516 B.C. shows us what would need to be done in order to re-install the first generation of priests at the tabernacle. In Ezra 2:62 we see an investigation was conducted on the genealogy of each man who applied to serve as a priest. And those who did not have valid genealogies were excluded from the priesthood.

Simple.

This means tabernacle leaders need to provide a "human resources" function similar to other human corporations. In this case, the initial appointment of priests in the reestablished religion of 516 B.C. required a thorough investigation into the background of each applicant.

In examining this topic further, let's assume our first generation of Levites have been appointed in the reestablished tabernacle.

Eventually, however, this first generation of Levites appointed would need to retire at age 50 (Num. 8:24-25). And they would they would be replaced by younger Levites (30 years old—or 25, as stated in the LXX).

So, let's say you have a brand-new Levite who just reached age 25 or 30. Surely you would not turn him loose in the tabernacle area. Rather, this new Levite would need to be *trained extensively*—most likely through an apprenticeship with an older Levite (Num. 8:26). (Although Levites were required to retire from physically carrying items at age 50, they were still permitted to oversee and lead younger Levites.)

And, like the new Levite, before <u>a new priest</u> could start serving at the tabernacle, he would need a few things. . . .

<u>First</u>, a new priest would need to have priestly garments issued to him. And the God-appointed leader would need to make several determinations—even in this first step. The God-appointed leader and high priest would need to keep an inventory of their stock of extra priestly garments. And, as certain items ran low in stock, they would need to coordinate with craftsmen to have new clothing articles made so they could be ready *when needed.*

Anyone who has led an organization is ever mindful of this principle: *It is better to have it and not need it, than to need it and not have it.*"

<u>Second</u>, once the God-appointed leader had an extra set of priestly clothing ready, he would need to "consecrate" the new priest—requiring planning to schedule the ceremony.

And, <u>third</u>, following his consecration, the new priest—like the new Levite—would need *extensive training* to help him master his duties.

Do you see the importance of *oversight*?

Even in the issue of clothing and simple priestly installation, it is necessary for leaders to think ahead, planning diligently to ensure tabernacle operations are never halted.

And, oversight continues further. Just because a priest is properly clothed and consecrated this does not mean he will always do things properly. In fact, the Law of Moses presents several "what if" scenarios, detailing what should be done in the case of priest misconduct or defilement (Lev. 21-22). And, from time to time, the God-appointed leader needs to challenge the decisions of the high priest to ensure things are done in the most proper way (Lev. 10:16-20).

Indeed, this model of tabernacle/temple oversight continues throughout all Scripture—where God always sends forth prophets after the order of Moses to challenge the actions of the priesthood and the people (Deu. 18:18). Perhaps a most notable example is found in the Lord Jesus' cleansing of the temple—demonstrating He was filling this Moses-based role of temple oversight (Deu. 18:18-19; Matt. 21:13)

Whenever an organization has employees, there will always be employees who break the rules. Certainly, this applies to the tabernacle—especially when all tabernacle operations are to be conducted with precise adherence to the written Law.

One such occurrence is found in Nehemiah 13:1-9—where Nehemiah discovered the misuse of rooms within the place of worship, where *prohibited items* were placed.

And, just as Nehemiah found, it is necessary to oversee the finances of the tabernacle to ensure the priests and Levites are properly compensated for their work (Neh. 13:10-13). Indeed, no matter how spectacular the rebuilding of a worship structure may be, if one lacks the ability to oversee its successful day-to-day operation, it will rapidly crumble. This is why *"Phase #3: Overseeing the Tabernacle"* is absolutely vital in the keeping of the Law of Moses.

Moreover, the tabernacle courtyard and surrounding areas would need to be policed—ensuring activity carried out within was acceptable. In the reestablishment of the Law of Moses, Nehemiah restricted commerce in the areas surrounding their central place of worship—prohibiting sales on the Sabbath (Neh. 7:3; 13:15-22).

Therefore, the God-appointed leader must have procedures in place to define how to deal with such rule-breaking. These are very simple "human resource" considerations, but they are vital nonetheless for any organization attempting to run a tight ship.

In conclusion, in order to keep the Law of Moses, you *must* have an effective system in place to administer and oversee tabernacle operations. It is not enough to just build the tabernacle. You must ensure it is perpetually operated according to the standards of the Lord given to Moses (Exo. 25:40).

Number of Priests & Levites

During the time of Moses, he originally appointed only one high priest (Aaron) and four normal priests (Nadab, Abihu, Eleazer and Ithamar) according to Exodus 28:1.

But the Levites were *very* numerous in comparison to the priests. In order to be eligible for tabernacle duties, a Levite man needed to be 25-50 years old (Num. 8:24-26). And during the time of Moses there were a total of 8,580 eligible Levite men, including 2,750 Kohathites, 2.630 Gershonites and 3,200 Merarites (Num. 4:36, 40, 44).

So, why were there so many eligible Levites?

Functionally it would make sense to have a large population to share duties—especially if the Lord called the people to transport the tabernacle *far away*. Moreover, having a large population of eligible Levites would allow the Levites to select men from among their population who were *best* fit to serve.

Later on, David used the large population of Levites to provide a new function at the house of the Lord. He directed the Levites to have a praise schedule—ensuring praise melodies arose from the Lord's house (1 Chr. 15:27; 16:4). After the reestablishment of God's house, we see this tradition carried forth with the installation of choirs—or bands of singers (Neh. 12:40).

Supervision of Levites

As the Levites carried out their duties they were under the direction of the priests. After the death of his first two sons, Nadab and Abihu, Aaron—the high priest—only had two other sons serving as priests, Eleazar and Ithamar.

As the tabernacle operated, the two priests Eleazar and Ithamar performed supervisory roles in addition to their normal duties as priests. The Bible tells us that Eleazar was in charge of the Kohathites—who carried the articles of the tabernacle (Num. 3:32; 4:16). Additionally, it was Eleazar's job to assist the high priest with the covering and uncovering of the tabernacle articles.

Considering Eleazar was now the eldest son of the high priest, it makes sense he would bear responsibility over the tabernacle. In fact, the Day of Atonement actually allows the incoming high priest to perform the steps of the entire ceremony (see page 185). This means the high priest would work closely with his eldest son for many years—ensuring he had opportunity to master all the duties of the high priesthood he would assume upon his father's death.

The other son of the high priest, Ithamar, was in charge of both the Gershonites and Merarites—who carried the curtains and structural pieces of the tabernacle tent, respectively (Exo. 38:21; Num. 4:28, 33; 7:8).

Moreover, in addition to the supervision provided by the priests, the Levites were also guided by the elder Levites. Even after attaining the age of 50, and being restricted from personally carrying objects, the elder Levites were expected to continue to provide apprenticeship to the younger Levites (Num. 8:24-26).

The Camps around the Tabernacle Area

Camping Locations around the Tabernacle Area

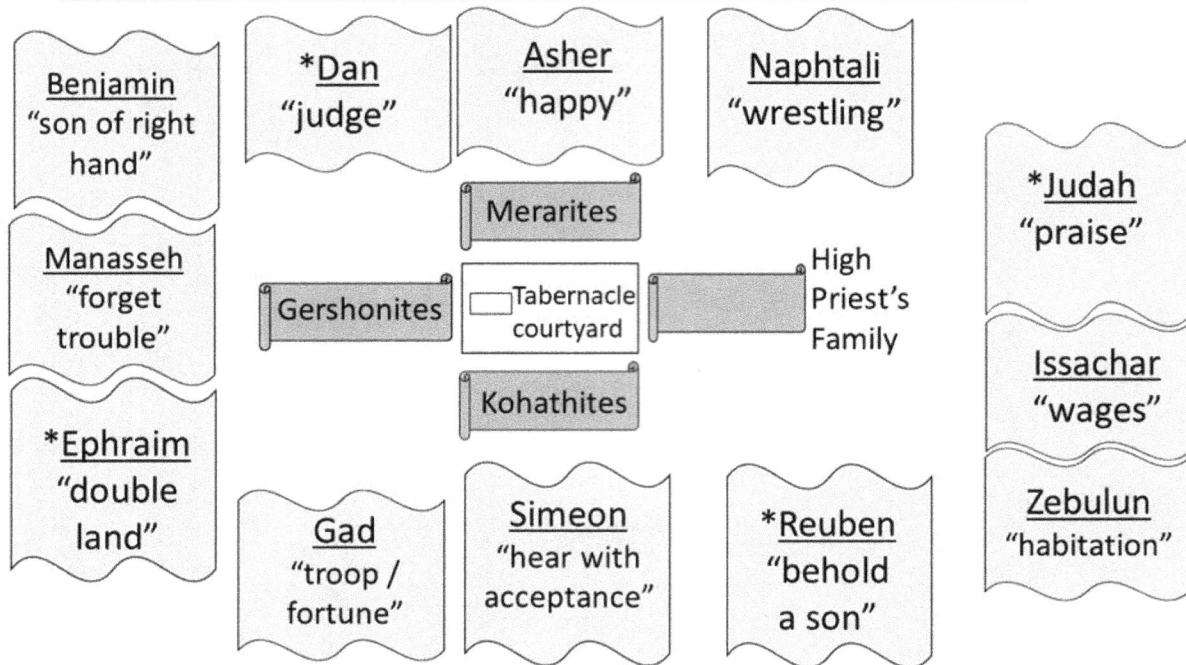

Benjamin "son of right hand"	***Dan** "judge"	**Asher** "happy"	**Naphtali** "wrestling"	
		Merarites		***Judah** "praise"
Manasseh "forget trouble"	Gershonites	[ ] Tabernacle courtyard	High Priest's Family	
		Kohathites		**Issachar** "wages"
*Ephraim "double land"	**Gad** "troop / fortune"	**Simeon** "hear with acceptance"	***Reuben** "behold a son"	**Zebulun** "habitation"

In the Law it states the God-appointed leader, <u>the high priest and his sons are to camp to the east of the tabernacle</u> (Num. 3:38). From this position they would ensure no unauthorized person was ever permitted to approach the tabernacle.

The <u>Kohathite clan was to perpetually camp south of the tabernacle</u> (Num. 3:29).

Then the <u>Gershonite clan was to perpetually camp west of the tabernacle</u> (Num. 3:23).

Last, the <u>Merarite clan was to perpetually camp north of the tabernacle</u> (Num. 3:35).

So, why is this important?

Well, for security reasons it was vital. These consecrated individuals would be prepared at all times to move the tabernacle whenever the Lord directed the God-appointed leader. Therefore, they were stationed in camps surrounding the tabernacle.

How would they be signaled?

Remember on page 48 we discussed the trumpets. Interestingly, the trumpet blasts which signal moving out correspond with the camp locations and the order in which the tabernacle area would be disassembled for transport. The trumpet blasts are as follows . . .

> *-Setting out blasts: When setting out, the first blast signals the tribes on the east to set out. Then, the second blast signals the tribes on the south to set out. LXX adds that the third blast signals the west to set out, and the fourth blast signals the north.*

Note how the first trumpet blast signals those encamped on the east—which would have been the high priest and his sons. Upon hearing the trumpet blast, the high priest and his sons would enter the tabernacle to cover all the holy articles—the ark, bread table, lampstand, incense altar, additional items, the altar table and the wash basin. As necessary, each of these items would have their carrying poles inserted (except for the ark which always had the carrying poles inserted). And, in the case of the lampstand and the additional articles, they would be placed upon a carrying frame.

Upon completing this process, the second trumpet blast would be sounded, signaling those who encamped on the south—which would have been the Kohathites. Upon hearing the second trumpet blast, the Kohathites would enter the tabernacle areas to carry the most holy articles which were covered and prepared for transport by the high priest and his sons. Then the Kohathites would set out on the road, following the pillar and the cloud of God's presence.

Then the third trumpet blast would be sounded, signaling those who encamped on the west—which would have been the Gershonites. Upon hearing the third trumpet blast, the Gershonites would enter the tabernacle area to remove all the curtains, placing them within their two carts. Then they would move onto the road—trailing behind the Kohathites.

Last, the fourth trumpet blast would be sounded—signaling those who encamped in the north—which would have been the Merarites. Upon hearing the fourth trumpet blast, the Merarites would move into the tabernacle area to remove all the posts, frames and bases—placing them into their four carts. Then they would move onto the road—trailing behind the Gershonites.

And, at the sounding of the trumpets, the tribes of Israel prepare to set out in order. As Numbers 1:52-2:34 explains, at the sounding of the trumpets, the tribes in the corresponding location would be ready to hit the road in trail of the respective portion of the tabernacle procession. So, following the tabernacle procession the tribes would march in order from those who camp on the east (Judah, Issachar, Zebulun), second the south (Reuben, Simeon, Gad), third is the west (Ephraim, Manasseh, Benjamin), last, the north (Dan, Asher, Naphtali). These camping locations around the tabernacle area are portrayed in the illustration on page 78.

As I detail in the diagrams on page 78, during their journey to the next location, the marching order would reverse—as the Gershonites pass the Kohathites, and the Merarites pass both the Kohathites and the Gershonites. This allows the tabernacle to be reassembled in reverse order upon reaching the new location.

So, where is the God-appointed leader, the high priest and his sons during this process?

Well, they would need to *supervise the entire process*—likely with one of them stationed alongside each of these groups as they perform their functions.

Why?

Like I said earlier, in the case of any operation you need supervisors to ensure things go according to plan, in addition to addressing emerging contingencies immediately. It is not enough to simply assume everything will go according to plan. Rather, a good leader will always "inspect what he expects." So, in all cases where the Levites were performing their functions it is likely that either the God-appointed leader, the high priest or one of the high priest's sons were standing aside to inspect and offer additional instructions.

Unexpected things occur. This is why *onsite* leadership is necessary.

For example, imagine the Kohathites are walking with the most holy items. Then in the jostling of steps, one of the utensils falls off the altar table onto the ground, or an item slips from the lampstand covering and falls off the carrying frame onto the ground.

What should the Kohathites do?

They are not authorized, *at any time*, to touch any of the most holy items. They are only permitted to touch the carrying poles.

Therefore, the only way in which this situation could be addressed within the parameters of the Law, would be for the high priest or one of his sons to pick up the item and re-secure it underneath the covering.

Or, if a carrying pole were to break, or a carrying pole ring were to become unattached on the road, only the high priest or one of his sons could remedy this situation—because it would require *touching* a most holy article.

Make sense?

Thus, we sense the great importance of oversight to all aspects of tabernacle operation. So, before you can have a fully operational tabernacle, the God-appointed leader must set in place oversight procedures—ensuring the high priest and his sons can appropriately address emerging contingencies.

<u>Camping Locations for the 12 Tribes (Num. 1:52-3:38)</u>

Outside the camps of the Levites, the rest of the tribes were instructed to camp in certain locations—as depicted in the below illustration . . .

Camping Locations around the Tabernacle Area

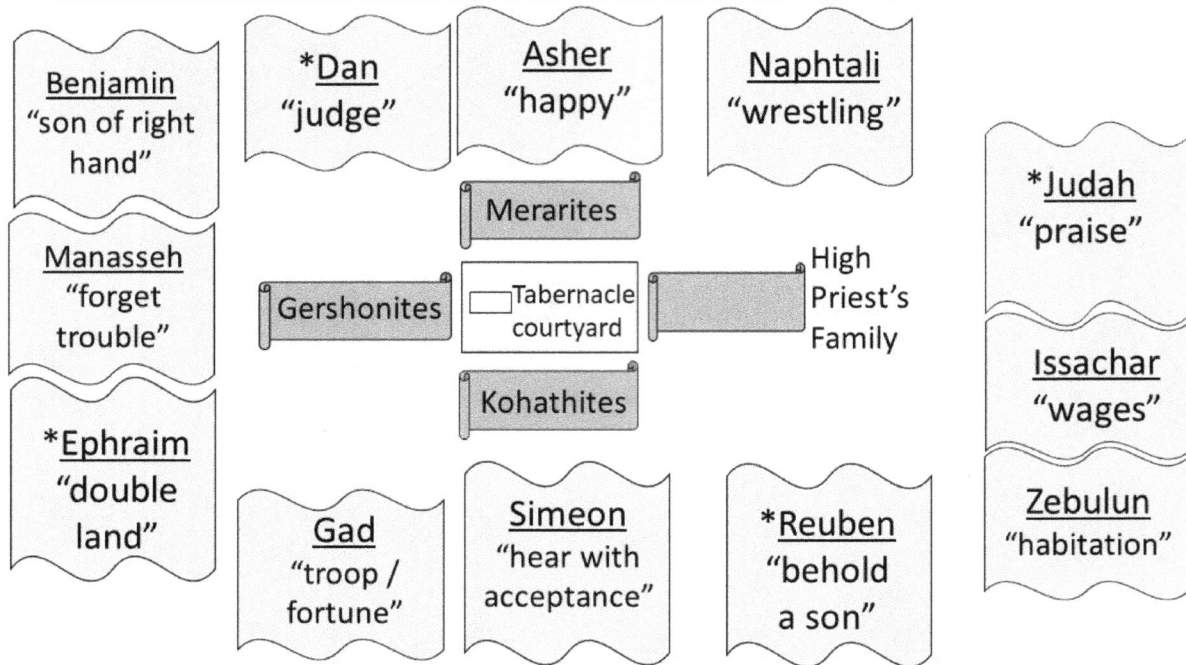

Benjamin "son of right hand"	***Dan** "judge"	**Asher** "happy"	**Naphtali** "wrestling"
Manasseh "forget trouble"	Gershonites	Merarites / Tabernacle courtyard	High Priest's Family / *Judah "praise"
*Ephraim "double land"		Kohathites	Issachar "wages"
	Gad "troop / fortune"	**Simeon** "hear with acceptance"	***Reuben** "behold a son" / Zebulun "habitation"

Numbers 1:52 explains each tribe set up *standards* to mark their camping locations, most likely with the use of banners. In the above illustration I include the meaning of each name—which can be found in the book of Genesis (specifically 29:31-30:24; 35:18; 41:51-52).

As explained above, the trumpets would be used to signal the tribes to be prepared to move out in order. And, when they would travel, they would do so in order—<u>east</u> (Judah, Issachar, Zebulun), <u>south</u> (Reuben, Simeon, Gad), <u>west</u> (Ephraim, Manasseh, Benjamin) then <u>north</u> (Dan, Asher, Naphtali).

When understanding the meaning of each name, it is likely the marching procession contains a coded message—perhaps helping us to see how we should follow after God's presence.

Look at the meaning of each name in the illustration.

Why do you think Moses had these tribes camp *in this order*?

If you are looking for a quick answer, begin by simply reflecting on the fact that Naphtali—meaning "wrestling"—comes last in the sequence, but each sequence begins with Judah—which is "praise." Simply put, when attempting to wrestle ourselves out of difficult situations, praise can be used for incredible benefit—helping us to begin the next stage of our journey.

Can you see more? I challenge you to further reflect on the meaning of the names in the marching procession.

Moreover, what I find interesting is that as the tribes moved westward following Judah's lead, this would cause all of them to pass around the central location counter-clockwise where the tabernacle was located—viewing the location from afar before trekking out to their new location in trail of the tribes before them. In fact, if moving out in the morning, looking directly ahead—to the east—would have been visually unbearable with the rising sun. So, as the tribes marched eastward in order to follow Judah, they would have been inclined to look north—to see the tribes across the old tabernacle location as they moved westward. Indeed, much can be said about this by a skilled teacher—ushering forth profound truths now forgotten in the ancient Law. And, something significant can be said in carefully considering where we have been in the past in preparation for where we will be in the future.

For the moment, however, I will digress—hopefully leaving you to examine these things for yourself. I mention these things to illustrate the power of the Law. Even in the most minute details we find a rich tapestry of instruction. Those who neglect the wisdom of God's Law miss out on all it has to teach us. So, I invite you most earnestly to look with intent into the perfect Law—faithfully searching it out, adding nothing to it and subtracting nothing from it, but simply seeing it exactly as it was delivered (Isa. 8:20). In this there is found ancient power.

Required Inventory

In order to maintain temple operations, the priests would need to keep an inventory of certain stock items, including, but not limited to the following . . .

#1 Water of Cleansing & Ashes of Red Heifer (Num. 8:7; 19:1-22; 31:23)

- Used during the Levite Consecration Ceremony for all new Levites (Num. 8:7) (see page 136).
- Used to cleanse those who were defiled by contact with a human corpse—being applied on the third day and seventh day after contact. Then the person to be cleansed would remain unclean until evening, then be clean (Num 19:11-13).
- Used to cleanse soldiers returning from battle, in addition to any plunder they took in battle (Num. 31:23). All plunder articles which can withstand fire are also put into fire before they are sprinkled with the "water of cleansing." Similar to Num. 19:11-13, soldiers would be sprinkled with the water of cleansing on both the third day and the seventh day. Then they would remain unclean until evening— then permitted to come into the camp.
- A priest would sprinkle the "water of cleansing" upon these individuals—but in doing so, the priest who sprinkled another would become unclean until evening, and need to wash his clothes (Num. 19:21).
- Water of cleansing is made with water and the ashes from a red heifer through these steps (Num. 19) . . .

-**Step 1**: Priest prepares the following items: (1) firewood, (2) cedar wood, (3) hyssop, and (4) scarlet wool.

-**Step 2**: A representative from God's people brings a red heifer who has never been under a yoke to the priest.

-**Step 3**: The priest takes the red heifer to a ceremonially clean place outside the camp—probably near the location where the ashes from the altar table are disposed.

-**Step 4**: Priest slaughters the red heifer.

-**Step 5**: Priest sprinkles blood seven times with his finger toward the tabernacle. (Whereas some English translations state the priest sprinkles it *toward* the tabernacle—as if to imply he remains in the same location as the red heifer's body; the LXX omits "finger" and says he must sprinkle the blood seven times in *front* of the tabernacle—as if to imply the priest goes back into the tabernacle area at this time with some blood. If it is the latter, the body of the red heifer would obviously remain guarded in his brief absence.)

-**Step 6**: Priest uses firewood (from Step #1) to burn the entire red heifer—and remains standing there to watch it burn.

-**Step 7**: As the red heifer burns, the priest places upon it the cedar wood, hyssop and scarlet wool from Step #1.

-**Step 8**: Priest leaves the red heifer under the watch of someone else. Priest washes his clothes and bathes himself outside the camp. Then he returns to the camp and secludes himself—because he will be unclean until evening.

-**Step 9**: The person who remains with the burning red heifer stays until burning is complete.

-**Step 10**: A third person arrives at the site where the red heifer was burned. At the arrival of the third person, the person who stayed with the burning red heifer leaves—washing his clothes and bathing himself outside the camp. The person who stayed with the burning red heifer remains unclean until evening.

-**Step 11**: The third person, gathers all the ashes of the red heifer and places them in a ceremonially clean area outside the camp—probably near the location where ashes from the altar table are disposed. The third person becomes ceremonially unclean until evening and must wash his clothes and bathe himself outside the camp.

-**Step 12**: Whenever necessary, a priest retrieves ashes from the red heifer and mixes them with water to create the "water of cleansing."

<u>Maintaining the Red Heifer's Ashes</u>

In Step #11 above, I note how the red heifer ashes are left outside the camp in a ceremonially clean place—most likely near the same location where the ashes from the altar table are disposed.

How were they kept?

The text doesn't say if the red heifer ashes were left uncovered, or if they were placed in a jar / container. Perhaps it would be best for them to be stored within a container to prevent them from being washed away by inclement weather or otherwise compromised.

It is important to remember here that the tabernacle was required to move—frequently, if necessary. This would present a problem with the red heifer ashes.

Why?

Well, the Bible passage does not say the priests were required to relocate the red heifer ashes. Yet, it might be improper to leave them behind. Thus, every time they prepared to move the tabernacle, the priests would need to make a decision concerning any red heifer ashes present outside the camp.

So, what were their choices?

I think they had two options . . .

First, if the priests chose to leave the red heifer ashes behind, they would need to ensure they were not compromised. In other words, they bore responsibility over the ashes—and they were something special. So, although the Bible does not require it, perhaps it would be best for the priest to mingle the remaining red heifer ashes with the disposed ashes from the altar table present in that location. Or, it might be proper to empty any container with red heifer ashes—rather than just leaving it there. This first choice might be the best option if there is only a small amount of red heifer ashes remaining. Of course, this first option would require the priests re-make red heifer ashes immediately upon reaching their new location.

Or, second, if the priests chose to bring the red heifer ashes with them, it would require a priest to become unclean during the day he carried the ashes. The high priest would need to make the decision whether or not it is proper for another person to carry the red heifer ashes in lieu of a priest. This second choice might be the best option if there are still a lot of red heifer ashes remaining.

What do you think would be the best option?

Purpose of the Water of Cleansing

In examination of the "water of cleansing," it is quite easy to see the parallels between the ceremony with the red heifer and other offerings. But, in this brief discussion, I want to point out what makes the red heifer ceremony special. This might give us insights about its purpose—and the message it conveys.

In many of the offerings and calendar festivals (discussed on pages 153-238), I note how people place their hands upon the heads of the animals offered. The placement of one's hand signifies a transfer—usually of guilt or sin—from the person onto the animal. Note, however, in the red heifer ceremony, no hand is laid upon the head of the red heifer.

Perhaps this is saying something about those who are sprinkled with the water of cleansing . . . that those people are not necessarily complicit participants who erred in something. Rather, their circumstances *happened* to make them unclean. When considering the circumstances of its use, it certainly seems this applies to the people for whom the water of cleansing is made—soldiers, Levites and those who came into contact with a human corpse.

Ignorance of Sacrifice

Note, in the "water of cleansing" ceremony, the sacrifice—that is the red heifer—is slaughtered separately and *without the direct knowledge of the person to be cleansed* with the water. This makes it different from other ceremonies and offerings—where the people would bring and have their animals slaughtered before them. In other words, those who are sprinkled with the water of cleansing carry with them the results of great sacrifice, yet an ignorance of what provided for the water.

Bear with me in this thought . . .

When considering how this water of cleansing is placed upon the soldiers—who fought for God's people—we recognize that the proper citizens of the community have an ignorance of the sacrifice made by the soldiers themselves. Therefore, the proper community does not *watch* the burning of the red heifer—they are *oblivious* to it.

Yet, the only time in which a proper citizen grasps the great sacrifice of the soldier is when the proper citizen receives a glimpse of human death. Hence, the proper citizen who touches a human carcass is required to undergo the same cleansing as the battle-tested soldier. In other words, the soldier is only understood by those who are touched by personal human loss—when they lose someone whom they love so closely they are willing to be defiled just to touch them one last time.

Uncleanliness which Compels Ministry

The water of cleansing is unique because, although it is used to make a person clean, it makes everyone unclean. Even the priest who sprinkles it becomes unclean just by sprinkling it on another person.

What does this mean?

Well, when considering the water of cleansing is used on soldiers, it serves to force priests who use it into an entire day of *intentionality*. In other words, a priest would need to "plan" to use the water of cleansing. He would have to block out an entire day—where he would be absolutely restricted from doing his normal activities. And, in essence, it would compel the priest to spend the *entire day* with either the soldiers or the grieving person whom he cleansed. Thus, a priest would need to have a deep desire to help a person—to be willing to become unclean for them. They couldn't begin the process of trauma counseling flippantly.

It is no wonder why the Lord Jesus had such a strong rebuke for the priest who was unwilling to take upon himself such compassion—when this compassion is absolutely required by the Law (Luke 10:31-32). When understanding the Levite Consecration Ceremony, this parable takes new light. Here the Levite—whose very consecration required a priest to be willing to become unclean for him (page 136)—was unwilling to become unclean for his fellow man.

So, by the requirement to use the water of cleansing on soldiers and those who were touched by loss, God's Law requires priests to clear their *day's schedule* to devote themselves to ministry and prayer for the ones to be cleansed.

Moreover, by using the water of cleansing, a priest would be prohibited from eating portions at the tabernacle. Thus, the use of the water of cleansing may have also spurred priests to "fast"—as they abstained from food for the entire day while they prayed with the person who was sprinkled.

Transition & Respite
Rather than compelling soldiers to immediately re-enter the camp and presume their normal lives, the requirement for them to be cleansed demanded they remain secluded first for one week. So, even if they were prepared to return to their homes, God's Law provided time for them to slowly readjust themselves following the terror of battle.

Compartmentalization of Battle
Rather than soldiers being left to deal with the aftermath of their combat experiences during their normal lives, the requirement to use the "water of cleansing" created a separation from their wartime experiences.

How so?

Well, immediately upon returning from war, soldiers were encouraged to label their experiences—referring to them as an "uncleanliness" from which they would be separated.

Get it?

They would not view their experiences as "themselves," but rather something to be washed from their minds. So, by labelling their experiences as unclean, this separation from these bad experiences may have enabled them to more readily dispose of some of the long-term effects of battle—such as PTSD. When understanding a key factor in PTSD development involves time and how long a war-scarred mind is left to ruminate and settle into new destructive patterns, a religious practice—like the "water of cleansing"—provided an immediate opportunity for returning soldiers to identify and separate themselves from their combat experiences.

Moreover, the use of the water of cleansing would likewise present a clear line of demarcation for those grieving with loss. Rather than being left to have grief endure without limit, the water of cleansing ritual would label the dark portions of that painful loss as "unclean." And, in this process, the person would be ushered into the ability to let go of their pain—along with that uncleanliness—after seven days. Choosing to let go of the dark portions, while retaining the good memories.

Water of Cleansing in Levite Consecration Ceremony

On page 136, I detail how the water of cleansing is used in the Levite Consecration Ceremony.

Now, when examining the above details of the water of cleansing, you may be asking yourself why the "water of cleansing" is used for Levite consecration. After all, it is not used for the consecration of priests.

Well, we are able to answer this question by examining commonalties between its uses . . .

In the Bible we see the water of cleansing is used for: (1) soldiers who return from battle, (2) people who touched a human corpse, and (3) for the Levite Consecration ceremony.

So, what do these three things have in common?

Simply this . . .

They all involve "loss" of human life. *In the first case*, soldiers in battle experience loss. *In the second case*, people experience the effects of loss. And, *in the third case*—the Levites are redeemed from their own deaths.

Remember, the Levites are "redeemed" as the firstborn of God's people. Whereas in Egypt all the firstborn died; God passed over His people. But in passing over His people, God did not give up His claim on the lives of the firstborn among His people.

So, rather than taking *every firstborn* from among His people, God demands all the Levites to be devoted to His service. (This is the purpose of the census taken before the Levite Consecration Ceremony.) Therefore, Levites have the "water of cleansing" sprinkled upon them because they are redeemed from death. In other words, they touch death on behalf of all the tribes of God's people. And, being redeemed from it, they are cleansed with the "water of cleansing" as if returning from the grave.

Cool, huh?

The use of the "water of cleansing" here is a reminder of the Passover. And it differs from the other uses of the "water of cleansing." In the cases of returning soldiers and those defiled with a human corpse, they are sprinkled on both the 3rd and 7th days. But in the case of Levite consecration, they are only sprinkled once—on the day before their consecration ceremony. Then they spend the day preceding their consecration as "unclean"—being separated from the people, devoting themselves to prayerful reflection on their redemption from the fate of the firstborn.

On the day of their consecration, the Levites are called forth from their prior day of uncleanliness and self-reflection. They are granted new life as from the grave—strikingly reminiscent of the Lord Jesus calling forth Lazarus (John 11:43).

This picture of redemption is furthered within the Levite Consecration Ceremony itself—when the high priest lifts the Levites to their feet, presenting them as a "wave offering" before the Lord (see page 136). By presenting them as a wave offering, this is an acknowledgement of God's possession of the Levites— similar to animals which are devoted to the fire of His altar (see page 236). Yet the Lord chooses instead to allow the priests to bring the Levites into their service at the tabernacle.

In these ways, the use of the "water of cleansing" lends powerful imagery to the consecration of Levites—compelling reflection on God's redemption.

Thus, we see within the Law of Moses powerful portrayals of grace and redemption. By reflecting on such things we gain marvelous insight on the teachings of the New Testament.

<u>Water of Cleansing & Christ Touching the Deceased</u>

Although beyond the scope of this book, I would like to address an issue which may be raised by an inquisitive mind. . . .

The Law of Moses requires those who come into contact with a corpse to be sprinkled.
And, Christ came into contact with corpses (Mark 5:41; Luke 7:14) . . .
So why wasn't Christ sprinkled with the water of cleansing?

Simple: The raising of the dead redeemed them from uncleanliness. In other words, the dead were no longer dead. And, as such, *upon the return of life to their bodies there was no need for cleansing*—because the problem was solved.

Consider Christ's resurrection: Technically, according to the Law, a corpse is unclean. But if the corpse is made alive, there is no longer a reason for cleansing. Thus, the resurrection of Christ confounds the Law. His life proclaims victory over the Law because His resurrection removes the need for ceremonial cleansing. And, in the place of the requirement for cleansing, there remains only praise. God is given glory for His miracle—and there remains nothing from which to be cleansed.

#2 Anointing Oil (Exo. 30:22-33)

- Made one batch at a time, when necessary. Recipe includes:
  (1) olive oil (one hin),
  (2) liquid myrrh (500 shekels),
  (3) cassia (500 shekels),
  (4) cinnamon (250 shekels),
  (5) calamus (250 shekels)

- Used in the Consecration Ceremony (pages 97)

#3 Sacred Incense (Exo. 30:34-38)

- Made from equal amounts of gum resin, onycha, galbanum, frankincense. LXX states the incense formula consists of sweetherb, stacte, onycha, sweet galbanum.
- Used on incense altar and bread table (see pages 40 & 44)

#4 Wood (Lev. 6:12-13)

- The priests would need to constantly keep wood for use on the altar table. This would require planning to ensure stock never ran low and it was always maintained.
- The wood would also need to be transported by God's people. Wood was not transported by priests or Levites.
- Used for altar fires and fires outside the camp

#5 Olive Oil (Exo. 35:8)

- Used for the lampstand (see page 42)

#6 Spares

- In the listing of tabernacle articles, it states on page 62 there were additional items kept in the tabernacle. On page 62, I discuss these items—which were likely extra parts and components to be used in the case other items were broken or damaged.

#7 Livestock

- In order to offer the required tabernacle sacrifices faithfully, the priests would need to know the location of the livestock to be used. In other words, at the beginning of the week they would already know whom would be bringing the lambs to be used on each day for the morning and evening offerings.

#8 Livestock Feed and Equipment

- Whenever you have livestock, it is necessary to plan to ensure you have food and other necessities to provide for them. Of course, the livestock would not be kept in the tabernacle itself. But the priests would need to be a part of planning—ensuring they constantly had livestock available.

Organizational Leadership Methods

A good leader always *"inspects what he expects."* So, the priests would by necessity be required to oversee all logistical concerns and planning considerations so that the sacrifices would be offered without fail. Therefore, it is most likely the high priest would conduct inspections and inventories to control what he had available. And, when necessary, he would give direction to increase the tabernacle stock.

What would be a good way to do this?

Well, during the time of Moses, there was the high priest, Aaron, and four priests under his leadership—Nadab, Abihu, Eleazar and Ithamar. So, a simple *division of labor* could ensure the accomplishment of these supervisory tasks.

In fact, I am quite intrigued by this topic. How indeed should the high priest lead tabernacle efforts, including the other priests and the Levites?

This is how I would do it . . .

Daily there would be a planning meeting. The high priest would sit down with each of the priests and a leader from each branch of the Levites. Each person would give a report in turn on relevant issues dealing with their assignments. And, upon receiving reports from these subordinate leaders, the high priest could delegate action to bring resolution.

For example, the leader from the Merarites might report that one of the courtyard posts has a crack in it. At this time, the high priest might instruct one of the priests to conduct an inspection on *all* the posts—looking them over carefully for cracks. The high priest might reason—quite accurately—that the post was somehow damaged during transportation. And, if one post was damaged, it is likely another post may have been damaged on the same cart.

And, while the high priest sends one of the priests to check for damaged posts, he may choose to send another priest to consult with a craftsman to determine the course of action if the post needs to be replaced. After all, it might take several days in order to procure the proper type of wood. So, planning would need to be quick.

To prevent future problems, the high priest may determine he wants the craftsman to prepare several extra posts to be kept on hand in inventory.

While the high priest sends off the subordinate leaders to each complete their own part of this task, the high priest may go with the Merarite leader to inspect the carts themselves—trying to figure out if there is a pinch point on one of them which could be the source of the problem. Before the high priest goes, however, he would need to instruct one of the other priests to stand watch at the tabernacle in his absence.

Of course, the above scenario is hypothetical. But it serves to illustrate the multi-tasking which would be absolutely required within tabernacle leadership. The high priest and other priests would need to provide this type of oversight leadership *constantly*—foreseeing problems and preparing solutions *ahead of time*.

This is why leadership oversight is absolutely critical to tabernacle operations. The high priest would need to have his finger upon the pulse of everything dealing with the operation of the tabernacle. And, as time went on, he would need to mentor one of his sons to replace him.

The Importance of Scheduling

Any good leader must develop plans and oversee others to make sure things happen according to plan. It is not good for a leader to *assume* something will happen.

Why?

Well, in the case of the high priest, God held him personally responsible for making sure the offerings were provided at the tabernacle without fail. Yet, as I discuss on page 163-164, the ceremonies for the morning and evening offerings <u>*required*</u> a *representative from God's people* to bring the lamb, grain, olive oil and drink to the high priest. In other words, the high priest couldn't just keep all those things at his own house. He was *required* to <u>receive these items daily from a representative</u> among God's people.

Unfortunately, as we leaders know, just because someone is *supposed to do something*, doesn't mean he will. In fact, people often forget. And, since God required the high priest to oversee the entire tabernacle, the high priest would need to develop a schedule and a system of verification to ensure everyday there would be no mistakes.

What do I mean?

Of course, the Law of Moses doesn't tell the high priest *exactly* how to make sure God's people always brought the required morning and evening offerings. But, to help you to understand, I offer the following as an example of how the high priest *should consider* scheduling the morning and evening offering ceremonies.

This is how I would do it . . .

(1) Call a monthly meeting with the representative heads from each tribe of God's people on about the 15th day of the month.
(2) During the meeting, have them each sign up for certain dates for the following month. Then make sure they each know exactly what they must bring on their assigned days. (The offerings vary on each day depending on whether it is a New Moon, Sabbath, festival day, etc. See pages 153-204.)
(3) The high priest should question them each to ensure they know the location from which they will bring the animals on their assigned dates.
(4) The high priest should delegate oversight to one of his subordinate priests. On the days leading up to each assigned date, the priest should send a message to ensure the respective representative will arrive on the planned date.
(5) Maintain a fallback plan. In the military, we called this a "supernumerary"—which is a person who was scheduled to immediately fill in for a particular duty if the assigned person had an emergency. For example, if a particular representative knew he would have extra items for the offerings available near the tabernacle for the month, then the high priest could assign him to quickly fill in—in the case the scheduled representative did not arrive on a particular day.

Easy, right?

Management & Leadership Aptitude

When considering all the above factors, it is clear to see that one of the most important characteristics of a priest is his ability to manage others, plan, track logistics, manage contingencies and lead people. In other words, the high priest and his priests were not simple people who just stood by the altar table waiting for people to do things.

Rather, the priests are called to be adept *managers*—similar to other great men of old, such as Joseph and Daniel. And, they were charged by God to administer the tabernacle in all things—ensuring the prescribed offerings were presented without fail. Therefore, before any priest would be consecrated it would be wise to assess his management and leadership aptitude.

Priest Procedures

As a final consideration, it should be recognized that the priests were required to perform certain functions and procedures to support God's people as they encountered various situations.

Whenever one of God's people had a complaint, they were required to go to a judge—who was appointed under the authority of the God-appointed leader (Exo. 18:13-26). Then, upon hearing a person, the judge would render a decision. The person was then charged to carry out the verdict in obedience.

Thus, a judge would decide on matters—and many of those decisions would require the person levying the complaint to go to a priest. So, within the Law, God's people were not required to render verdicts for themselves. Rather they relied on the judges, and the judges would refer them to the priests in certain cases which necessitated the action of the priests.

Make sense?

So, what were some of the basic things judges would discuss with people?

These are some of them . . .

Specific Rules (this list is also found on page 261)

-Animals (Exo. 23:12; Lev. 19:19, 26; 24:18-21; 27:9-13, 26-27; Deu. 15:19-23; 22:1-4, 6-7; 22:10; 27:21)
-Camp (Num. 5:1-3; Deu. 23:9-14)
-Childbirth (Lev. 12:1-8)
-Circumcision (Gen. 17:9-14; Exo. 4:24-26)
-Cities of Refuge (Num. 35:6-34; Deu. 4:41-43; 19:1-13)
-Clothing / Adornment (Lev. 19:19, 27-28; Num. 15:37-41; Deu. 6:4-9; 14:1; 22:5, 11-12)
-Dedicating / Devoting (Lev. 27:1-29; Num. 18:14-19)
-Diet (Lev. 7:22-27; 11:1-47; 17:1-16; 19:26; 20:25; Deu. 12:15-16, 20-25; 14:3-21)
-Discharges (Lev. 15:1-33; Num. 5:1-3; Deu. 23:9-14)
-Exclusion from Assembly (Deu. 23:1-8)
-Fallen Religions (Exo. 34:12-17; Lev. 19:26, 31; 20:1-6, 23, 27; Deu. 4:15-31; 6:14-15, 7:25-26; 12:2-3, 30-31; 13:1-18; 16:21-22; 17:2-7; 18:10-11, 14; 23:17; 29:16-18)
-Farming (Exo. 23:10-11; 34:21; Lev. 19:9-10, 19, 23-25; 25:1-7; Num. 18:12-13; Deu. 11:18; 22:9-10; 23:24-25; 24:19-22; 25:4)
-Firstborn (Deu. 21:15-17)
-House (Deu. 6:4-9; 11:20; 22:8)
-Inheritance (Num. 36:7-9; Deu. 25:5-10)
-Injury (Exo. 21:12-36; Lev. 24:19-20)
-Justice and Mercy (Exo. 23:1-9; Lev. 19:15; Deu. 10:17-19; 21:22-23)
-King (Deu. 17:14-20)
-Marriage / Engagement (Deu. 22:13-30; 24:1-5)
-Mold (Lev. 13:47-59; 14:33-57)
-Nazirite (Num. 6:1-21)
-Parenting (Exo. 13:14; Deu. 6:4-9, 20-25; 11:19; 29:29)
-Property Protection and Restitution (Exo. 22:1-15; Num. 5:5-10; Deu. 19:14)
-Rebellious Son (Deu. 21:18-21)
-Sabbath (Exo. 23:10-13; 31:12-17; 34:21; 35:1-3; Lev. 23:3; Num. 15:32-36)
-Servants (Exo. 21:2-11; 23:12; Lev. 19:20-22; Deu. 15:12-18; 23:15-16)
-Sacrifices (Lev. 22:17-30)
-Sex (Lev. 18:1-30; 19:20-22, 29; 20:10-21; Deu. 27:20-23)
-Skin Disorders (Lev. 13:1-46; 14:1-32; Num. 5:1-3; Deu. 24:8-9)
-Social Behavior (Exo. 22:16-31; Lev. 19:12-14, 16, 32-36; Deu. 23:19-20, 24-25; 24:6-7, 10-18; 25:11-16; 27:18-19, 24-25)
-Ten Commandments and Enforcement (Lev. 20:9; 24:15-17, 19-22)
-Unfaithful Wife Test (Num. 5:11-31)
-Unsolved Murder (Deu. 21:1-9)
-Vows / Oaths (Num. 30:1-15; Deu. 6:13; 12:26-27; 23:8, 21-23)
-War (Deu. 20:1-20; 21:10-14; 24:5; 25:17-19)
-Witnesses (Deu. 19:15-21)
-Worship (Deu. 12:4-7)

Rather than specifically outline the *exact steps* for each of the scenarios—which would become quite lengthy—I decided to simply provide this list. An acting judge could simply consult this list when hearing a complaint. After reading the respective Bible passages, considering other factors and mitigating circumstances, the judge would provide the person with *steps* to resolve his complaint.

For example, if a judge heard a complaint about an animal, he would read the sections of the Law which discuss "animals." Then he would make a decision which would incorporate these basic principles.

And, if in another case, a judge was to hear about "mold" in a person's home, he would read sections of the Law which discuss "mold." (*See above.*) Since this scenario, and many others detailed above, require the action of priests, the judge could choose to send the person levying the complaint directly to the tabernacle to speak with a priest. Or if more appropriate, the judge could send a letter or go to the priest in person. Either way, however, it is clear the judges are intended to work along with the priests in providing spiritual instruction and practical support to God's people.

Of course, the priests and judges would need to develop a means of cooperation and mutual support. This is how the Law was designed.

For more information on "judges" see Phase #7 (page 239).

Blemish-Free Animals

As a planning consideration, *all* festival celebrations, sacrifices and offerings use "blemish-free" animals. Priests would need to verify in all cases that animals presented are blemish-free.

Conclusion

Well, I hope this Phase has done well in demonstrating the vital importance of tabernacle leadership. Indeed, we are left to wonder if many of the "temple" problems were a result of lack of leadership.

For example, during the Lord Jesus' earthly ministry, the temple officials erred by allowing for commerce to be conducted within the temple areas (Matt. 21:12-13). Perhaps, this was a result of leadership errors—where priests failed to properly schedule representatives to bring required sacrifices.

Of course, we cannot know for sure, but we know this is true: Organizations need good leaders. And, certainly the tabernacle is no exception.

Therefore, priests *must* develop and implement effective procedures for *everything* dealing with the tabernacle. Through detailed planning, priests ensure tabernacle operations continue without interruption. Nothing is left to chance. Everything is planned and carried out with diligence.

For this reason, the demeanor of the high priest and priests should be similar to Joseph and Daniel—leaders with aptitude for detailed administration of all things under their charge.

How to Keep the Law

Phase 4

Consecration

When complete with the leadership and management considerations discussed in Phase #3, the God-appointed leader can begin Phase #4—*consecrating the first generation of priests and Levites to serve at the tabernacle*.

Before any services can be offered at the tabernacle, consecration *must* be accomplished—according to the Law of Moses. So, to allow you to understand this process, I will provide notes on each step to prepare everything for tabernacle services.

Consecration of the High Priest, Priests & the Tabernacle
(Exodus 29:1-46 & Leviticus 8:1-36)

So, how does the consecration begin?

Remember at the beginning of the book when we discussed the importance of the "God-appointed leader?" Well, when it is time to consecrate the high priest, we see once again the vital role of the God-appointed leader. In fact, nothing can be accomplished if there is not such a leader who has been directed by God to fill this "Moses" role.

Why?

Well, in order for the man to become the high priest, someone in authority *must* appoint him. The Bible is clear in this—specifically stating that no one can take upon himself the authority of a priest, but he must be appointed by God (Heb. 5:1-4). Therefore, if you do not have the God-appointed leader it is impossible to reestablish the *legitimate* high priest. Keep this in mind as you view the steps of consecration for the high priest: The God-appointed leader is *required* to initiate the process of consecration *as God directs*.

So, exactly how does the God-appointed leader consecrate the high priest and the other priests?

Below I detail the process of consecration in a series of steps (according to Exo. 29:1-46 & Lev. 8:1-36). Then, to assist you in visualizing these steps, I include a series of illustrations—which "show" pertinent details for each step (such as location or other helpful diagrams).

So, let's get started . . .

Consecration Ceremony
Day 1

-**Step #1**: The God-appointed leader prepares unleavened, fine wheat flour bread (in loaves kneaded with oil and cakes spread with oil), and places them in a basket.

-**Step #2**: The God-appointed leader prepares anointing oil for the ceremony.
- Recipe batch includes (Exo. 30:22-33):
  (1) olive oil (one hin),
  (2) liquid myrrh (500 shekels),
  (3) cassia (500 shekels),
  (4) cinnamon (250 shekels),
  (5) calamus (250 shekels)

-**Step #3**: The God-appointed leader brings the bread basket, the anointing oil, a young bull (without defect) and two rams (without defect) to the *new* tent of meeting—the tabernacle—and sets them aside.
-[Note: *To fit with Exo. 29:23, it would be best for the God-appointed leader to place the bread basket upon the "bread table" within the tabernacle—until he retrieves it in Step #22 below. See diagram of detailing location of the "bread table" on page 49.*]

-**Step #4**: The God-appointed leader gathers all God's people at the tabernacle to view the ceremony and briefly addresses them before the next step (Lev. 8:4-5). [*Note: It is likely the people are gathered by sounding blasts on the trumpet, as explained on page 48.]

-**Step #5**: The God-appointed leader washes the high priest and his sons with water at the entrance to the *temporary* tent of meeting.
-[*Note that the high priest and his sons do not wash themselves. Rather, the God-appointed leader performs the activity—likely pouring water upon them, and perhaps washing their hands and feet. As unconsecrated, the high priest and his sons do not yet possess authority to wash themselves using the wash basin.*]

-**Step #6**: The God-appointed leader dresses the high priest.
-[*Note that the high priest does not dress himself—because as yet he does not possess authority to place any of these items upon himself. Therefore, the items are placed upon the high priest by the God-appointed leader. For more details on how the high priest is dressed in order, please see page 51 of this book.*]

-**Step #7**: The God-appointed leader anoints the tabernacle and its articles with the anointing oil, then sprinkles the altar table seven times, its utensils and the wash basin (Lev. 8:10-11). (In the LXX, the God-appointed leader sprinkles anointing oil on the altar table seven times and its utensils, then the wash basin, then the tabernacle and the articles within it.)

-**Step #8**: The God-appointed leader pours anointing oil on the head of the dressed high priest.

-**Step #9**: The God-appointed leader dresses the high priest's sons—who will become the "priests."
-[*Note that the high priest's sons do not dress themselves—because as yet they do not possess authority to place any of these items upon themselves. For more details on how the high priest's sons are dressed in order, please see page 50 of this book—which describes their garments as those of the "normal priests."*]

-**Step #10**: The God-appointed leader brings the bull to the entrance of the tent of meeting. Then he tells the high priest and his sons to place their hands upon its head.

-**Step #11**: The bull is slaughtered at the entrance to the tent of meeting by the God-appointed leader.

-**Step #12**: The God-appointed leader takes some of the bull's blood. With his finger, he puts blood on the horns of the altar table. The remaining blood is poured out at the base of the altar table.

-**Step #13**: The God-appointed leader removes the belly fat, liver and kidneys, and their fat, from the bull and places them upon the altar table. He burns them.

-**Step #14**: The God-appointed leader gathers the remaining flesh of the bull, including the hide, offal and dung. He transports them outside the camp—where they are burned as a "sin offering." (For more information on "sin offerings," see page 226.)
-[*Note: The high priest and his sons must remain at the entrance of the tent of meeting for the entire seven-day period—sleeping there as well (Lev. 8:35). They are not permitted to leave for any reason, so they cannot follow the God-appointed leader as he transports the bull carcass outside the camp.*]

-**Step #15**: The God-appointed leader brings the first ram to the entrance of the tent of meeting. Then he tells the high priest and his sons to place their hands upon its head.

-**Step #16**: This first ram is slaughtered at the entrance of the tent of meeting by the God-appointed leader.

-**Step #17**: The God-appointed leader takes some of the first ram's blood and sprinkles it on the altar table on all sides. [*Note: LXX says to "pour" it—which causes blood to be upon the altar table inside the rim for use in Step #22 below.]

-**Step #18**: The God-appointed leader butchers the first ram, cutting it into pieces and washing them as necessary. [*Note: The LXX says in Lev. 8:19 that it is butchered by separating the legs, head and fat, and that only the belly and feet of the animal are washed.] Then, he places these pieces upon the altar table. He burns the entire ram.

-**Step #19**: The God-appointed leader brings the second ram to the entrance of the tent of meeting. Then he tells the high priest and his sons to place their hands upon its head.

-**Step #20**: This second ram is slaughtered at the entrance of the tent of meeting.

-**Step #21**: The God-appointed leader takes some of the second ram's blood and puts it on the tips/lobes of their right ears, right thumb and right big toe of the high priest and his sons. [*Note: The LXX and KJV say "tips" of right ears, but some other translations favor "lobe."]

-**Step #22**: The God-appointed leader takes some of the blood from the altar table (from the first ram) and mixes it with some anointing oil. The God-appointed leader takes this blood-anointing oil mixture and sprinkles it on the high priest, his sons and all their garments. Then the remaining blood is poured out on all sides of the altar table. [***Note: Exo. 29:21 states this step is performed here—after the second's ram blood is placed upon the right ears, right thumbs and right big toes of the high priests and his sons, in Step #21 above. But Lev. 8:29-30 states this step is performed rather right before the remaining portions of the second ram are cooked and the high priest and his sons begin eating. In determining the best position for this step, perhaps it would be better to favor the Exodus account because Exodus contains the instructions delivered by God; whereas the Leviticus account is a report of what Moses actually did.]

-**Step #23**: The God-appointed leader butchers the second ram—removing the fat, rump (fat tail), belly fat, the liver, the kidneys and their fat, and the right thigh/shoulder. (The LXX says in Lev. 8:24 these butchered portions are the fat, rump, belly fat, liver and kidneys with their fat, and the right shoulder—which would denote the entire right leg.)

-**Step #24**: The God-appointed leader removes one bread loaf and one bread cake from the basket upon the "bread table" in the tabernacle.

-**Step #25**: The God-appointed leader places all the ram portions from Step #23 and the bread from Step #24 into the hands of the high priest and his sons. Then the high priest and his sons "lift up" these items—similar to how an item might be held up in the air as an act of reverence. In the Bible this is called a "wave offering," but this simply denotes "lifting up" an item—not jiggling it back and forth as "wave" in English tends to indicate. (For more information on "wave offerings," see page 236.)

-**Step #26**: The God-appointed leader takes these portions from the second ram and the bread from the hands of the high priest and his sons. Then the God-appointed leader burns the bread and second ram portions on the altar table—as *God's portion*. In other words, these portions from Step #22-24 are viewed as God's portion (see Lev. 21:6, 8, 17, 21-22; 22:25).

-**Step #27**: The God-appointed leader removes the breast and a shoulder from the second ram and lifts them up as a wave offering, for *the God-appointed leader's portion*.
   ****See Note of Step #22.*

-**Step #28**: The remaining portions of the second ram are cooked at the entrance to the tent of meeting—as the *portion of the high priest and his sons*. (The LXX says they are to be boiled.) Then, the God-appointed leader brings out the bread basket from the bread table. The God-appointed leader eats the breast portion from Step #27—as his own portion. And the high priest and his sons eat the rest of the second ram and the bread. Everything must be eaten at the entrance to the tent of meeting throughout that day and evening. No one else is permitted to eat it.

-**Step #29**: The following morning, all remaining ram meat and bread is burned. No one else is permitted to eat it.

<u>Tending the Altar Table Fire</u>

As needed, the God-appointed leader adds firewood to the altar table and rearranges pieces to keep the fire burning.

As necessary, during the Consecration Ceremony week, the God-appointed leader relocates ashes from altar table—placing them in a pile east of the altar table (Lev. 1:16). To dispose of the ash pile, the God-appointed leader, although differing from a priest, would need to somehow align to the general steps prescribed for ash-disposal by priests: (1) changing his clothes, putting on unspecified clothing—leaving behind his normal clothes, (2) God-appointed leader relocates the ashes to a ceremonially clean place outside the camp—most likely *near* the same location where he burns the carcass of the sin offering in Step#14 above, and (3) upon his return to the tabernacle area, the God-appointed leader changes his clothes, clothing himself again with his normal clothes (Lev. 6:10-11). Due to the high priest and priests being (as yet) unconsecrated, the God-appointed leader would bear responsibility for this task on their behalf.

The God-appointed leader leaves offerings smoldering on the altar table all night during every day of the Consecration Ceremony. The altar table fire is tended so it never goes out.

To assist you in visualizing the above 29 Steps of the Consecration Ceremony, I will now provide you with a series of illustrations detailing those same steps. This will help you to understand where each step takes place within the tabernacle area . . .

Consecration Ceremony
Step #1
Bread prepared and placed in basket

The God-appointed leader prepares unleavened, fine wheat flour bread (in loaves kneaded with oil and cakes spread with oil), and places them in a basket.

Consecration Ceremony
Step #2
Anointing oil prepared

The God-appointed leader prepares anointing oil for the ceremony.
- Anointing oil is made one batch at a time, when necessary (Exo. 30:22-33).
- Recipe includes:
    (1) olive oil (one hin),
    (2) liquid myrrh (500 shekels),
    (3) cassia (500 shekels),
    (4) cinnamon (250 shekels),
    (5) calamus (250 shekels)

Consecration Ceremony
Step #3
Bread basket, anointing oil, 1 bull and 2 rams brought to tabernacle

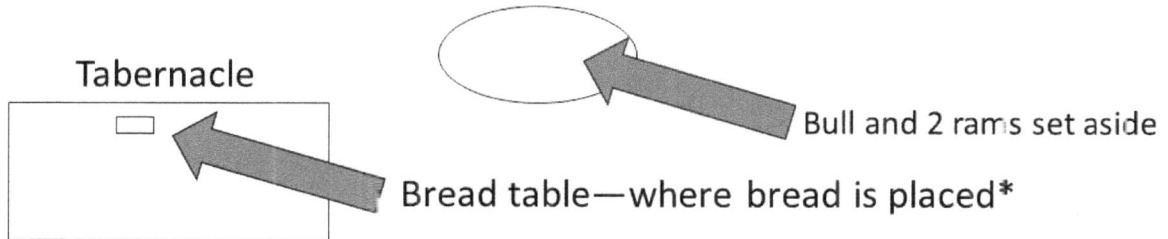

Tabernacle

Bull and 2 rams set aside

Bread table—where bread is placed*

*For detailed illustration of the tabernacle interior and the tabernacle courtyard, see pages 18 & 33.

    The God-appointed leader brings the bread basket, the anointing oil, a young bull (without defect) and two rams (without defect) to the *new* tent of meeting—the tabernacle—and sets them aside.
-[Note: *To fit with Exo. 29:23, it would be best for the God-appointed leader to place the bread basket upon the "bread table" within the tabernacle—until he retrieves it in Step #22 below. See diagram of detailing location of the "bread table" on page 40.*]

Consecration Ceremony
Step #4
People gathered by trumpet blasts

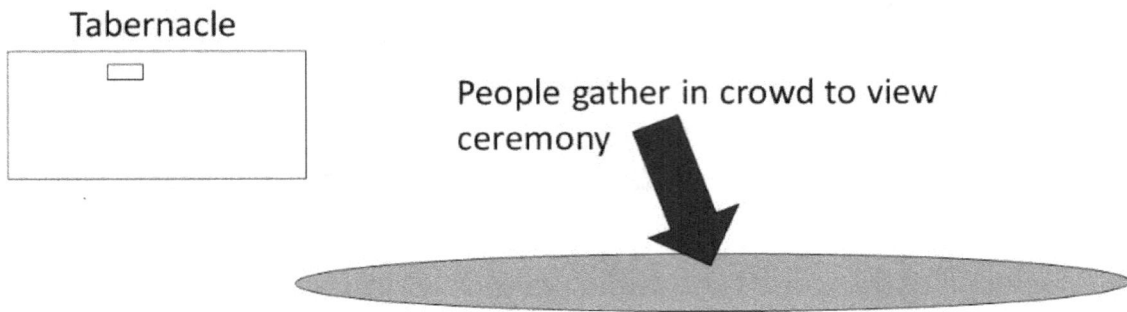

Tabernacle

People gather in crowd to view ceremony

The God-appointed leader gathers all God's people at the tabernacle to view the ceremony and briefly addresses them before the next step (Lev. 8:4-5). [*Note: It is likely the people are gathered by sounding blasts on the trumpet, as explained on page 48.]

Consecration Ceremony
Step #5
God-appointed leader washes the high priest and his sons at the wash basin

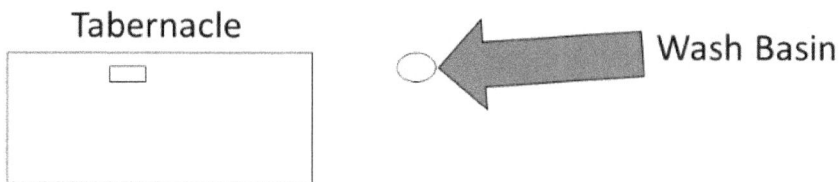

Tabernacle

Wash Basin

The God-appointed leader washes the high priest and his sons with water at the entrance to the *temporary* tent of meeting.

-[*Note that the high priest and his sons do not wash themselves. Rather, the God-appointed leader performs the activity—likely pouring water upon them, and perhaps washing their hands and feet. As unconsecrated, the high priest and his sons do not yet possess authority to wash themselves using the wash basin.*]

Consecration Ceremony
Step #6
God-appointed leader dresses the high priest

Tabernacle

High priest dressed at
tabernacle entrance

The God-appointed leader dresses the high priest.
-[*Note that the high priest does not dress himself—because as yet he does not possess authority to place any of these items upon himself. Therefore, the items are placed upon the high priest by the God-appointed leader. For more details on how the high priest is dressed in order, please see page 51 of this book.*]

Consecration Ceremony
Step #7
God-appointed leader uses anointing oil to anoint tabernacle, tabernacle articles and the altar table

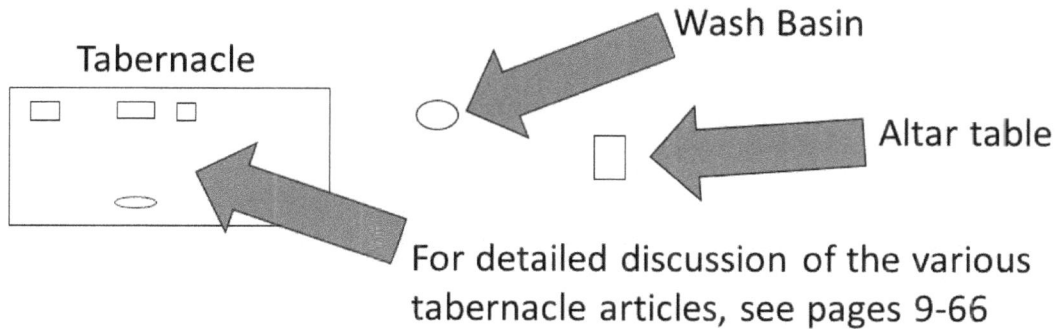

Tabernacle

Wash Basin

Altar table

For detailed discussion of the various tabernacle articles, see pages 9-66

The God-appointed leader anoints the tabernacle and its articles with the anointing oil, then sprinkles the altar table seven times, its utensils and the wash basin (Lev. 8:10-11). (In the LXX, the God-appointed leader sprinkles anointing oil on the altar table seven times and its utensils, then the wash basin, then the tabernacle and the articles within it.)

Consecration Ceremony
Step #8
God-appointed leader pours oil on high priest's head

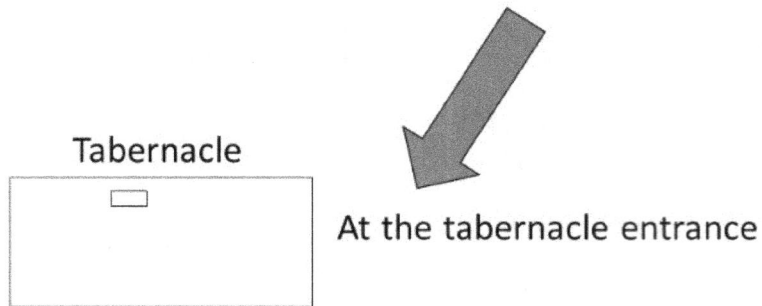

Tabernacle

At the tabernacle entrance

The God-appointed leader pours anointing oil on the head of the dressed high priest.

Consecration Ceremony
Step #9
God-appointed leader dresses the high priest's sons

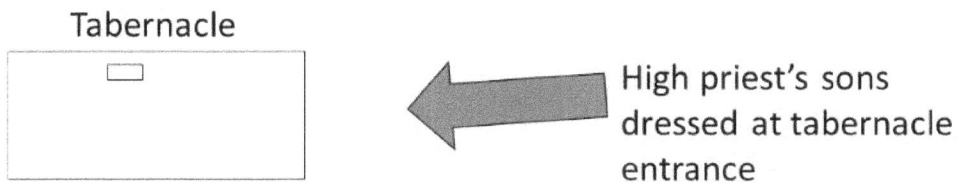

Tabernacle

High priest's sons dressed at tabernacle entrance

The God-appointed leader dresses the high priest's sons—who will become the "priests." -[*Note that the high priest's sons do not dress themselves—because as yet they do not possess authority to place any of these items upon themselves. For more details on how the high priest's sons are dressed in order, please see page 50 of this book—which describes their garments as those of the "normal priests."*]

Consecration Ceremony
Step #10
God-appointed leader brings the bull to the tabernacle entrance

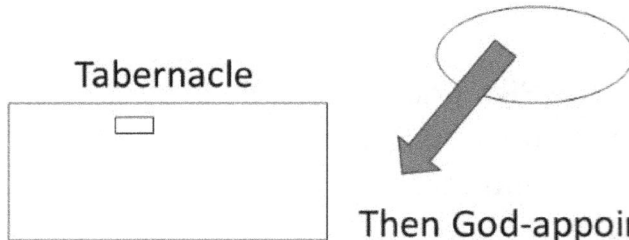

Tabernacle

Then God-appointed leader tells high priest and his sons to place their hands on the bull's head

The God-appointed leader brings the bull to the entrance of the tent of meeting. Then he tells the high priest and his sons to place their hands upon its head.

Consecration Ceremony
Step #11
God-appointed leader slaughters the bull

Tabernacle

At tabernacle entrance

The bull is slaughtered at the entrance to the tent of meeting by the God-appointed leader.

Consecration Ceremony
Step #12
God-appointed leader puts bull's blood on altar horns with his finger

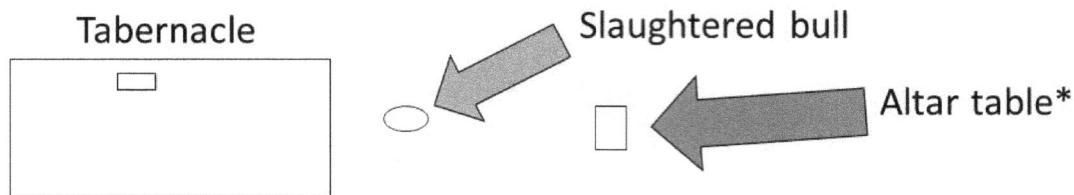

Tabernacle   Slaughtered bull

Altar table*

Remaining bull's blood is poured out at the base of the altar table.

*For a detailed illustration of the altar table, see page 20.

The God-appointed leader takes some of the bull's blood. With his finger, he puts blood on the horns of the altar table. The remaining blood is poured out at the base of the altar table.

Consecration Ceremony
Step #13
God-appointed butchers bull: Removing belly fat, liver and kidneys

Belly
Fat

Kidneys

Liver

The God-appointed leader removes the belly fat, liver and kidneys, and their fat, from the bull and places them upon the altar table. He burns them.

Consecration Ceremony
Step #14
God-appointed leader alone transports remaining bull carcass outside the camp to be burned

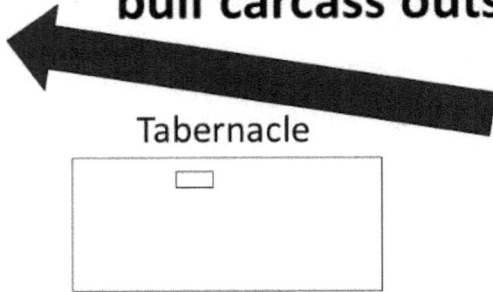

Tabernacle

The God-appointed leader gathers the remaining flesh of the bull, including the hide, offal and dung. He transports them outside the camp—where they are burned as a "sin offering." (For more information on "sin offerings," see page 226.)

-[Note: *The high priest and his sons must remain at the entrance of the tent of meeting for the entire seven-day period—sleeping there as well (Lev. 8:35). They are not permitted to leave for any reason, so they cannot follow the God-appointed leader as he transports the bull carcass outside the camp.*]

Consecration Ceremony
Step #15
God-appointed leader brings the first ram to the tabernacle entrance

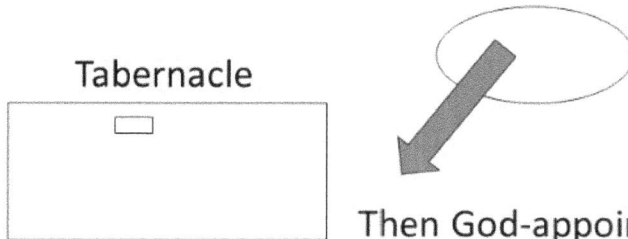

Tabernacle

Then God-appointed leader tells high priest and his sons to place their hands on the ram's head

The God-appointed leader brings the first ram to the entrance of the tent of meeting. Then he tells the high priest and his sons to place their hands upon its head.

Consecration Ceremony
Step #16
God-appointed leader slaughters the first ram

Tabernacle

At tabernacle entrance

This first ram is slaughtered at the entrance of the tent of meeting by the God-appointed leader.

Consecration Ceremony
Step #17
God-appointed leader sprinkles/pours the first ram's blood on the altar table

Tabernacle   Slaughtered ram

Altar table*

*For a detailed illustration of the altar table, see page 20.

    The God-appointed leader takes some of the first ram's blood and sprinkles it on the altar table on all sides. [*Note: LXX says to "pour" it—which causes blood to be upon the altar table inside the rim for use in Step #22 below.]

Consecration Ceremony
Step #18
God-appointed butchers the first ram: First washing the feet and belly, then separating the legs, head and fat. The pieces are placed on altar and burned.

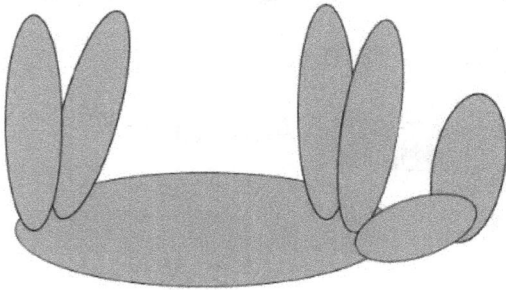

The God-appointed leader butchers the first ram, cutting it into pieces and washing them as necessary. [*Note: The LXX says in Lev. 8:19 that it is butchered by separating the legs, head and fat, and that only the belly and feet of the animal are washed.] Then, he places these pieces upon the altar table. He burns the entire ram.

Consecration Ceremony
Step #19
God-appointed leader brings the second ram to the tabernacle entrance

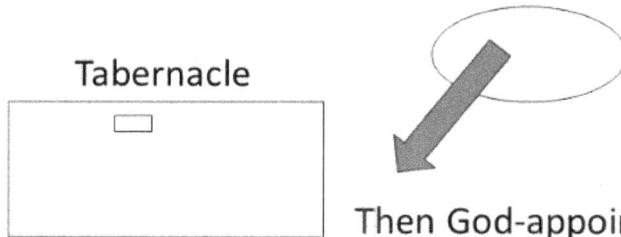

Tabernacle

Then God-appointed leader tells high priest and his sons to place their hands on the ram's head

The God-appointed leader brings the second ram to the entrance of the tent of meeting. Then he tells the high priest and his sons to place their hands upon its head.

Consecration Ceremony
Step #20
God-appointed leader slaughters the second ram

Tabernacle

At tabernacle entrance

This second ram is slaughtered at the entrance of the tent of meeting.

Consecration Ceremony
Step #21
God-appointed leader puts some of the second ram's blood on the high priest and his sons—ear lobes, right thumbs and big right toes

Tabernacle

At tabernacle entrance

The God-appointed leader takes some of the second ram's blood and puts it on the tips/lobes of their right ears, right thumb and right big toe of the high priest and his sons. [*Note: The LXX and KJV say "tips" of right ears, but some other translations favor "lobe."]

Consecration Ceremony
Step #22
God-appointed leader removes some of the first ram's blood from the altar table and mixes it with some anointing oil.

Tabernacle

Altar table

Then the God-appointed leader sprinkles the high priest and his sons and all their garments. Any remaining blood/oil mixture is poured out at the base of the altar table.

The God-appointed leader takes some of the blood from the altar table (from the first ram) and mixes it with some anointing oil. The God-appointed leader takes this blood-anointing oil mixture and sprinkles it on the high priest, his sons and all their garments. Then the remaining blood is poured out on all sides of the altar table. [***Note: Exo. 29:21 states this step is performed here—after the second's ram blood is placed upon the right ears, right thumbs and right big toes of the high priests and his sons, in Step #21 above. But Lev. 8:29-30 states this step is performed rather right before the remaining portions of the second ram are cooked and the high priest and his sons begin eating. In determining the best position for this step, perhaps it would be better to favor the Exodus account because Exodus contains the instructions delivered by God; whereas the Leviticus account is a report of what Moses actually did.]

Consecration Ceremony
Step #23
God-appointed butchers the second ram: Removing its fat, rump, belly fat, liver, kidneys and right shoulder.

The God-appointed leader butchers the second ram—removing the fat, rump (fat tail), belly fat, the liver, the kidneys and their fat, and the right thigh/shoulder. (The LXX says in Lev. 8:24 these butchered portions are the fat, rump, belly fat, liver and kidneys with their fat, and the right shoulder—which would denote the entire right leg.)

Consecration Ceremony
Step #24
God-appointed leader retrieves one bread loaf and one bread cake from the basket on the bread table

Tabernacle

Bread table—where bread basket
was placed earlier

*For detailed illustration of the tabernacle interior and the tabernacle courtyard, see pages 18 & 33.

The God-appointed leader removes one bread loaf and one bread cake from the basket upon the "bread table" in the tabernacle.

Consecration Ceremony
Step #25
God-appointed leader puts all the second ram pieces and the bread from Steps #23 & 24 in the hands of the high priest and his sons

Tabernacle

At tabernacle entrance

Then the God-appointed leader tells the high priest and his sons to "lift" up these items.

The God-appointed leader places all the ram portions from Step #23 and the bread from Step #24 into the hands of the high priest and his sons. Then the high priest and his sons "lift up" these items—similar to how an item might be held up in the air as an act of reverence. In the Bible this is called a "wave offering," but this simply denotes "lifting up" an item—not jiggling it back and forth as "wave" in English tends to indicate. (For more information on "wave offerings," see page 236.)

Consecration Ceremony
Step #26
God-appointed leader takes the second ram's pieces and the bread from the hands of the high priest and his sons

Tabernacle

Altar table

The God-appointed leader places these pieces from the second ram and the bread upon the altar table to be burned. This is viewed as God's portion.

The God-appointed leader takes these portions from the second ram and the bread from the hands of the high priest and his sons. Then the God-appointed leader burns the bread and second ram portions on the altar table—as *God's portion*. In other words, these portions from Step #22-24 are viewed as God's portion (see Lev. 21:6, 8, 17, 21-22; 22:25).

Consecration Ceremony
Step #27
God-appointed removes the breast and a shoulder/leg from the second ram. This is viewed as the God-appointed leader's portion.

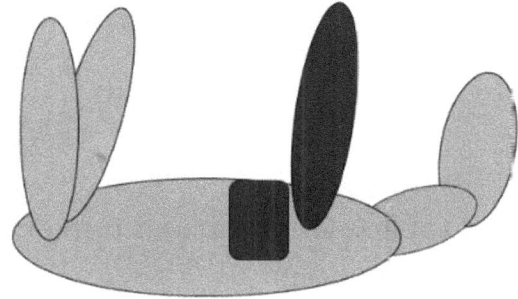

The God-appointed leader removes the breast and a shoulder from the second ram and lifts them up as a wave offering, for *the God-appointed leader's portion*.

*** *See Note of Step #22.*

Consecration Ceremony
Step #28

The rest of the second ram is boiled and eaten by the high priest and his sons at the tabernacle entrance along with the remaining bread. This is their portion.

Tabernacle

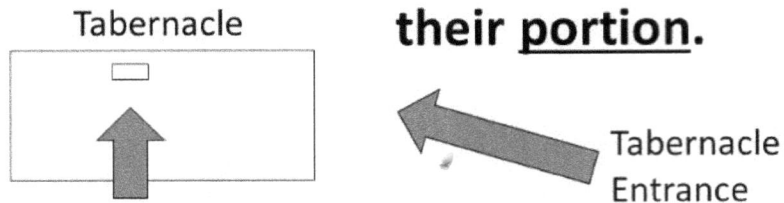

Bread table—where bread basket
was placed earlier

Tabernacle
Entrance

The remaining portions of the second ram are cooked at the entrance to the tent of meeting—as the *portion of the high priest and his sons*. (The LXX says they are to be boiled.) Then, the God-appointed leader brings out the bread basket from the bread table. The God-appointed leader eats the breast portion from Step #27—as his own portion. And the high priest and his sons eat the rest of the second ram and the bread. Everything must be eaten at the entrance to the tent of meeting throughout that day and evening. No one else is permitted to eat it.

Consecration Ceremony
Step #29
The following morning any remaining parts from the second ram and remaining bread is burned

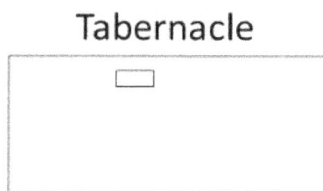

Tabernacle

The following morning, all remaining ram meat and bread is burned. No one else is permitted to eat it.

Tending the Altar Table Fire

As needed, the God-appointed leader adds firewood to the altar table and rearranges pieces to keep the fire burning.

As necessary, during the Consecration Ceremony week, the God-appointed leader relocates ashes from altar table—placing them in a pile east of the altar table (Lev. 1:16). As necessary, to dispose of the ash pile, the God-appointed leader, although differing from a priest, would need to somehow align to the general steps prescribed for ash-disposal by priests: (1) changing his clothes, putting on unspecified clothing—leaving behind his normal clothes, (2) God-appointed leader relocates the ashes to a ceremonially clean place outside the camp, and (3) upon his return to the tabernacle area, the God-appointed leader changes his clothes, clothing himself again with his normal clothes (Lev. 6:10-11). Due to the high priest and priests being (as yet) unconsecrated, the God-appointed leader would bear responsibility for this task on their behalf.

The God-appointed leader leaves offerings smoldering on the altar table all night.

Consecration Ceremony
Days 2-7

-Each day, repeat Steps #1-29 of Day 1 (Exo. 29:35-37).

-On Day 6, the God-appointed leader's last ceremonial action is sprinkling the Levites to be consecrated with the "water of cleansing" (see Step #4 of the Levite Consecration Ceremony on page 135). Therefore, the God-appointed leader will need to complete all activities on Day 6 to coordinate it with the steps of the Levite Consecration Ceremony.

-At the completion of Steps #1-29 on Day 7, the altar will be most holy and the high priest and his sons will be capable of performing services. Following the completion of the steps of the Consecration Ceremony on Day 7, the God-appointed leader completes the Levite Consecration Ceremony (Steps #5-6 on page 135).

Note: During the entire seven-day ordination process, the high priest and his sons must remain at the entrance to the tent of meeting. They are not permitted to leave the entrance for any reason whatsoever.

Replacing the High Priest

When the high priest is replaced, the new high priest to be anointed is to bring an offering on the day he is anointed (Lev. 6:20-21). The offering is one-tenth ephah fine flour, kneaded thoroughly, then prepared with oil on a griddle. Then the incoming high priest is to break it in pieces—offering half in the morning and the other half in the evening.

Unlike the other "grain offerings," where the priest could eat a portion (see page 217), this offering had to be burned completely. The priests were not authorized to eat any portion of the grain offering for the anointing of the new high priest (Lev. 6:22-23).

In Num. 20:25-29, Moses simply removes the high priest's clothing from Aaron and places it upon his son, Eleazar, who would succeed him. And, in doing so, Eleazar became the new high priest.

So, what is the implication?

Well, perhaps, because Eleazar was previously consecrated by this elaborate Consecration Ceremony, he didn't need an *additional* consecration. Rather, the God-appointed leader—Moses—merely placed the clothing of the high priest upon him and Eleazar immediately became the new high priest.

What do you think is the most "proper" way to install a new high priest? Should the new high priest be required to perform all the above steps of the Consecration Ceremony? Or, do you think Moses' actions in Num. 20:25-29 set precedent for new high priest installation through a simple removal and placement of clothing?

If it is the latter, perhaps the simple bringing of the grain offering and the simple transfer of clothing serve to impart humility to the incoming high priest. Just as the Lord Jesus is the Bread of Life, so also the new high priest approaches—bearing nothing but a simple loaf of bread, which he breaks and offers: A fitting picture of both the old and new high priests—who are offered in turn in the morning and the evening.

Who Actually Slaughtered the Animals?

When viewing the above steps in the Consecration Ceremony, we see a major trend. Being yet unconsecrated, the high priest and other priest relied on Moses to perform *everything* for them. Being yet unconsecrated, the high priest and priest were not even permitted to wash or clothe themselves—rather they relied on Moses to do so *for them*.

Why does this matter?

Well, it is demonstrating to us the importance of consecration. Without consecration, a man could not take upon himself the honors of the priesthood.

And, this principle extends well beyond the Consecration Ceremony itself—into all the other calendar events, festivals and offerings. Those who were not consecrated were not permitted to do the things of the priesthood. Only the priests—who were consecrated—could do those things required for their atonement.

Reflect on this.

Therefore, when considering who slaughters the sacrificial animals, the most straightforward answer is the Law of Moses placed this responsibility upon the priests—who were consecrated to move about the tabernacle area freely. Therefore, it is most likely within the parameters of the Law of Moses that only priests were intended to slaughter and butcher sacrificial animals on behalf of the people.

I explain this because there is some confusion in regard to some of the other offerings and whether or not normal (that is unconsecrated) people were required to slaughter their own sacrificial animals. The standard answer is "no"—they would bring the animals to the priests and lay their hands on the animals' heads as instructed, when necessary. But the priests would slaughter the animals—just as Moses slaughtered the animals on behalf of the high priest and his sons before they were consecrated.

Beyond this, it might be permissible in the case of freewill offerings or fellowship offerings—and certainly the Law does not prohibit people from slaughtering their own animals in those cases. But, in the case of the calendar events, festivals, guilt offerings, sin offerings and burnt offerings, the precedent established here in the Consecration Ceremony is for the unconsecrated person to stand passively as atonement is wrought on his behalf.

Get it?

After all, permitting unconsecrated people to perform slaughtering could have a disastrous outcome— for which the priest who permits it is unprepared.

For example, let's say the priest permits a person to slaughter his own animal, and he chooses to do so with some unusual cruelty. Or, imagine the person is unskilled, resulting in their own injury. Remember, priests *bore responsibility* for guarding the sanctity of the tabernacle area—even sleeping in shifts to ensure those holy things were never compromised in any way. Therefore, do you imagine it reasonable that such a skilled priest would freely permit visitors to perform his holy rites for which he has been entrusted to carry out with precision before God?

Thus, you could conclude—most reasonably—that common, unconsecrated people do not slaughter their own sacrificial animals. Nor would they be required to do so. Atonement was a function performed by a priest *for* the people. It was not a function priests demanded normal people to do *for themselves*.

Why Priests Wash and Clothe Themselves Before the People

In the above steps for the Consecration Ceremony, you may have noticed how the priests are washed and dressed before the people. Moreover, in many ceremonies, events and offerings priests would routinely wash themselves—and even dress themselves—before the assembled people.

Of course, we know this was done with modesty—shielding nakedness. But barring immodesty, it was important for the people to see the priests carrying out these steps of personal cleansing.

Why?

Well, the priests served in roles where they provided atonement for the people. And, a prerequisite for atonement is honesty about one's sin and confession. So, to lead people in such a religious venture, the priests needed to *set the example*.

Priests were not expected to strut about—as if perfected, untouchable beings. Rather, they were to show forth their humanity—demonstrating they too required cleansing. Rather than shying away from their uncleanliness, or hiding away from the assembly to rid themselves of it, the washing and clothing of the priests allowed the people to see a picture of the importance of grappling with one's own sin—choosing to confess it and thus break its power.

So, the thought would be: Since this priest was courageous enough to put himself and his body on display, then all the people in the crowd should be likewise willing to come forward to confess to his own faults. And, in this way, he who is clean can help others to become clean as well (John 13:3-15).

Levite Consecration Ceremony
On Day 7—After the "Consecration Ceremony"

Simply stated, in order to transport the tabernacle articles, the curtains and the posts and frames, there needed to be people who were consecrated for the task.

So, who were the people who were assigned these tasks?

The Levites.

And, within the tribe of the Levites, there were three divisions (Kohathites, Gershonites and Merarites). Each group was assigned a specific task in carrying the tabernacle articles, curtains and posts. After all, whenever it was time for the tabernacle to move, the movers were not given authorization to move *whatever*. Instead the process of transporting the tabernacle was an *orderly* process. (*If you would like to see detailed diagrams showing how the tabernacle was moved, see page 57.*)

Since the Levites were called as tabernacle servants, they were required to go through a process which made them holy for their occupation. This process included the following steps . . .

<u>Levite Consecration Ceremony (Num. 3:5-51; 8:5-22)</u>

-[*Note: After the final step of the Consecration Ceremony on Day 7—when the consecration of the high priest, priests and tabernacle is complete—the Levite Consecration Ceremony is conducted (Steps #5-6 below). But leading up to the Levite Consecration Ceremony, (Steps #1-3 below) are completed <u>weeks in advance</u>. Then Step #4 below is completed the <u>day prior</u> to the ceremony day.*]

-[*Note: Steps #1-3 below are completed **<u>weeks in advance</u>**.*]

-**Step #1**: God-appointed leader conducts a census of all the first-born males among God's people—one-month old or older.

-**Step #2**: God-appointed leader conducts a census of the Levite tribe to record total numbers of the clans of the Kohathites, Gershonites and Merarites.

-**Step #3**: The two numbers are compared (from Step #1 and Step #2). If there are more Levites than the first-born males, then collect a five-shekel tax for each Levite that exceeds the population of the first-born males. [*Note: *What is the purpose of this "five-shekel tax?" Simply stated, to financially support the tabernacle employees, there would need to be sufficient revenue from God's people. Therefore, if there were too many Levites, then the Law of Moses ensured adequate finances were received at the beginning to cover the additional employees. So, by levying an initial tax from God's people this ensured the additional Levites would be provided for from the tabernacle treasury in the case of later lack of funding. This measure was important because without adequate funding, the priests and Levites would have felt pressured to abandon their tabernacle responsibilities—as illustrated in Neh. 13:10-13. This tax further illustrates the vital importance of tabernacle oversight prior to the establishment of the tabernacle—as discussed in detail in Phase #3 of this book.*]

-[*Note: Step #4 below is completed **<u>one day before the ceremony day</u>**.*]

-**Step #4**: <u>On the day before the ceremony</u>, the God-appointed leader sprinkles "the water of cleansing" on the Levites to be consecrated. Then the God-appointed leader tells them to shave their whole bodies and wash their clothes (Num. 8:5-22). [*-Note: By using the water of cleansing, the God-appointed leader <u>makes himself unclean until evening</u> and must go into seclusion (Num. 19:21). Likewise, by having the water of cleansing sprinkled on them, the Levites to be consecrated <u>are made unclean until evening</u>. For this reason, the God-appointed leader must ensure all his required ceremonial activities are complete before he takes the "water of cleansing" in hand. In other words, the <u>last</u> activity performed by the God-appointed leader on this day will be sprinkling the Levites. (Perhaps, in making himself unclean in this way, it serves as a reminder to the God-appointed leader to spur him to prayer for the Levites during his seclusion throughout the day.) For more information on the "water of cleansing," see page 80.*]

-[Note: *Steps #5-6 below are completed **on the ceremony day**.*]

-**Step #5**: Levites to be consecrated bring two bulls and a grain offering of fine flour mixed with oil to the tabernacle entrance (Num. 8:5-22). The bulls and grain offering are set aside. (The LXX says the bulls must be one year old.)

*-[Note: *Although unstated, it is likely the grain offering here is sixth-tenths ephah total—following the proportions common elsewhere—where each bull is typically matched with three-tenths ephah (Num. 15:9; 28:12; 29:3).*]

-**Step #6**: Ceremony is conducted (Num. 8:5-22) . . .

-(A) The God-appointed leader uses the trumpets to gather the entire assembly. (For more information on the trumpets, see page 48.)

-(B) The God-appointed leader calls the assembly of God's people to the tabernacle entrance and tells them to place their hands on the heads of the Levites to be consecrated. (Most likely, the Levites kneel.) The LXX specifies only the males of God's people lay their hands on their heads.

-(C) The high priest makes these Levites a "wave offering." The LXX says the Levites to be consecrated are made a "gift" to the Lord.

[*Note*: *On page 236, I explain the activity involved in a wave offering is "lifting up" the thing which is offered. So how would the high priest do this? Simple: If the Levites kneel in (B) above as God's people lay their hands upon them, then the high priest would make the Levites a wave offering by approaching them and "lifting" them up—helping them to their feet. This is why it is important to understand what is simply meant by "wave"—which is to "lift." It would be incorrect to suppose the high priest had to hold the Levites over his head to jiggle them back and forth—as the English word "wave" implies. So, all the high priest does in this step is approach the kneeling Levites and help them to their feet. Make sense?*]

-(D) The God-appointed leader could simply read Num. 3:7-13 and Num. 4:1-33. In these passages, the justification and duties of the Kohathites, Gershonites and Merarites are explained to the assembled people.

-(E) The Levites to be consecrated lay their hands on the heads of the bulls.

-(F) The high priest accepts the Levites to be consecrated by performing sacrifices with the bulls: one a sin offering and the other a burnt offering (Num. 8:21). After the completion of this final step, the Levites to be consecrated are permitted to carry out their duties under the supervision of the priests (Num. 8:22). For specific "burnt offering" and "sin offering" procedures, see pages 207 & 230, respectively.

Required Gifts from the Leaders of God's People: Day 7-18
(Num. 7:1-88)

After the above ceremonial week (Day 1-7), one tribal leader from God's people is to bring gifts for the altar *each day* (Num. 7:11). The first gift occurs <u>at the completion of the Levite Consecration Ceremony steps on Day 7</u>.

This order is necessary because in order for the tribal leaders to present the carts and oxen to the Levites, the Levites must be consecrated. And, before the Levites can be consecrated, the high priests, priests and tabernacle articles must be consecrated. Thus, following the completion of *both* the consecration ceremonies on Day 7, the tribal leaders begin bringing their required gifts. Make sense?

On **Day 7**, the tribal leaders from God's people bring forth the six carts and twelve oxen for service by the Levites (Num. 7:1-3). The newly consecrated Levites receive the six carts and twelve oxen. And, the leader from Judah brings his gifts to the high priest (Num. 7:12).

On **Day 8**, the Issachar leader brings his gifts (Num. 7:18).

On **Day 9**, the Zebulun leader brings his gifts (Num. 7:24).

On **Day 10**, the Reuben leader brings his gifts (Num. 7:30).

On **Day 11**, the Simeon leader brings his gifts (Num. 7:36).

On **Day 12**, the Gad leader brings his gifts (Num. 7:42).

On **Day 13**, the Ephraim leader brings his gifts (Num. 7:48).

On **Day 14**, the Manasseh leader brings his gifts (Num. 7:54).

On **Day 15**, the Benjamin leader brings his gifts (Num. 7:60).

On **Day 16**, the Dan leader brings his gifts (Num. 7:66).

On **Day 17**, the Asher leader brings his gifts (Num. 7:72).

On **Day 18**, the Naphtali leader brings his gifts (Num. 7:78).

On each day gifts are received and the newly consecrated high priest and priests perform the sacrifices.

So, what is each leader <u>required</u> to bring?

Each leader is responsible to bring *exactly* what is listed below:

- 1 bull
- 2 oxen*
- 6 rams
- 6 male goats
- 6 one-year-old male lambs
- 1 silver plate, weighing 130 shekels, with fine flour & olive oil upon it
- 1 silver bowl, weighing 70 shekels, with fine flour & olive oil in it
- 1 gold dish, weighing 10 shekels, with <u>frankincense</u> upon it**
- 1.08 hin wine to accompany the burnt offerings (Num 7:87)
- Six-tenths ephah flour to accompany the burnt offerings (Num 7:87)

*-[Note: *In the above, two oxen are listed. These are not the oxen presented to pull the carts of the Levites. Rather, the oxen listed here are to be used in fellowship offerings—as stated in Num. 7. So, on Day 7 above, the representative from the tribe of Judah would bring two oxen with him for offerings. These two oxen are in addition to the oxen presented to pull the carts.*]

**-[Note: *Concerning the incense, remember no one is permitted to make the prescribed sacred formula—except the God-appointed leader and the priests (Exo. 30:9; Num. 16:40). Therefore, it should be understood that a representative from God's people is bringing <u>only frankincense</u>—as described in the "grain offering" procedures on pages 217. (Since the representatives only bring frankincense, it is placed <u>on the altar table with the grain offering</u>—as detailed in the grain offering procedures. The priests <u>cannot place frankincense on the incense altar</u> because only sacred incense is authorized.*]

The high priest and priests then perform offerings with the above gifts <u>on each day</u> when they are received, as follows . . .

-<u>Grain offering</u>: Consisting of all the flour on the silver plate and bowl. (See page 217 for procedures.)
-<u>Burnt offering</u>: Consisting of one bull, ram, lamb, 1.08 hin wine, six-tenths ephah flour. (See page 207.)
-<u>Sin offering</u>: Consisting of one goat. (See page 230 for procedures.)
-<u>Fellowship offering</u>***: Consisting of two oxen, five rams, five goats, five lambs. (See page 212.)

***-[Note: *When following the "fellowship offering" procedures for the above daily offerings, omit the steps which detail accompanying flour offerings and drink offerings—which typically go with an animal offered as a "fellowship offering." During each of these daily offerings, the representatives from each tribe <u>omit</u> the flour offering and drink offering normally associated with the fellowship offerings.*]

Day 19 and Every Day Thereafter (Exo. 29:38-42)

Following the above Consecration Ceremony, Levite Consecration Ceremony and gift presentations on Day 1-18, the high priest would implement the Ceremonial Calendar, discussed in Phase #5. This calendar involves morning and evening offerings, sabbath offerings, new moon offerings, in addition to the festivals. (For more information on the calendar, see pages 153-204.)

Consecration of God's People (Exodus 19:10-15)

Although God's people are not permitted within the tabernacle itself, the Law of Moses shows it is necessary for people in the vicinity to be consecrated.

So, how should the community of God's people be consecrated?

When planning to be in the vicinity of God's presence—whether upon Mount Sinai or the tabernacle, God's people should take action to prepare themselves, *beginning two days prior to an event.*
In Exo. 19:10-15, it says the people should begin consecrating themselves two days prior to being within God's presence . . .

First, they abstain from sexual relations for two days prior to the event and during the day of the event.

Second, they wash their bodies for two days prior to the event.

Third, they wash their clothes for two days prior to the event.

And, when the third day arrives, God's people are prepared—having focused on cleansing themselves for two days.

Last, on the third day, the God-appointed leader fixes limits and instructs God's people where they cannot cross. As Exo. 19:13 explains, once God's presence withdraws from a location, the limits should be removed—and then the people can move about in that location freely. This fits well with the concept of the tabernacle. Once God's presence in the pillar and cloud departed from a region, and once the tabernacle articles left and followed, the people would be free to move in the location where the tabernacle was located.
In other words, a physical location was not intended to be perpetually sacred or restricted. It is God's presence which is holy—not the mountain or the location itself. [*-Note: *This has implications for the foreign idea that the worship of God is dependent on a specific location anywhere. In fact, the tabernacle was designed to be set up wherever the Lord directed. It is God's presence which is holy—not a particular location. By understanding this a person becomes capable of removing himself from teachings which are foreign to the Law of Moses. The Law does not demand a specific location. Rather, the location of the tabernacle could be anywhere as the Lord directs.*]

Make sense?

Concerning the consecration of God's people in preparation to be in God's presence . . .

Any individual who has not properly prepared himself following the above steps should remain away from the assembly on the appointed day—similar to a person who is ceremonially unclean.

Consecration of the God-Appointed Leader

Now, in reading the extensive measures taken to consecrate the high priest and his sons, you may be wondering what steps are necessary for the *God-appointed leader* to be consecrate himself.

Well, looking to Moses as the example of the "God-appointed leader," we see he is consecrated by his close contact with God.

First, the God-appointed leader is consecrated by removing his sandals. In Exo. 3:5, Moses was required to take off his sandals when in the presence of God. And, beyond this, during his many meetings with God, it is said Moses met with the Lord face-to-face.

Second, the God-appointed leader is consecrated by God's presence. The effect of these face-to-face meetings were significant. The Bible tells us that Moses' face would shine as a result of being in God's presence (Exo. 34:33-35). Moreover, although the high priest and all others needed to shield themselves at all times from the ark—even approaching on the Day of Atonement veiled by incense smoke, God called Moses to the most holy place before the ark frequently (Exo. 25:22; Num. 7:89).

On page 37, I note how the high priest himself was restricted from viewing the ark—even when preparing it for transport, using the shielding curtain to block his vision as he approached and backed away from it. But Moses had no such restrictions.

Note especially the reversal of Moses' connection with those around him. Rather than being veiled before God, Moses was bare before Him. And, over time, Moses began to relate more closely to God—choosing rather to veil himself before other humans, while removing his veil when before God (Exo. 34:33-35). Incredibly, Moses became more comfortable with God than he was with his fellow men.

Third, as explained in my discussion of the lampstand on page 42, we know the lamps are designed to project their holy light forward. And, when we consider that the lampstand contains 22 bowls which reflect light forward—entirely bathing the most holy curtain with golden light, Moses would have been cleansed as the light searched him from every angle during his steps closer to the most holy place. And, once stepping through the veil before the ark, Moses' eyes would adjust to the change in lighting—turning his attention inward upon the true condition of his spirit.

Fourth, in Exo. 33:18-34:8, God causes His presence to pass before Moses. Perhaps this event has an effect of "consecration" upon Moses.

So, what does it mean when it says God's glory passed before Moses?

Well, in the verses above we see it is not a personal, "face to face" type of appearance as seen elsewhere when Moses would speak to the Lord face-to-face before the ark. Rather, the "glory" of Exo. 33:18 might be best understood as an effect of the Holy Spirit—as He localized His power before Moses. In other words, God gave Moses a glimpse of His intense ability to control the Earth's environment—similar to the parting of the Red Sea and the plagues in Egypt.

Fifth, and last, it might be best to consider that Moses *did* have a consecration ceremony upon Mount Sinai.

After all, Moses was upon the mount for forty days with the Lord (Exo. 34:28). And, more interestingly, we know that when Moses was upon the mount, the Lord showed him the Heavenly tabernacle (Exo. 25:40; Heb. 8:5). Therefore, it would be reasonable to conclude the Lord consecrated Moses within the Heavenly tabernacle, somewhat similar to how Aaron and his sons were consecrated.

Cool, huh?

Of course, we cannot know for sure, but it would definitely provide a basis for Moses' long stay on Sinai—as the Lord performed a consecration ceremony on his behalf.

Is there more support for this view?

Perhaps . . .

In Matt. 17:1-8 & Mark 9:2-8, we read about the transfiguration of the Lord Jesus. During this event—upon a high mountain—Moses and Elijah appear, speaking with the Lord Jesus. Remarkably, this is not the first meeting between the Lord and Moses upon a mountain. Rather, this transfiguration follows that same pattern established on Sinai—when the Lord appeared to Moses: Whereas upon Sinai, the Father sent forth the Son to meet with Moses; now the Father sends forth Moses to meet with the Son.

Get it?

In other words, the Lord provides consecration for His prophet, Moses, within the Heavenly tabernacle and by special interaction—placing upon him a call to specific activity and empowering him with His Holy Spirit.

When you understand this, the office of the prophet makes sense. Whereas the priests were those ordained for Earthly ministry, through consecration in the Earthly tabernacle; a prophet is a person who is transcendent to those restrictions. The prophets had authority because they followed after the order established by Moses. And, when the Lord places His Spirit upon a prophet, He grants the prophet transcendent authority to direct even the high priest and priests.

This system of priests and prophets provide a mutually-supportive system to accomplish God's work on the Earth. Without the prophet, the first group of priests cannot be consecrated. As the tabernacle system continues in its operation, the arrival of future prophets is intended by the Law to provide insights and guidance to the priesthood (Deu. 18:18). Without prophets, the tabernacle would quickly degrade and the focus of the priesthood would become detached from the people. Thus, prophets serve in a vital role—preventing tabernacle priests from degrading into an echo chamber, elitist society. Therefore, Moses told the priests and people to always expect the Lord's prophet—in every generation—arriving to provide instruction and demanding obedience (Deu. 18:18)

In some generations, as seen in the book of Judges, the prophet sent forth was called a "judge." And, in other cases, the prophet could be called "king"—as in the case of David. But the Lord was ever faithful to send forth people to serve within the prophetic office of Moses—leading through transcendence.

Although some prophets were also priests, the full unification of the two offices awaited Christ. The Lord Jesus is sent forth from the Father as the angel (that is "messenger") of the Lord—serving as the ultimate fulfillment of Deu. 18:18. And, the book of Hebrews details how the Christ also serves as the High Priest within the Heavenly tabernacle, offering His blood once for the sins of the world (Heb. 9:11-12).

<u>Importance of the God-Appointed Leader</u>

Consider carefully the many activities of the God-appointed leader in the Consecration Ceremony (page 97). Notice throughout the steps the God-appointed leader is the one *performing the steps.*

Why?

Well, the high priest's lack of consecration precludes him from doing the steps. The high priest must await the completion of the entire ceremony before he is consecrated—and thus capable of serving near the tabernacle. So, the God-appointed leader acts under God's authority to initiate and complete all these steps, while the man who is selected to serve as high priest and his sons *stand passively.* The high priest and his sons stand passively—as the God-appointed leader washes, dresses and anoints them.

The only action required by the high priest and his sons is <u>obedience</u>. In Steps #10, 15 and 19 of the Consecration Ceremony, the God-appointed leader commands the high priest and his sons to place their hands upon the head of each of the animals to be slaughtered—the bull and the two rams. Then in Step #25, the God-appointed leader commands the high priest and his sons to hold out their hands to receive the portions of ram and bread he places in their hands. Then he tells them to lift them up as a wave offering to the Lord.

This entire ceremony is a powerful picture of the activity of God on behalf of His people. The God-appointed leader signifies the *transcendent* activity of God Himself—as He prepares and accomplishes activity while we stand passively in simple obedience. No one can consecrate himself. Rather, consecration is received by the activity of God.

And, while in the process of consecration, the one to be consecrated must allow God to wash him, to place portions in his hands to be lifted up in thanksgiving. And, he must be willing to place his hands in obedience upon the animal which purchases his atonement.

In all this, the one to be consecrated watches as the God-appointed leader *strives*—physically struggling through the tasks of slaughtering and butchering, and moving various items. This is a powerful picture of the strivings of Christ—as He moved with incredible effort to offer Himself for our atonement. And, as Christ moves for us, we can only stand passively—in reverence, humility and reflection—as He accomplishes for our consecration what we cannot do on our own.

So, how would the high priest and his sons *feel*?

Perhaps they would feel similar to Peter, who was aghast at the Lord's insistence to wash his feet. Surely Peter thought he could wash himself. And, nothing is more humbling than to be denied the right to care for our own bodies in that intimate way. Yet, the Lord shows only He can ceremonially cleanse to prepare a person for a life of consecration. Therefore, anyone to be cleansed by the Lord must be capable of standing passive—receiving the simple kindness extended by God as He washes us.

The high priest and his sons may have felt guilt as they watch the God-appointed leader striving, sweating and straining as he slaughters, butchers and moves the heavy portions of the sacrificial animals. They might have felt compelled to offer assistance. Yet, they cannot. The act of consecrating an individual is one performed by God—and this ceremony illustrates this fact. Despite feeling compelled to offer assistance, no one lacking initial consecration is able to participate in the actions necessary for their own consecration.

Thus, the high priest and his sons are humbled—having to witness the physical strivings necessary for their own establishment under God's authority.

Thus, when viewing Christ upon the cross, purchasing salvation to the one who believes—one is left to simply view in humble reflection the physical strivings necessary for their own consecration. One cannot add to it. But in its completion, Christ commands us to simply hold out our hands to receive the flesh and bread which has been provided by great effort for us. And we are commanded to lift it up in reverent thankfulness—having received a portion completely given in grace.

As a sign of our new relationship with the Lord, He graciously provides within our hands a large portion—capable of sustaining us. And, the day ends as we enjoy fellowship in His presence—eating with Him—being filled physically and spiritually.

<u>Remaining at the Entrance for Seven Days & The Development of Empathy</u>

In Lev. 8:35, it states the high priest and his sons are to remain at the entrance to the tent of meeting for the entire seven-day period of the Consecration Ceremony.

They are not permitted to leave the entrance *for any reason* whatsoever.

So, why is this a requirement?

Well, I have some reflections to share . . .

First, being required to remain in this specific location would have allowed the minds of the high priest and his sons to be completely immersed in the events of their consecration. In other words, this would have prevented them from being distracted by anything. Therefore, their minds would have been fully captured by their calling.

When Christ prepared to go to the cross, He looked to His calling with a focused mind. Even when asked questions during the days leading up to His crucifixion, Christ shows His mind was honed in upon the accomplishment of the mission given to Him by the Father (John 12:20-36).

Second, within the activities of their consecration, the high priest and his sons would be reminded of their basic physical nature as humans. This is significant and cannot be understated.

During the seven days, they would need to sleep. And, they would sleep at the entrance to the tent of meeting.

They would need to eat, and they would eat at the entrance to the tent of meeting.

They would need to wash, and they would wash and be re-dressed at the entrance to the tent of meeting.

And, perhaps a point from which you may retract, they would need to relieve themselves—and they would need to do so discreetly at the tent of meeting, likely in a pot which would be carried outside the camp by the God-appointed leader.

Of course, one could reject such thoughts as improper or embarrassing. But if the reader instead carefully considers what is happening within this requirement, there is a beautiful picture of faith to be found within it. At times in life one can be so humbled that they are reduced to mere physical existence. And priests were called to have an intimate connection to the physical humanity of their people. After all, they would need to be accustomed and comfortable with things which were abhorrent to others (Lev. 14:1-32). In fact, priests were called to cleanse lepers, so if they were not comfortable with their own humanity—capable of operating past their own intimate embarrassment—how could they ever muster compassion in the midst of the gruesome physical conditions which afflicted some of God's people?

So, if your mind is incapable of understanding, seek wisdom. If your heart recoils at such thoughts, allow yourself to move out of those thoughts which hold your mind captive. Understand the basic human condition. See for yourselves the physical maladies encountered by countless humans. Learn compassion. Then you will see the power contained within intimate care for the body of your fellow man. The God-appointed leader is foremost a "shepherd," and thus he begins by "shepherding" the high priest and priests—waiting on them in compassion (John 13:3-17).

You must understand this. Priests were called to be used in God's service to heal and to offer compassion—serving as conduits for God's power. So, they needed to be accustomed to blood and other base aspects of physical existence. And, in the midst of such situations they needed to master things from which others would recoil.

On the first day, it might be possible that the men would not understand the purpose of laying their hands upon the heads of the three animals to be slaughtered. But as the week moved forward, and as these men were commanded to place their hands upon the heads of the animals—animal after animal—they would find a transformation occurring within their hearts. Whereas on the first day, they would have been detached from the animals; in the following days they would have developed a *connection* to the sacrificial animals themselves. They would find themselves being drawn into the eyes of each animal—thinking of it in compassion, recognizing in their base physical form there is nothing which separates them from the animals being sacrificed. Both they and the animals were brought and remained at the entrance at the direction of the God-appointed leader. Both they and the animals had the same physical needs which were attended by the God-appointed leader. Yet they were *spared continually*; while the animals *perished*.

Do you understand?

Please tell me you understand.

Dear friend, you must understand.

A faithful person must develop such a view of God—as continually saving, moment after moment, setting in motion events to help him.

Moreover, by the God-appointed leader providing and attending to all the basic physical necessities of the high priest and his sons, it offered them a powerful picture of faith. One must not be embarrassed before God—realizing that He sees and knows everything about our basic human form. Before God all are naked and bare—being incapable of pretending to be something we are not. And, God attends to us in our most basic physical form—helping us as we truly are, in sincerity.

The requirement for the high priest and priests to remain at the tabernacle so deprived their minds of external stimulation that they were able to deeply reflect on each animal. And, they would peer into their eyes. And those eyes would serve as mirrors into their own souls.

Then, as the sacrifices became more real—their hearts broke for the animals. They felt the pain. And, only in that breakthrough moment—they finally understood atonement and sacrifice. Compassion is the gateway to understanding any of these things. And to learn compassion, one must have the discipline to strip away distractions to focus on God's economy.

Eating with God

In Steps #23-28 of the Consecration Ceremony (on page 97), we see there are different portions given from the second ram and the bread basket. Why?

Well, to simplify things, the <u>first portion</u> is God's portion—which is burned on the altar table. This includes the fat portions, the liver and kidneys, rump, right shoulder, one bread loaf and one bread cake as discussed in Steps #23-24.

Throughout Leviticus, these types of fat portions which are offered are thought of as the "food of God" (Lev. 21:6, 8, 17, 21-22; 22:25). Interestingly, the idea of the Lord eating or receiving such offerings in this way is found elsewhere in the Old Testament (Gen. 18:5; Judg. 6:20-21).

Then, the <u>second portion</u> is Moses' portion, the breast of the second ram—which the God-appointed leader eats once it is boiled.

Last, the <u>third portion</u> is the portion of the high priest and his sons. This final portion consists of all the remaining meat of the second ram and the remaining bread within the bread basket.

So, why is this concept of eating with God portrayed in the Consecration Ceremony?

From a New Testament perspective, it was important to condition God's people to the fact that the Son would bear human form—needing to eat food. Therefore, the imagery of the tabernacle itself serves as a type for Christ—with the ark itself being approached as the very physical presence of the Lord. This concept is carried further within the tabernacle, where the bread table was made to hold daily provisions thought to be needed by the Lord.

This is why there is such a strong prohibition against eating fat (Lev. 7:25). Since the fat was considered as the portion "eaten" by God through the fire of the altar, eating the fat was prohibited. Whenever one would eat, he would be conscious of God's presence among him by refusing to eat the fat.

The Ephod & the Butchering the Bull and Second Ram

In Steps #13 and #23 of the Consecration Ceremony (see page 97), we see the butchering instructions for the bull and the second ram.

Now, you may wonder why those parts are selected for this ceremony. Worry not, for I am here to offer an explanation . . .

As seen in the case of the bull in Step #13, the liver, kidneys and belly fat are removed. And in the case of the second ram in Step #23, the liver, kidneys, belly fat are also removed—with the additions of the rump (fat tail) and the right leg (shoulder/thigh).

So, what's the deal?

Why the *liver* and the *kidneys*? Why not the heart, or the brain?

Well, the first thing we notice is that the portions removed from these animals provide a mirrored picture of the high priest's ephod articles. As shown in the illustration on page 51, the two glossy kidneys would correspond with the two jewels upon the ephod should piece. The liver—the largest internal organ would correspond to the yoke of the ephod shoulder piece, which stretches across the upper back of the high priest. And, the belly fat would correspond to the position of the ephod itself and the ephod waistband.

Moreover, consider the functions of the liver, kidneys and fat within an animal. The liver and kidneys *filter* things which enter the body. In essence, the liver and kidneys are the natural means through which the body *discerns* from the good and bad things which enter it.

Get it?

The high priest was called to be *discerning*—and to assist him in that calling, he bore within the ephod the Manifestation and Truth, also known as the Urim and Thummim. Even these names make sense within this explanation—as the liver and kidneys perform the function of "discernment" in the body, which is akin to the determination of "truth" in the world around us.

And, concerning the fat—which was melted and burned away on the altar table—this corresponds to the ephod itself. The ephod served as a touchpoint which linked the high priest to the Holy Spirit. And, just as the Lord Jesus told us in John 3:8, the Holy Spirit moves ethereally and unseen in mysterious ways. Thus, the high priest was to reverence the special power which abode upon his own belly—as a symbol of God's power transferring itself from the supernatural to within the natural world.

Moreover, within an animal, the fat in essence is a record of the animal itself. The amount of fat within an animal shows how it was treated during its life—whether fattened and treated well or if it was malnourished. And, within the fat of the animal is stored past nutrients and accumulations of whatever it ate.

So, in a biological sense, the fat of an animal is a snapshot on its entire life. The fat of an animal can be analyzed to determine the life and diet of the creature.

Furthermore, when reading Bible passages, such as Psalm 104:27-30, which describe how God sustains all life upon the Earth, it is no wonder why the fat—which is a testament of the animal's sustenance would belong to the Lord God. For this reason, the fat is commanded to be delivered to transcendence—being transformed from solid to liquid and finally to gas—as it returns to the Lord who gave it.

Expanding further in our understanding of the Manifestation and the Truth within the ephod, the belly fat—which was transformed upon the altar from solid (fat) to liquid, melted fat, and finally to smoke is the ultimate demonstration of <u>transcendence</u>. And, whereas the <u>discernment</u> of the liver and kidneys correspond to the <u>Truth</u> within the ephod; the <u>transcendence</u> of the fat corresponds to <u>Manifestation</u> within the ephod.

Cool, huh? Read this again to make sure you get this. It is important.

Over-Emphasis on Fat

When reading the butchering instructions for the bull and second ram during the Consecration Ceremony, you may have noted the multiple emphases on "fat"—with it being listed several times.

Why?

It was very important *any* extra fat found within the animal would be butchered and removed so it could be offered to God. So, as the God-appointed leader, and the priests in later sacrifices, would butcher animals they would look at the carcass—locating extra fat to be removed.

There are so many different angles from which this could be discussed. Specifically, when we consider the role of fat in an animal, it is the means of the animal to sustain itself during periods without food. Yet, theologically we believe it is God who sustains (Psa. 104:27-30). This means when one trusts in God, he can depend on Him for provision through faith.

Moreover, before God all creatures are bare—having had all embellishments stripped away Therefore, no one can approach God in pretension or guise—as if to fool Him. Just as the rich man's wealth was stripped away on the day he made a prideful proclamation about it, so also as each creature approaches God any devise they have stored for their benefit will be of no use in deterring God's righteous appraisal.

And, since God sustains all creatures, then the fat through which they are naturally sustained is an accurate record of how He has cared for them throughout their natural lives (Psa. 104:27-30). To gain fat an animal must eat in excess. And excess is at times a testament of God's abundant blessing.

Perhaps further, the removal of fat is a call to live disciplined lives—where we avoid excess. After all, God takes care to provide from His abundance for all creatures. So, rather than us feasting on our abundance we should follow His example—faithfully providing and assisting those who are in need (Matt. 25:34-40). In this way, a faithful servant of God should not arrive at the end of his days with abundant treasures unused—when there are so many in need. And, since God calls for the removal of all such fat, His servants should be diligent in this life to "lift up" and dedicate all abundances to His service—caring for those who are in need.

Do you agree?

We entered this world naked, and naked we will depart. Be mindful of this. Search for extra "fat" within your life and be faithful to dedicate it unto the Lord.

For all these reasons, the fat of animals is dedicated unto the Lord (Lev. 7:25). This is why fat is so important.

How to Keep the Law

Phase 5

Calendar

Having completed Phases #1-4, your next step will be to reinstitute the annual "calendar"—observing *all* the required festivals.

To "keep the Law of Moses," one *must* keep the required festivals. This is shown clearly in the book of Ezra—where the people reinstituted the religious calendar as soon as the altar was reconstructed (Ezra 3:4-6). Therefore, anyone venturing to keep the Law of Moses must keep the festivals, offerings and sacrifices prescribed.

So, if you desire to keep the Law of Moses, I will explain to you *in detail* what you must do to observe the festivals and required sacrifices.

To make this simple, I carefully explain the basics of every festival below—adding nothing to the Law. There is no nonsense and no "fluff." To present this Law calendar, I will begin by showing you a sample annual calendar. Then, I will explain every tabernacle occurrence and festival in detail. But before I do this, let's discuss a couple matters first . . .

Emphasis on New Moons in the Law

When reading the Law of Moses, you might have noticed the emphasis upon *new moons*.

Why?

Simply stated, from a 21st Century perspective, the moon cycle itself should determine the end and beginning of months. But instead of using the moon cycle, people in the 21st Century use a numbered calendar—where each month has a certain name, and each month has a certain number of days, with the exception of leap years. All this is done to make sure our days match up with the full year.

However, the Law of Moses uses the moon cycles.

How does it do this?

Simple: To determine where an annual calendar begins, you would start by identifying the evening of the first new moon in spring. The following day would be "the 1st day of the 1st month."

Got it?

From that 1st day of the 1st month in spring, all the required festivals and special offering days can be placed on an annual calendar.

So, how would this correspond to our 21st Century calendar?

Well, the dates of specific events would vary. This is why "Easter" is always on different days of the month from year to year.

To make this easier when reading this Phase, forget about the 21st Century way of doing things. See things from this "new moon" perspective instead and everything will make sense to you.

As a disclaimer, when reading the below calendar, there will be varying numbers of weeks and some other numerical disparities due to the moon cycle. But simply begin with the first "new moon" in spring, and it is easy to plug in all the required festival dates. Beyond this, to implement the calendar, all that would need to be added are the exact days on which "new moon offerings" are completed and the days on which "sabbath offerings" are completed.

But I am confident if you understand all Phases described prior to this one, this discussion on the calendar should be quite simple to master. I believe you can figure this out for yourself—so I will provide you with a basic sample below.

To simplify this, I will plot twelve new moons for the year below. And, to simplify the seasons, I will put down thirteen weeks in each season (even though this can vary). This will allow you to see a <u>sample</u> year. (For the below calendar, I use the "new moon" calendar for 2020.) Of course, when making your own tabernacle calendar, the exact numbers of new moons, weeks and so on will vary for you. But this sample calendar below should give you a great start in understanding how this works . . .

Tabernacle Calendar

Abbreviations

M/E = Morning Offering / Evening Offering

Sabb. = Sabbath Offering

NewM1-12 = New Moon / Monthly Offering

PassOPrep = Passover Preparation (10th Day of 1st Month)

Passover = Passover (14th Day of 1st Month)

UnL.1-7 = Festival of Unleavened Bread (15th-21st Days of 1st Month)

P2Prep = Make-up Passover Preparation (10th Day of 2nd Month)

PassO2 = Make-up Passover (14th Day of 2nd Month)

HFFF = Harvest Festival of First Fruits (Ceremony every 1st Day of Week throughout entire Summer and Fall)

W/Pent = Festival of Weeks / Pentecost (50 Days after First Fruits began)

Trump = Festival of Trumpets (1st Day of 7th Month)

Atone = Day of Atonement (10th Day of 7th Month)

TabPrep = Tabernacles Preparation (14th Day of 7th Month)

Taber1-8 = Festival of Tabernacles (15th to 22nd Days of 7th Month)

Ingather = Festival of Ingathering (End of harvesting season)

Spring

		SPRING BEGINS	M/E	M/E	M/E	M/E Sabb.
M/E	M/E NewM1	M/E	M/E	M/E	M/E	M/E Sabb.
M/E	M/E	M/E	M/E PassOPrep	M/E	M/E	M/E Sabb.
M/E Passover	M/E UnL.1	M/E UnL.2	M/E UnL.3	M/E UnL.4	M/E UnL.5	M/E Sabb. UnL.6
M/E UnL.7	M/E	M/E	M/E	M/E	M/E	M/E Sabb.
M/E	M/E	M/E NewM2	M/E	M/E	M/E	M/E Sabb.
M/E	M/E	M/E	M/E	M/E P2Prep	M/E	M/E Sabb.
M/E	M/E PassO2	M/E	M/E	M/E	M/E	M/E Sabb.
M/E	M/E	M/E	M/E	M/E	M/E	M/E Sabb.
M/E	M/E	M/E	M/E	M/E NewM3	M/E	M/E Sabb.
M/E	M/E	M/E	M/E	M/E	M/E	M/E Sabb.
M/E	M/E	M/E	M/E	M/E	M/E	M/E Sabb.
M/E	M/E	M/E	M/E	M/E	M/E	

Summer

						M/E Sabb.
					SUMMER BEGINS	
M/E NewM4	M/E	M/E	M/E	M/E	M/E	M/E Sabb.
M/E HFFF	M/E	M/E	M/E	M/E	M/E	M/E Sabb.
M/E HFFF	M/E	M/E	M/E	M/E	M/E	M/E Sabb.
M/E HFFF	M/E	M/E	M/E	M/E	M/E	M/E Sabb.
M/E HFFF	M/E NewM5	M/E	M/E	M/E	M/E	M/E Sabb.
M/E HFFF	M/E	M/E	M/E	M/E	M/E	M/E Sabb.
M/E HFFF	M/E	M/E	M/E	M/E	M/E	M/E Sabb.
M/E HFFF	M/E	M/E	M/E	M/E	M/E	M/E Sabb.
M/E HFFF W/Pent	M/E	M/E NewM6	M/E	M/E	M/E	M/E Sabb.
M/E HFFF	M/E	M/E	M/E	M/E	M/E	M/E Sabb.
M/E HFFF	M/E	M/E	M/E	M/E	M/E	M/E Sabb.
M/E HFFF	M/E	M/E	M/E	M/E	M/E	M/E Sabb.
M/E HFFF	M/E	M/E	M/E	M/E NewM7 Trump	M/E	M/E Sabb.

Fall

FALL BEGINS	M/E	M/E	M/E	M/E	M/E	M/E Sabb. Atone
M/E HFFF	M/E	M/E	M/E TabPrep	M/E Taber1	M/E Taber2	M/E Sabb. Taber3
M/E HFFF Taber4	M/E Taber5	M/E Taber6	M/E Taber7	M/E Taber8	M/E	M/E Sabb.
M/E HFFF	M/E	M/E	M/E	M/E NewM8	M/E	M/E Sabb.
M/E HFFF	M/E	M/E	M/E	M/E	M/E	M/E Sabb.
M/E HFFF	M/E	M/E	M/E	M/E	M/E	M/E Sabb.
M/E HFFF	M/E	M/E	M/E	M/E	M/E	M/E Sabb.
M/E HFFF	M/E	M/E	M/E	M/E	M/E NewM9	M/E Sabb.
M/E HFFF	M/E	M/E	M/E	M/E	M/E	M/E Sabb.
M/E HFFF	M/E	M/E	M/E	M/E	M/E	M/E Sabb.
M/E HFFF	M/E	M/E	M/E	M/E	M/E	M/E Sabb.
M/E HFFF	M/E	M/E	M/E	M/E	M/E	M/E Sabb.
M/E NewM10 Ingather	M/E	M/E	M/E	M/E	M/E	M/E Sabb.

Winter

M/E	M/E	M/E	M/E	M/E	M/E	M/E Sabb.
M/E	M/E	M/E	M/E	M/E	M/E	M/E Sabb.
M/E	M/E	M/E	M/E	M/E	M/E	M/E Sabb.
M/E	M/E NewM11	M/E	M/E	M/E	M/E	M/E Sabb.
M/E	M/E	M/E	M/E	M/E	M/E	M/E Sabb.
M/E	M/E	M/E	M/E	M/E	M/E	M/E Sabb.
M/E	M/E	M/E	M/E	M/E	M/E	M/E Sabb.
M/E	M/E	M/E	M/E NewM12	M/E	M/E	M/E Sabb.
M/E	M/E	M/E	M/E	M/E	M/E	M/E Sabb.
M/E	M/E	M/E	M/E	M/E	M/E	M/E Sabb.
M/E	M/E	M/E	M/E	M/E	M/E	M/E Sabb.
M/E	M/E	M/E	M/E	M/E	M/E	M/E Sabb. NewM.
M/E	M/E	M/E	M/E	M/E	M/E	M/E Sabb.

Easy, right?

To keep the ceremonial calendar, the high priest would simply fill out the annual calendar with all the ceremonies. From there, to keep the calendar, the priests would simply follow the calendar—being sure to complete each ceremony according to the detailed procedures.

To elucidate each ceremony, I include notes on <u>all</u> of them below. I trust these notes will be helpful—guiding you to seeing the various ceremonies of the Law in a fresh way.

Let's begin with the Morning and Evening Offerings . . .

Morning Offering
(Num. 28:1-8)

- In morning (exact time not specified)
- **Step 1**: A scheduled representative from God's people delivers the following four items to the high priest: (1) one blemish-free, one-year old lamb, (2) one-tenth ephah fine flour, (3) one-quarter hin olive oil, and (4) one-quarter hin fermented drink.
  -[Note: *In Num. 28, it says God's people bring these things to the Lord. So, the first step in the ceremony is for the presentation of these items to the high priest. This is significant because the high priest and the priests do not keep livestock or these items which are used for morning and evening offerings. They can, however, record and schedule the offering ceremonies—where they ensure the required representatives in turn each arrive with the required items at a predetermined time. The precedent for this planning is seen in the initial provision of the six carts and twelve oxen for the service of the tabernacle—where the tribes of God's people each coordinated with one another to share the responsibility (see page 138). Likewise, in the daily provision of items for the morning and evening offerings, the tribes of God's people would need to maintain a schedule—where each knew in turn when it was his turn to bring the items and participate in the offering ceremony. Make sense? If you would like to read more about this topic, see page 138.*]
- **Step 2**: The above lamb and flour offering are burned by the high priest or a priest at the altar as an aroma unto the Lord. Follow "burnt offering" procedures on page 207.
- **Step 3**: As specified in the "burnt offering" procedures on page 207, the aforementioned wine is poured out upon the bread table in the tabernacle by the high priest or a priest (see page 40 for more information on the bread table). And the olive oil is used for the lampstand.
  -[Note: In the morning, the high priest/priests must tend the articles of the tabernacle, including: (1) Lampstand—tending to ensure still lit, (2) Incense altar—ensuring incense lit, (3) Bread table—replacing old showbread with fresh showbread on the table along with salt and incense, and (4) Altar table—adding firewood and rearranging smoldering pieces from the previous day, ensuring the fire never goes out (Lev. 6:12). (For more information on the lampstand, incense altar, bread table, or altar table, see pages 20 & 40-44.)]

Evening Offering
(Num. 28:1-8)

- At twilight
- **Step 1**: A scheduled representative from God's people delivers the following four items to the high priest: (1) one blemish-free, one-year old lamb, (2) one-tenth ephah fine flour, (3) one-quarter hin olive oil, and (4) one-quarter hin fermented drink. [-*Note: In Num. 28, it says God's people bring these things to the Lord. So, the first step in the ceremony is for the presentation of these items to the high priest. This is significant because the high priest and the priests do not keep livestock or these items which are used for morning and evening offerings. They can, however, record and schedule the offering ceremonies—where they ensure the required representatives in turn each arrive with the required items at a predetermined time. The precedent for this planning is seen in the initial provision of the six carts and twelve oxen for the service of the tabernacle—where the tribes of God's people each coordinated with one another to share the responsibility (see page 138). Likewise, in the daily provision of items for the morning and evening offerings, the tribes of God's people would need to maintain a schedule—where each knew in turn when it was his turn to bring the items and participate in the offering ceremony. If you would like to read more about this topic, see page 138.*]
- **Step 2**: The above lamb, flour offering and olive oil are burned by the high priest or a priest at the altar as an aroma unto the Lord. Follow "burnt offering" procedures on page 207.
- **Step 3**: As specified in the "burnt offering" procedures on page 207, the aforementioned fermented drink is poured out upon the bread table in the tabernacle by the high priest or a priest (see page 40 for more information on the bread table). And the olive oil is used for the lampstand.
  -[Note: In the evening, the high priest/priests must tend the articles of the tabernacle, including: (1) Lampstand—tending to ensure still lit, (2) Incense altar—ensuring incense lit, (3) Bread table—replacing old showbread with fresh showbread on the table along with salt and incense, and (4) Altar table—adding firewood and rearranging smoldering pieces from the previous day, ensuring the fire never goes out (Lev. 6:12). (For more information on the lampstand, incense altar, bread table, or altar table, see pages 20 & 40-44.)]

Sabbath Offering
(Num. 28:9-10)

- In morning (exact time not specified)
- **Step 1**: A scheduled representative from God's people delivers the following three items to the high priest or a priest: (1) two blemish-free, one-year old lambs, (2) two-tenths ephah fine flour mixed with olive oil, and (3) one-quarter hin wine. [-*Note: In Num. 28, it says God's people bring these things to the Lord. So, the first step in the ceremony is for the presentation of these items to the high priest. This is significant because the high priest and the priests do not keep livestock or these items which are used for offerings. They can, however, record and schedule the offering ceremonies—where they ensure the required representatives in turn each arrive with the required items at a predetermined time. The precedent for this planning is seen in the initial provision of the six carts and twelve oxen for the service of the tabernacle—where the tribes of God's people each coordinated with one another to share the responsibility (see page 138). Likewise, in the provision of items for offerings, the tribes of God's people would need to maintain a schedule—where each knew in turn when it was his turn to bring the items and participate in the ceremony. If you would like to read more about this topic, see page 138.*]
- **Step 2**: The above lambs and flour offering is burned by the high priest or a priest at the altar as an aroma unto the Lord. Follow "burnt offering" procedures on page 207.
- **Step 3**: As specified in the "burnt offering" procedures on page 207, the aforementioned wine is poured out upon the bread table in the tabernacle by the high priest or a priest (see page 40 for more information on the bread table).
- **Morning & Evening of the Sabbath:** Conduct a normal "morning offering" and "evening offering" as specified on pages 163-164. Note in Num. 28:9, that the sabbath offering is only on the "sabbath *day*."

[-*Note: In some English translations it is stated that the Sabbath offering is "in addition" to the morning offering. So, on the morning of a Sabbath, <u>both</u> the Sabbath offering and the morning offering are performed. How do we know this is the case? Simple: Note in the description of the morning and evening offerings that both include olive oil for the lampstand. This means the morning offering must be made <u>every day</u>—because apart from it, there would be no olive oil provided for the lampstand.*]

The sabbath offerings are intended to follow the example of God's double giving of manna to His people. In Exo. 16:29, we see God would give to His people a double portion of manna before every sabbath. Therefore, on the sabbath, His people were called to bring a double portion offering. Cool, huh?

New Moon / Monthly Offering
(Num. 28:11-15)

- In morning of the first day following the evening with the new moon (exact time not specified)
- **Step 1**: Trumpets sounded to gather God's people (Num. 10:10)
- **Step 2**: A scheduled representative from God's people delivers the following six items to the high priest or a priest: (1) two young bulls, (2) one ram, (3) one male goat, (4) seven male lambs one-year-old, (5) one and a half ephahs of fine flour mixed with olive oil, and (6) 3.08 hins of wine. [-*Note: In Num. 28, it says God's people bring these things to the Lord. So, the first step in the ceremony is for the presentation of these items to the high priest. This is significant because the high priest and the priests do not keep livestock or these items which are used for offerings. They can, however, record and schedule the offering ceremonies—where they ensure the required representatives in turn each arrive with the required items at a predetermined time. The precedent for this planning is seen in the initial provision of the six carts and twelve oxen for the service of the tabernacle—where the tribes of God's people each coordinated with one another to share the responsibility (see page 138). Likewise, in the provision of items for offerings, the tribes of God's people would need to maintain a schedule— where each knew in turn when it was his turn to bring the items and participate in the offering ceremony. If you would like to read more about this topic, see page 138.*]
- **Step 3**: The goat is set aside.
- **Step 4**: The other items are used as burnt offerings, offered by the high priest at the altar as an aroma unto the Lord. When performing the burnt offerings, the <u>bulls</u> are each matched with three-tenths ephah of flour and a half hin of wine; the <u>ram</u> is matched with two-tenths ephah of flour and a third hin of wine; and each <u>lamb</u> is matched with one-tenth ephah of flour and a quarter hin of wine. Follow "burnt offering" procedures on page 207.
- **Step 5**: As specified in the "burnt offering" procedures on page 207, the aforementioned wine is poured out upon the bread table in the tabernacle by the high priest or a priest (see page 40 for more information on the bread table).
- **Step 6**: The above goat is presented as a sin offering by the high priest or a priest (Num. 28:15). Follow "sin offering" procedures, titled, "A Leader's Sin Offering" on page 230.
- **<u>Morning & Evening of the New Moon</u>:** Conduct a normal "morning offering" and "evening offering" as specified on pages 163-164. So, on the morning of the New Moon, *both* a "morning offering" and a "New Moon offering" will be conducted.

Passover & Festival of Unleavened Bread
(Exo. 12:1-23, 43-51; 13:3-14; 23:14-19; 34:18-25; Lev. 23:4-8; Num. 9:9-14; 28:16-25; Deu. 16:1-8)

10th Day of the 1st Month

- Preparation for Passover
- **Step 1**: On the 10th day of the 1st month, every family plans for the upcoming feast by getting and caring for a year-old lamb. They determine the amount of lamb needed for their household and any guests—planning accordingly with the appropriate amount of meat (Exo. 12:2-11).
- **Step 2**: Perhaps at this time people begin removing all leaven from their homes in preparation for the Passover and Festival of Unleavened Bread (Exo. 12:18-19). All yeast must be removed from homes.

14th Day of the 1st Month

- Passover
- **Step 1**: The people in the household dress themselves—cloaks tucked into belts, sandals on feet and staffs in hands.
- **Step 2**: At twilight on the evening of the 14th day of the 1st month, each household slaughters their lamb (Exo. 12:2-11).
- **Step 3**: Blood is put on the sides and tops of the doorframes where the lambs are eaten. A basin and hyssop are used to apply the blood. No one is permitted to leave the home where they ate lamb.
- **Step 4**: The lamb meat is roasted over fire with bitter herbs and served with unleavened bread. It is eaten in haste.
- **Step 5**: Evening: All remaining parts of sacrificial animals must not remain until morning (Exo. 34:25). Remaining parts must be burned (Exo. 12:2-11).

15th Day of the 1st Month

- First day of Festival of Unleavened Bread
- The first "sacred assembly" is held on the 15th day of the 1st month (Num. 28:16-25; Exo. 12:16). All males among God's people must appear before the tabernacle (Exo. 23:17; 34:24). No one is permitted to work on this day (Exo. 12:16).
- **Step 2A-E**: Offerings presented on the 15th day of the 1st month (Lev. 23:8), following these specific steps (A-E below) . . .
  A: Trumpets sounded to gather God's people (Num. 10:10)
  B: A scheduled representative from God's people delivers the following five items to the high priest: (1) two young bulls, (2) one ram, (3) one male goat, (4) seven male lambs one-year-old and (5) one and a half ephahs of fine flour mixed with olive oil. [-*Note: In Num. 28, it says God's people bring these things to the Lord. So, the first step in the ceremony is for the presentation of these items to the high priest. This is significant because the high priest and the priests do not keep livestock or these*

items which are used for offerings. They can, however, record and schedule the offering ceremonies—where they ensure the required representatives in turn each arrive with the required items at a predetermined time. The precedent for this planning is seen in the initial provision of the six carts and twelve oxen for the service of the tabernacle—where the tribes of God's people each coordinated with one another to share the responsibility (see page 138). Likewise, in the provision of items for offerings, the tribes of God's people would need to maintain a schedule—where each knew in turn when it was his turn to bring the items and participate in the offering ceremony. If you would like to read more about this topic, see page 138.]

C: The goat is set aside.

D: The other items are used as burnt offerings, offered by the high priest at the altar as an aroma unto the Lord. When performing the burnt offerings, the <u>bulls</u> are each matched with three-tenths ephah of flour; the <u>ram</u> is matched with two-tenths ephah of flour; and each <u>lamb</u> is matched with one-tenth ephah of flour. Follow "burnt offering" procedures on page 207.

E: The above goat is presented as a sin offering by the high priest. Follow "sin offering" procedures, titled, "A Leader's Sin Offering" on page 230.

16th Day of the 1st Month

- Second day of Festival of Unleavened Bread
- **Step 1A-E**: Offerings presented on the 16th day of the 1st month (Lev. 23:8), following these specific steps (A-F below) . . .

A: Trumpets sounded to gather God's people (Num. 10:10)

B: A scheduled representative from God's people delivers the following five items to the high priest: (1) two young bulls, (2) one ram, (3) one male goat, (4) seven male lambs one-year-old and (5) one and a half ephahs of fine flour mixed with olive oil. [-*Note: In Num. 28, it says God's people bring these things to the Lord. So, the first step in the ceremony is for the presentation of these items to the high priest. This is significant because the high priest and the priests do not keep livestock or these items which are used for offerings. They can, however, record and schedule the offering ceremonies—where they ensure the required representatives in turn each arrive with the required items at a predetermined time. The precedent for this planning is seen in the initial provision of the six carts and twelve oxen for the service of the tabernacle—where the tribes of God's people each coordinated with one another to share the responsibility (see page 138). Likewise, in the provision of items for offerings, the tribes of God's people would need to maintain a schedule—where each knew in turn when it was his turn to bring the items and participate in the offering ceremony. If you would like to read more about this topic, see page 138.*]

C: The goat is set aside.

D: The other items are used as burnt offerings, offered by the high priest at the altar as an aroma unto the Lord. When performing the burnt offerings, the <u>bulls</u> are each matched with three-tenths ephah of flour; the <u>ram</u> is matched with two-tenths ephah of flour; and each <u>lamb</u> is matched with one-tenth ephah of flour. Follow "burnt offering" procedures on page 207.

E: The above goat is presented as a sin offering by the high priest. Follow "sin offering" procedures, titled, "A Leader's Sin Offering" on page 230.

17th Day of the 1st Month

- Third day of Festival of Unleavened Bread
- **Step 1A-E**: Offerings presented on the 17th day of the 1st month (Lev. 23:8), following these specific steps (A-F below) . . .
  A: Trumpets sounded to gather God's people (Num. 10:10)
  B: A scheduled representative from God's people delivers the following five items to the high priest: (1) two young bulls, (2) one ram, (3) one male goat, (4) seven male lambs one-year-old and (5) one and a half ephahs of fine flour mixed with olive oil. [-*Note: In Num. 28, it says God's people bring these things to the Lord. So, the first step in the ceremony is for the presentation of these items to the high priest. This is significant because the high priest and the priests do not keep livestock or these items which are used for offerings. They can, however, record and schedule the offering ceremonies— where they ensure the required representatives in turn each arrive with the required items at a predetermined time. The precedent for this planning is seen in the initial provision of the six carts and twelve oxen for the service of the tabernacle—where the tribes of God's people each coordinated with one another to share the responsibility (see page 138). Likewise, in the provision of items for offerings, the tribes of God's people would need to maintain a schedule—where each knew in turn when it was his turn to bring the items and participate in the offering ceremony. If you would like to read more about this topic, see page 138.*]
  C: The goat is set aside.
  D: The other items are used as burnt offerings, offered by the high priest at the altar as an aroma unto the Lord. When performing the burnt offerings, the <u>bulls</u> are each matched with three-tenths ephah of flour; the <u>ram</u> is matched with two-tenths ephah of flour; and each <u>lamb</u> is matched with one-tenth ephah of flour. Follow "burnt offering" procedures on page 207.

  E: The above goat is presented as a sin offering by the high priest. Follow "sin offering" procedures, titled, "A Leader's Sin Offering" on page 230.

18th Day of the 1st Month

- Fourth day of Festival of Unleavened Bread
- **Step 1A-E**: Offerings presented on the 18th day of the 1st month (Lev. 23:8), following these specific steps (A-F below) . . .
  A: Trumpets sounded to gather God's people (Num. 10:10)
  B: A scheduled representative from God's people delivers the following five items to the high priest: (1) two young bulls, (2) one ram, (3) one male goat, (4) seven male lambs one-year-old and (5) one and a half ephahs of fine flour mixed with olive oil. [-*Note: In Num. 28, it says God's people bring these things to the Lord. So, the first step in the ceremony is for the presentation of these items to the high priest. This is significant because the high priest and the priests do not keep livestock or these items which are used for offerings. They can, however, record and schedule the offering ceremonies— where they ensure the required representatives in turn each arrive with the required items at a*

169

predetermined time. The precedent for this planning is seen in the initial provision of the six carts and twelve oxen for the service of the tabernacle—where the tribes of God's people each coordinated with one another to share the responsibility (see page 138). Likewise, in the provision of items for offerings, the tribes of God's people would need to maintain a schedule—where each knew in turn when it was his turn to bring the items and participate in the offering ceremony. If you would like to read more about this topic, see page 138.]

C: The goat is set aside.

D: The other items are used as burnt offerings, offered by the high priest at the altar as an aroma unto the Lord. When performing the burnt offerings, the <u>bulls</u> are each matched with three-tenths ephah of flour; the <u>ram</u> is matched with two-tenths ephah of flour; and each <u>lamb</u> is matched with one-tenth ephah of flour. Follow "burnt offering" procedures on page 207.

E: The above goat is presented as a sin offering by the high priest. Follow "sin offering" procedures, titled, "A Leader's Sin Offering" on page 230.

19th Day of the 1st Month

- Fifth day of Festival of Unleavened Bread
- **Step 1A-E**: Offerings presented on the 19th day of the 1st month (Lev. 23:8), following these specific steps (A-F below) . . .

A: Trumpets sounded to gather God's people (Num. 10:10)

B: A scheduled representative from God's people delivers the following five items to the high priest: (1) two young bulls, (2) one ram, (3) one male goat, (4) seven male lambs one-year-old and (5) one and a half ephahs of fine flour mixed with olive oil. [-*Note: In Num. 28, it says God's people bring these things to the Lord. So, the first step in the ceremony is for the presentation of these items to the high priest. This is significant because the high priest and the priests do not keep livestock or these items which are used for offerings. They can, however, record and schedule the offering ceremonies— where they ensure the required representatives in turn each arrive with the required items at a predetermined time. The precedent for this planning is seen in the initial provision of the six carts and twelve oxen for the service of the tabernacle—where the tribes of God's people each coordinated with one another to share the responsibility (see page 138). Likewise, in the provision of items for offerings, the tribes of God's people would need to maintain a schedule—where each knew in turn when it was his turn to bring the items and participate in the offering ceremony. If you would like to read more about this topic, see page 138.*]

C: The goat is set aside.

D: The other items are used as burnt offerings, offered by the high priest at the altar as an aroma unto the Lord. When performing the burnt offerings, the <u>bulls</u> are each matched with three-tenths ephah of flour; the <u>ram</u> is matched with two-tenths ephah of flour; and each <u>lamb</u> is matched with one-tenth ephah of flour. Follow "burnt offering" procedures on page 207.

E: The above goat is presented as a sin offering by the high priest. Follow "sin offering" procedures, titled, "A Leader's Sin Offering" on page 230.

20th Day of the 1st Month

- Sixth day of Festival of Unleavened Bread
- **Step 1A-E**: Offerings presented on the 20th day of the 1st month (Lev. 23:8), following these specific steps (A-F below) . . .
  A: Trumpets sounded to gather God's people (Num. 10:10)
  B: A scheduled representative from God's people delivers the following five items to the high priest: (1) two young bulls, (2) one ram, (3) one male goat, (4) seven male lambs one-year-old and (5) one and a half ephahs of fine flour mixed with olive oil. [-*Note: In Num. 28, it says God's people bring these things to the Lord. So, the first step in the ceremony is for the presentation of these items to the high priest. This is significant because the high priest and the priests do not keep livestock or these items which are used for offerings. They can, however, record and schedule the offering ceremonies— where they ensure the required representatives in turn each arrive with the required items at a predetermined time. The precedent for this planning is seen in the initial provision of the six carts and twelve oxen for the service of the tabernacle—where the tribes of God's people each coordinated with one another to share the responsibility (see page 138). Likewise, in the provision of items for offerings, the tribes of God's people would need to maintain a schedule—where each knew in turn when it was his turn to bring the items and participate in the offering ceremony. If you would like to read more about this topic, see page 138.*]
  C: The goat is set aside.
  D: The other items are used as burnt offerings, offered by the high priest at the altar as an aroma unto the Lord. When performing the burnt offerings, the <u>bulls</u> are each matched with three-tenths ephah of flour; the <u>ram</u> is matched with two-tenths ephah of flour; and each <u>lamb</u> is matched with one-tenth ephah of flour. Follow "burnt offering" procedures on page 207.
  E: The above goat is presented as a sin offering by the high priest. Follow "sin offering" procedures, titled, "A Leader's Sin Offering" on page 230.

21st Day of the 1st Month

- Seventh day of Festival of Unleavened Bread
- **Step 1A-E**: Offerings presented on the 21st day of the 1st month (Lev. 23:8), following these specific steps (A-F below) . . .
  A: Trumpets sounded to gather God's people (Num. 10:10)
  B: A scheduled representative from God's people delivers the following five items to the high priest: (1) two young bulls, (2) one ram, (3) one male goat, (4) seven male lambs one-year-old and (5) one and a half ephahs of fine flour mixed with olive oil. [-*Note: In Num. 28, it says God's people bring these things to the Lord. So, the first step in the ceremony is for the presentation of these items to the high priest. This is significant because the high priest and the priests do not keep livestock or these items which are used for offerings. They can, however, record and schedule the offering ceremonies— where they ensure the required representatives in turn each arrive with the required items at a predetermined time. The precedent for this planning is seen in the initial provision of the six carts and twelve oxen for the service of the tabernacle—where the tribes of God's people each coordinated with*

one another to share the responsibility (see page 138). Likewise, in the provision of items for offerings, the tribes of God's people would need to maintain a schedule—where each knew in turn when it was his turn to bring the items and participate in the offering ceremony. If you would like to read more about this topic, see page 138.]

C: The goat is set aside.

D: The other items are used as burnt offerings, offered by the high priest at the altar as an aroma unto the Lord. When performing the burnt offerings, the <u>bulls</u> are each matched with three-tenths ephah of flour; the <u>ram</u> is matched with two-tenths ephah of flour; and each <u>lamb</u> is matched with one-tenth ephah of flour. Follow "burnt offering" procedures on page 207.

E: The above goat is presented as a sin offering by the high priest. Follow "sin offering" procedures, titled, "A Leader's Sin Offering" on page 230.

- **Step 2**: The second "sacred assembly" is held on the 21st day of the 1st month (Exo. 12:16). Trumpets sounded to gather God's people (Num. 10:10). All males among God's people must appear before the tabernacle (Exo. 23:17; 34:24). No one is permitted to work on this day (Exo. 12:16). A festival is observed on the evening of the 21st day of the 1st month of Aviv—after seven days without yeast (Exo. 13:6).

- **Step 3**: All men among God's people must bring lamb offerings from their households to the high priest (Exo. 13:6-14). All firstborn lambs must be offered. Firstborn sons and donkeys must be redeemed by offering a lamb on their behalf during the final festival day. (For all these offerings of firstborn animals, follow "freewill offering" procedures on page 214. However, due to the absence of flour or drink offering requirements in Exo. 13:6-14, consider omitting the requirement for God's people to bring flour/drink in Step #1 of "freewill offerings." They are <u>only</u> required to bring the animals, not flour or drink.)

–[Note: *In the context of Exo. 13:6-14, these final offerings of the firstborn lambs should take place following the entire week of Unleavened Bread. Therefore, the lamb offerings are presented on the 21st of the 1st month.*]

Why Are there No Drink Offerings Listed?

You might have noticed the above discussed Bible passages do not list wine as a requirement for the offerings on the 15th to the 21st days.

Why?

Well, perhaps they are not included in the Bible references because—as you may guess—wine and fermented drink can contain things *similar* to leaven. And, since leaven is forbidden, it is not permitted to be used during the festival of unleavened bread.

Of course, that is one theory.

Another theory, which I think is quite intriguing, is to connect the lack of wine to the Lord's Supper. During the Lord's Supper, Christ compares wine to His blood which would be shed on the cross for the sins of the world (Matt. 26:28).

Over the countless years which the Passover offerings were completed, God intended for people to always reflect on why wine was not offered. Then, in the fulfillment of the Law with the arrival of Christ, it would be clearly seen they were all this time awaiting the "wine" which was to come down from Heaven—the sacrifice of the Christ, who offered Himself on their behalf.

However, I think it is likely—due to the mirroring of the animals and flour amounts with the new moon offering, that drink offerings might also be permitted for the offerings on the 15th to the 21st. So, it might be wise to simply borrow from the requirements listed for the new moon offering (page 166) and include 3.08 hins of wine for drink offerings on each day (Num. 28:11-14).

After all, we know from later in Scripture the Lord received drink during the Passover (Matt. 26:28). So, it would make sense the Lord would still require drink offerings to be poured out upon the bread table during these offerings.

Therefore, I conclude perhaps Moses omitted the listing of wine on the offerings of the 15th to the 21st to make future generations mindful of what they put within the wine to be offered, or to make them mindful of the blood placed upon their doorframes. During the observed offerings of the festival of unleavened bread, God's people need to avoid bringing drink to be offered which contains anything similar to leaven.

So, what do you think? . . .

Were the drink offerings for the Festival of Unleavened Bread the same as the drink offerings of the new moon (Num. 28:11-14)? (It seems Num. 15:3 indicates *all* the festival sacrifices *required* animals to be offered along with the prescribed drink and flour offerings in Num. 15:3-12.)

Or, were drink offerings *forbidden* during the Passover offerings either to make people mindful of excluding leaven, or mindful of the blood of the Messiah?

Passover for the Unclean and Journeying

If a person/family is unclean or away on a journey during the 1ˢᵗ month, they would follow these steps . . .

10ᵗʰ Day of the 2ⁿᵈ Month

- Preparation for Passover (make-up)
- On the 10ᵗʰ day of the 2ⁿᵈ month, those families would plan for their Passover by getting and caring for a year-old lamb. They determine the amount of lamb needed for their household and any guests—planning accordingly with the appropriate amount of meat (Exo. 12:2-11).

14ᵗʰ Day of the 2ⁿᵈ Month

- Passover (make-up)
- **Step 1**: The people in the household dress themselves—cloaks tucked into belts, sandals on feet and staffs in hands.
- **Step 2**: At twilight on the evening of the 14ᵗʰ day of the 2ⁿᵈ month, each of these households slaughter their lambs (Exo. 12:2-11).
- **Step 3**: Blood is put on the sides and tops of the doorframes where the lambs are eaten. A basin and hyssop are used to apply the blood. No one is permitted to leave the home where they eat lamb.
- **Step 4**: The lamb meat is roasted over fire with bitter herbs and served with unleavened bread. It is eaten in haste.
- **Step 5**: Evening: All remaining parts of lamb must not remain until morning (Exo. 34:25). Remaining parts must be burned (Exo. 12:2-11).

Harvest Festival of First Fruits
(Exo. 23:14-19; 34:23-24; Lev. 23:9-14; Num. 18:12-13)

Every 1ˢᵗ Day of the Week throughout Summer & Fall

- Harvest Festival of First Fruits (begins after first harvest week, then every first day of week throughout summer and fall***)
  –[***Note: *The exact dates of this festival would vary regionally because the time of harvest varies in different regions. Therefore, the plotting of every week in the summer and fall on the calendar is hypothetical and might be plotted differently depending on time of harvest. But if you have figured out everything up to this point, I am confident you can figure this out as well.*]
- **Step 1**: Trumpets sounded on the day after the sabbath (for multiple weeks**) to gather God's people who are ready to offer their first fruits (Num. 10:10). [*All males among God's people must appear before the tabernacle with their harvest first fruits (Exo. 23:17; 34:24). After harvesting his fields, every man is required to journey to the tabernacle with his first fruits—being prepared for the sounding of the trumpet on the day after the sabbath.*]
- **Step 2**: Upon hearing the trumpets, the men with first fruit offerings bring them to the priests. Each man who is bringing an offering must bring the following items: (1) a sheaf* of the first grain he harvested, (2) a year-old lamb, (3) two-tenths ephah of fine flour mixed with olive oil, and (4) quarter hin of wine.
- **Step 3**: Upon receiving the items from each man, the priest "lifts up" the received "sheaf" as a "wave offering." The priest sets the sheaf aside for use by his own family (Num. 18:12-13). For more information on "wave offering," see page 236.
- **Step 4**: The priest offers the lamb and two-tenths ephah as a burnt offering. Follow "burnt offering" procedures on page 207.
- **Step 5**: As specified in the "burnt offering" procedures on page 207, the aforementioned wine is poured out upon the bread table in the tabernacle by the high priest or a priest (see page 40 for more information on the bread table).
- **Step 6**: Although unrequired, it would make sense given the context of the blessing passage for each priest to send away each man with the blessing (Num. 6:22-27). (This is one of the rare opportunities where the priests would have direct interaction with individuals among God's people—so they should be intentional to send out each man with the Lord's blessing upon him and his family.)

Upon completion of the above steps, the family of the man who offered the sheaf*, lamb, flour and wine are authorized to eat what they harvested. Families are not permitted to eat anything from their harvests until the men from their families complete the below steps. Only then is a family authorized to eat *anything* they harvested (Lev. 23:14).

*What if I Don't Farm Grain?

This is a good question.

All men from among God's people were required to appear before the tabernacle during the Harvest Festival with what was their first fruits and a lamb, flour and wine for their required offering.

In Num. 18:12-13, it states the Lord gives to the priests all the first fruits brought to them—including olive oil, new wine and grain. Interestingly, Lev. 2:11-12 even says a person could bring a first fruit offering of yeast or honey. In other words, the "sheaf" which the men brought were not always "sheaves." In some cases, depending on what they farmed/made, they might have brought olive oil (if they grew olives), or wine (if they grew grapes).

Therefore, it is best to avoid getting too stuck on the word "sheaf." The concept is that when God blessed His people in their occupations, the Harvest Festival called them to bring the first part of their family's profits to the tabernacle to be given to the priests.

Make sense?

So, what if I don't farm grain?

Then I would bring a "sheaf" of *whatever* I farm/make—along with a lamb, flour and some wine.
Easy peasy, right?

Multiple Days of the Harvest Festival

In the above steps of the Harvest Festival and the passage, *"What if I Don't Farm Grain?"* I point out the different meanings of the word "sheaf"—stating specifically the men might bring as their first fruits different things—such as grain, olive oil, wine, honey or even yeast. Deuteronomy even speaks of the fleece of sheep in this context—commanding these to be brought as first fruits (Deu. 18:4). And, of course, depending on what they farmed/made, they would be able to bring different things from these as well.

This being the case, it is important we understand the implications for the tabernacle calendar. Since different things were able to be presented during the Harvest Festival, this means they would have been harvested on different dates (because not all plants are ready to be harvested at the same time).

Therefore, the tabernacle calendar would need to be made to accommodate men who needed to present their "first fruits" throughout the entire summer and fall (because different types of plants are harvested at different times).

Make sense?

So, how could this be done?

Simple: As stated in Step #1 of the Harvest Festival (page 175), on the first day after the sabbath for multiple weeks throughout the summer and fall,*** the trumpets would be sounded to signal the priests were ready to receive those who were prepared to bring first fruit offerings. And, of course, during some days they would have *many* men who arrived with offerings. But during other days there would have been *less* men with offerings. Nevertheless, on every day after the sabbath—*throughout the entire summer and fall*—the priests would have needed to sound the trumpets, being prepared to receive anyone who arrived with an offering. If they did not, then it might result in some of the men being incapable of offering their first fruits to fulfill their requirements.

Got it?

So, for the purpose of utility, it would have been necessary for the Harvest Festival of First Fruits to extend over *many weeks*—even though it might have only been discussed as a single event on a single day, likely the day in which the first offerings were received.

Often there are many conflicting things presented concerning the Harvest Festival's dates. To combat this, simply follow what Moses wrote and forget all the extra stuff which has been attached to his words (Deu. 4:2).

But when understanding the basic outline of this festival, and its purpose, it is easy to plot it correctly on a calendar depending on *local* harvest timelines. In other words, you would need to determine the dates of harvest for your region, then extend the Harvest Festival over that entire harvesting period. Thus the Harvest Festival was intended to extend over many weeks to allow people to bring the many different types of "first fruits" from their various labors.

Festival of Weeks / Pentecost
(Exo. 34:22-23; Lev. 23:15-22; Num. 28:26-31; Deu. 16:9-12)

Fifty days after the first day of the Harvest Festival, on day after sabbath

- Festival of Weeks / Pentecost
- **Step 1**: Trumpets sounded to gather God's people (Num. 10:10). All people are forbidden from working on this day.
- **Step 2**: A scheduled representative from God's people delivers the following seven items to the high priest/priest: (1) two loaves bread, made from two-tenths ephah flour—*without* leaven, mingled with at least a small portion of grain from this year's harvest,* (2) two young bulls,** (3) one ram.** (4) one male goat, (5) seven male lambs one-year-old, (6) one and a half ephahs of fine flour mixed with olive oil, and (7) 3.08 hins of wine.
- **Step 3**: The two loaves of bread, the goat and two lambs are set aside.
- **Step 4**: The other items are used as burnt offerings, offered by the high priest/priest at the altar as an aroma unto the Lord. When performing the burnt offerings, the <u>bulls</u> are each matched with three-tenths ephah of flour and a half hin of wine; the <u>ram</u> is matched with two-tenths ephah of flour and a third hin of wine; and each <u>lamb</u> is matched with one-tenth ephah of flour and a quarter hin of wine. Follow "burnt offering" procedures on page 207.
- **Step 5**: The goat (previously set aside in Step #3) is presented as a sin offering by the high priest/priest. Follow "sin offering" procedures, titled, "A Leader's Sin Offering" on page 230.
- **Step 6**: The high priest offers the two lambs (previously set aside in Step #3) as a fellowship offering. Follow "fellowship offering" procedures on page 212.
- **Step 7**: As detailed in "fellowship offering" procedures on page 212, the same two lambs in the above step are waved by the high priest/priest as a wave offering. For more information on wave offerings, see page 236.
- **Step 8**: The high priest/priest "lifts up" the two loaves of bread (previously set aside in Step #3) as a wave offering. For more information on wave offerings, see page 236.
- **Step 9**: The priests invite the men present among God's people to bring forward their freewill offerings as they desire (Lev. 16:10-11). The priests stand by to receive freewill offerings from the men, sending them each away with a blessing (Num. 6:22-27). For all offerings brought forth, follow "freewill offering" procedures on page 214.

*Leaven and Yeast Forbidden

Depending on your interest in this topic, I have something for you to consider . . .

In several passages, it states clearly that no yeast or leaven is to be contained in an offering presented to the Lord (Exo. 23:18; 34:25; Lev. 2:11; 6:17).

Before you read further, look up those passages.

Now that you see this for yourself, consider Lev. 23:17—which in many English translations states that *leavened* bread is to be presented.

So, what's the deal?

Well, it is clear God was *not* calling his people to present offerings with yeast—because that is forbidden in Exo. 23:18; 34:25; Lev. 2:11 and 6:11.

So, what is Lev. 23:17 saying?

Just this . . .

The flour offering of Lev. 23:17 is to "include" or be "mingled with" some of the grain made from the flour taken in the current harvesting year. In other words, when this flour offering is presented, it is to include at least a small portion of flour made from *this year's* harvest.

To be more specific, let's say you were preparing the flour offering to be presented. Lev. 23:17 is telling you to make sure the flour you prepare contains at least a little bit of flour made from this year's grain. In other words, the offering of Lev. 23:17 cannot just be made from flour in a jar that was stored from previous harvesting years. For the Festival of Weeks, God told His people to make the flour offering out of some of the fresh grain harvested in the *current* year.

Get it?

Lev. 23:17 isn't telling God's people to add yeast and leaven to the flour offering. Rather, Lev. 23:17 is telling God's people to ensure their flour offering is mingled with at least a small portion of flour from that year's harvest—similar to how a small amount of yeast is added to bread.

Hopefully you understand this—because it is important.

**How Many Bulls and Rams?

In Step #2 above, there is a disparity between the two Bible passages which prescribe the number of bulls and rams. In Num. 28:27, it states there are *two bulls* and *one ram*; whereas in Lev. 23:18, it states there is *one bull* and *two rams*.

So, which is it?

To keep with the prescribed number of animals used in the New Moon offerings and the Passover sacred assembly on the 15th of the 1st month, I choose to include the numbers listed in Lev. 23:18—*one bull* and *two rams*—in my above list for the Festival of Weeks.
This allows the numbers of animals on these lists to agree with one another.

Do you agree?

If not, perhaps a better way would be to simply err "on the safe side." For your observance of the Festival of Weeks, you could choose to offer *two bulls* and *two rams*—so you would be covered if Num. 28:27 is the preferred passage to be used. If that is the case, then you would need to simply increase your list of items in Step #4 to include an additional two-tenths ephah of flour and a third hin wine to offer along with the ram. Easy peasy.

Festival of Trumpets
(Lev. 23:23-25; Num. 29:1-6)

The 1st Day of the 7th Month

- Festival of Trumpets
- **Step 1**: Trumpets sounded to gather God's people (Num. 10:10). People forbidden from working on this day (Lev. 23:24).
- **Step 2**: A scheduled representative from God's people delivers the following five items to the high priest/priest: (1) one young bull, (2) one ram, (3) one male goat, (4) seven male lambs one-year-old, and (5) one and two-tenths ephahs of fine flour mixed with olive oil.* [-*Note: In Num. 28, it says God's people bring these things to the Lord. So, the first step in the ceremony is for the presentation of these items to the high priest. This is significant because the high priest and the priests do not keep livestock or these items which are used for offerings. They can, however, record and schedule the offering ceremonies—where they ensure the required representatives in turn each arrive with the required items at a predetermined time. The precedent for this planning is seen in the initial provision of the six carts and twelve oxen for the service of the tabernacle—where the tribes of God's people each coordinated with one another to share the responsibility (see page 138). Likewise, in the provision of items for offerings, the tribes of God's people would need to maintain a schedule—where each knew in turn when it was his turn to bring the items and participate in the offering ceremony. If you would like to read more about this topic, see page 138.*]
- **Step 3**: The goat is set aside.
- **Step 4**: The other items are used as burnt offerings, offered by the high priest/priest at the altar as an aroma unto the Lord. When performing the burnt offerings, the <u>bulls</u> are each matched with three-tenths ephah of flour; the <u>ram</u> is matched with two-tenths ephah of flour; and each <u>lamb</u> is matched with one-tenth ephah of flour. Follow "burnt offering" procedures on page 207. [-*Note: The drink offerings are omitted from the burnt offering procedures.*]
- **Step 5**: The above goat is presented as a sin offering by the high priest/priest. Follow "sin offering" procedures, specifically the section titled, "A Leader's Sin Offering" on page 230.

*Why Are there No Drink Offerings Listed?

You might have noticed the above discussed Bible passages do not list wine or fermented drink as requirements for the offerings during the Festival of Trumpets. Interestingly, this is similar to the Festival of Unleavened Bread—which is discussed on page 167.

So, why are there no drink offerings listed for the Festival of Trumpets?

Good question.

Perhaps this is done to link this festival to the Festival of Unleavened Bread—helping people to be intentionally mindful of purpose. The dry offerings may have made the people more mindful of the blood of the Passover lamb which initiated the festival—symbolizing the blood of the Messiah (see page 173).

Likewise, the offerings during the Festival of Trumpets could have been intentionally dry due to its close proximity to the Day of Atonement—just nine days later. By having the offerings remain dry during the Festival of Trumpets, this festival would be similar to Passover & the Festival of Unleavened Bread. God's people were called to be focused and mindful of those things which would secure their atonement. Thus, when leading up to the somber, most powerful propitiation memorialized on the Day of Atonement, the special offerings during the Festival of Trumpets omitted drink.

What do you think?

Do you think the Festival of Trumpets had intentionally dry offerings—without wine?

Or, do you think the offerings during this festival simply borrowed from the same amounts listed for other festivals? (It seems Num. 15:3 indicates *all* the festival sacrifices *required* animals to be offered along with the prescribed drink and flour offerings in Num. 15:3-12.)

If the latter is true, then the required list in Step #2 would require a simple addition of 2.58 hins of wine to allow for the standard measurements—including a half hin for the bull, a third hin for the ram, and a quarter hin for each lamb.

Purpose of the Festival of Trumpets (Num. 10:1-10)

Whereas the other required festivals have meaning assigned to them, there is nothing noting the special significance of the Festival of Trumpets—except the trumpets are to be sounded.

So, what's the deal?

Well, perhaps we can understand more by reflecting on what we know about the trumpets themselves.

In Scripture we see these trumpets were made out of hammered silver in the service of the tabernacle. The God-appointed leader, high priest and priests used them to signal the community. As noted on page 48, the trumpets could be used to call assemblies of tribal leaders and the entire community. They were also used to signal the setting out of the tribes to the east, south, west and north. And, the trumpets were used during the festivals where burnt offerings and fellowship offerings were presented.

Interestingly, in Numbers 10:9, it states the trumpets are to be sounded before the army of God's people goes out in battle against their enemies.

And, within these things, we find the purpose of the Festival of Trumpets. During this assembly, the high priest could likely speak to the assembled people about the trumpets and their purpose in Numbers 10. In this way, the Festival of Trumpets would be a special time of reflection—where the people could be mindful of the many past occasions of God's provision . . . particularly when He went ahead of them in battle, led them in procession throughout the wilderness and directed leaders to step forth to serve the community.

So, during this festival, the trumpets would blast their signals—being discussed in turn, helping the people to be mindful of God's protection over His people. And, in this, the Festival of Trumpets would be a powerful ceremony leading to the upcoming Day of Atonement nine days later, and the Festival of Tabernacles fourteen days later. Just as God moved powerfully through the trumpets to break down mighty walls in the past, so also the people would be invited to tune their hearts to the overwhelming surge from these divinely-powered instruments.

Day of Atonement
(Lev. 16:1-34; Num. 29:7-11)

The 10ᵗʰ Day of the 7ᵗʰ Month

- Day of Atonement
- **Step 1**: Trumpets sounded to gather God's people (Num. 10:10). People are forbidden from working at all on this day (Lev. 16:29).
- **Step 2**: High priest* washes himself with water near the tabernacle (most likely at the wash basin).
- **Step 3**: The high priest enters the tabernacle and removes his regular garments and the ephod articles. He dresses himself only with: (1) linen undergarments, (2) linen tunic, (3) linen sash and (4) linen turban. His regular clothing articles are left in the tabernacle. [*Other priests and Levites are forbidden from entering the Tabernacle on the Day of Atonement for any reason (Lev. 16:17). Only the high priest* can enter the tabernacle on the Day of Atonement.*]
- **Step 4**: At the tabernacle entrance, the high priest's own household presents him with a bull. He slaughters the bull at the tabernacle entrance and follows "sin offering" procedures, titled, "The High Priest's Sin Offering" on page 226. He sets aside some of the slaughtered bull's blood.
- **Step 5**: At the tabernacle entrance, a scheduled representative from God's people presents the high priest with the following: (1) one bull, (2) one ram, (3) two male goats, (4) seven one-year-old male lambs, (5) one and two-tenths ephahs flour mixed with olive oil. The bull, ram, lambs, and flour are set aside. -[Note: *The high priest does not touch this bull, ram, lambs or the flour because he touched his sin offering in Step #4.*]
- **Step 6**: High priest brings both goats to the tabernacle entrance. He casts lots to determine the "scapegoat." The other goat is designated as the sin offering to be later offered. Then he sets aside the two live goats.
- **Step 7**: The high priest takes a censer of burning coals from the altar table.
- **Step 8**: The high priest places upon the censer with the coals two handfuls of incense—most likely from the incense altar inside the tabernacle. (For more information on the incense formula, see page 44.)
- **Step 9**: The high priest places the smoldering censer inside the shielding curtain with the ark. The purpose here is to set down the censer and leave it so the most holy place fills with smoke to obscure the ark.** He completely avoids looking at the ark while setting down the censer (Lev. 16:12-13). [-Note: *The censer used here is left within the most holy place—even after it burns out. It is not moved until the next time the tabernacle is relocated. This is why Hebrews 9:4 mentions the presence of the censer always in the most holy place—since at the time of the New Testament, the tabernacle was transformed into the stationary temple.*]
- **Step 10**: While the most holy place fills with smoke from the smoldering censer, the high priest goes to the tabernacle entrance to get some of the slaughtered bull's blood.

- **Step 11**: The high priest goes into the most holy place with some of the bull's blood. He approaches the ark while averting his eyes through the incense smoke. He uses his finger to sprinkle the blood on the atonement cover and also in front of the atonement cover seven times—while avoiding touching the ark.

  [-Note: *The LXX says the high priest sprinkles the blood on the atonement cover "eastward." This seems to indicate that the high priest should approach the ark on an angle, rather than directly so that he is standing slightly to the ark's south-west corner. Perhaps this is emphasized as it is the first approach with blood in the ceremony; whereas when he sprinkles the goat's blood in Step #13 below he can stand <u>directly in front</u> of the ark—being covered by the blood of the bull. What do you think?*]

- **Step 12**: The goat previously determined by lot as the sin offering in Step #6 is slaughtered at the north side of the altar table. He sets aside some of the slaughtered goat's blood. Follow "sin offering" procedures, titled, "A Leader's Sin Offering" on page 230.

- **Step 13**: The high priest goes into the most holy place with some of the goat's blood. He approaches the ark while averting his eyes through the incense smoke. He uses his finger to sprinkle the blood on the atonement cover and also in front of the atonement cover seven times—while avoiding touching the ark.

- **Step 14**: The high priest mixes some of the blood from the slaughtered bull and the slaughtered goat at the tabernacle entrance. He uses his finger to place some of that blood mixture on each of the horns of the altar table. Then he uses his finger to sprinkle the blood mixture on the altar table seven times. For more information on the "altar table," see page 20.

- **Step 15**: The goat previously designated as the scapegoat in Step #6 is brought by the high priest to the tabernacle entrance. He places both hands on the scapegoat's head as he confesses the wickedness and rebellion of God's people. (The LXX says the high priest shall confess the unrighteousness and sins of God's people.)

- **Step 16**: The goat previously determined by lot as the scapegoat is taken by someone whom the high priest designates into a solitary place in the wilderness—where it is released. The designated man must wash himself and his clothes in the wilderness before he re-enters the camp (Lev. 16:26).

- **Step 17**: The carcasses of the bull and the goat at the tabernacle entrance are taken outside the camp by someone whom the high priest designates—where they are burned. The designated man is instructed to wash himself and his clothes outside the camp before he re-enters the camp (Lev. 16:26).

- **Step 18**: As specified in the "sin offering" procedures on page 226, The high priest washes himself with water near the tabernacle (most likely at the wash basin). He enters the tabernacle and removes the (1) linen turban, (2) linen sash, (3) linen tunic and (4) linen undergarments. Then he clothes himself with his regular clothing articles and the ephod articles—as shown on page 50. The clothing articles he wore during the previous steps are left in the tabernacle—until the next Day of Atonement, when he will use them again.

- **Step 19**: Now washed from the two sin offerings, and dressed with his normal high priestly clothing, the high priest performs burnt offerings using the bull, ram, seven lambs and flour set aside in Step #5. Follow "burnt offering" procedures on page 207. -[Note: *In the LXX translation of Num. 29:7-11, it uses both the phrases, "burnt offering" and "whole burnt offering" to describe the offerings of this bull, ram and the seven lambs. As I explain on page 238, a "whole burnt offering" is a burnt offering where the priests, Levites and the people refuse their meat portions—instead choosing for them to be burned upon the altar table as the Lord's portion. Therefore, with the offering of this bull, ram and the* lambs, those entitled to portions are free to decide for themselves. They can either receive their assigned portions or abstain from their portions. Why? Well, this is the Day of Atonement—and the priests and Levites are invited to search their hearts. God invites them to fast from their portions if they feel inclined to do so. And in the case where any priest or Levite decides to fast from his portion, that portion should be delivered to the fire of the altar table. Thus, just as the high priest was called to examine his own sin when he sacrificed the first bull at the beginning of the ceremony, so also at the end of the ceremony, the priests and Levites are beckoned to search their own hearts as they choose to either receive or abstain from their assigned portions. This is why I think the LXX uses both the terms "whole burnt offering" and "burnt offering." What do you think?]

*-[Note: *Once the replacement for the high priest has been identified, this son of the high priest is authorized to perform the entire Day of Atonement ceremony in lieu of his father—who is currently serving as the high priest (Lev. 16:32-33). Why? Well, consider the fact stated in Step #3—that when performing the steps within the tabernacle no one else was permitted to step within it. Therefore, in order to properly train his replacement, the high priest needed to teach him and allow him to do it for himself. In this way, the Day of Atonement is different from other ceremonies. For the other sacrifices it was always possible for the high priest to stand next to his sons to ensure they were performing their priestly duties properly. But on the Day of Atonement, no one could walk with the high priest or his replacement into the tabernacle, nor the most holy place.*]

**-[Note: *Hebrews 9:4 mentions the presence of incense burning within the Most Holy Place next to the Ark. Unfortunately, many English translations of Hebrews 9:4 state that the "incense altar" was placed behind the shielding curtain with the Ark. However, when understanding the Day of Atonement, we conclude Hebrews 9:4 is most likely a reference to the special censer used by the High Priest on the Day of Atonement to fill the Most Holy Place with smoke. The incense altar itself was placed in the main tabernacle room near to the bread table and lampstand—where they were each tended twice daily. For more information on this topic, please see pages 40-44. Therefore, Hebrews 9:4 cannot be referring to the actual "incense altar" because placing it within the most holy place would make it inaccessible for the priests during the morning and evening offerings. Make sense?*]

The High Priest's Son

Interestingly, in Lev. 16:32-33, it states either the high priest himself or his son who was anointed to replace him could perform all the steps on the Day of Atonement. In the first "note" on page 187, I explain this was necessary because the Day of Atonement precluded training because no one was permitted to enter the tabernacle with the one who was performing the steps. In other words, the high priest would have needed to teach his replacement on the proper steps—and allow him opportunity to do it for himself before he passed away.

But is there more to this?

I certainly think so.

As seen in Scripture, there is an emphasis on the Son. And, similar to how the Son of God would bear upon Himself the sins of the world—moving in His own mighty power to the throne to do away with sins, so also the designated son of the high priest is called when anointed to do the same. He is sent by his father alone into the most holy place—bearing upon himself the full weight of his people's sin.

The son strips away all regalia—approaching in complete sincerity, moving through the smoke to sprinkle the blood upon and before the seat of mercy.

Get it?

This is an absolute picture of the relationship of the Father and Son. One could even say—quite rightly so—that the overwhelming smoldering smoke within the most holy place represents the Holy Spirit, who shielded the body of the Son in His human approach to the highest throne of the Father.

Of course, people may have difficulty grasping such things. But perhaps it would help to understand when Lucifer attempted a similar approach to the highest throne of the Father—the glory of the Almighty blazed upon his pride as he drew nearer (Isa. 14:14-15). However, as the Son approached in complete righteousness, also being shielded by the presence of the Holy Spirit, He accomplished what no other could: He took His seat at the right hand of the Father. And, from that most exalted position the Son receives all glory, honor and power (Rev. 5:7).

So, suffice it to say, the son of the high priest—when anointed—was called upon to move in similar fashion to the presence of the Lord upon the mercy seat.

And, this is why the Law of Moses is so important: The Law of Moses gives us powerful glimpses of the Heavenly pattern (Exo. 25:40; Heb. 8:5).

The Sequence of Blood Placement & the Ark

As noted above, the LXX states in Lev. 17:14 the High Priest sprinkles blood on the Ark "eastward." I explained in the note how this indicates the High Priest does not approach the Ark directly with the bull's blood, but on a diagonal. He stands offset on the Ark's south-west corner so he can sprinkle the blood "eastward."

Now, we might think this is going a little too far. But the LXX often includes helpful information. And, this small inclusion of "eastward" carries with it the concept of "covering."

Think about it this way . . .

In discussion of the Ark, it is continually stated the Ark must not be looked upon, nor touched. During the Day of Atonement, the High Priest needs to even obscure his vision with smoke from smoldering incense. And, the curtain which was ever before the Ark is called the "shielding curtain." For these reasons, it would make perfect sense that the High Priest would offset himself from the Ark—avoiding approaching it directly at first.

But, once the blood of the bull is applied, and the High Priest returns with the blood of the goat, he no longer needs to offset himself to sprinkle "eastward." In other words, the blood of the bull grants the High Priest a measure of grace. And, although his vision still remains obscured by the smoke and he must avert his eyes from the Ark, he can approach it directly with the blood of the goat.

You may also be thinking, "Why is blood sprinkled both on the atonement cover and also on the ground in front of it?"

Good question.

To arrive at that answer, we must think about what happened within the Most Holy Place. In this area, before the Ark, the God-appointed leader, Moses, was instructed to meet the Lord face-to-face. And, it is likely Moses knelt down in reverence on the ground before the Ark.

Therefore, blood was placed on the atonement cover to influence God's vision of Moses before Him. And, the blood was placed on the ground to grant grace to Moses as he knelt before the Lord. The blood beneath Moses would keep him centered on his mission—to serve in ushering God's people to complete atonement.

And, as Moses would rise the blood sprinkled on the ground beneath him would cling to his clothing—giving color to the threads, reminding him always the blood of atonement should ever guide his steps while travelling amongst God's people. In this way, God honored Moses by making it so the blood of atonement would remain on them both—thereby demonstrating their shared responsibility over the people.

Moses was the servant of the Lord who was faithful in all God's house. The blood which remained upon him gave him grace to kneel in the presence of the Almighty. The Lord would be mindful of the blood upon Moses and would listen to him as he offered intercession for His people.

If this blood touched Moses' garment, he would be required to wash it (Lev. 6:27). But within the threads of his garment, the deep stain of applied blood would remain—ever reminding both the Lord and

Moses of the atonement. In other words, the blood sprinkled before the ark made certain the prophet would remain ever mindful of his atonement. The blood was shed for him—behind the veil—just as the Lord Jesus shed His blood for us.

Different Clothing for the High Priest

You may have noticed in Step #3 above, the high priest removes all his special clothing and ephod articles when conducting his duties on the Day of Atonement. In fact, the high priest doesn't even dress himself as a "normal priest"—because he does not wear a robe as the normal priests would (see page 51).

Why?

Well, it would seem at first that on the only day where the high priest is commanded to go into the "most holy place" to appear before the ark, he should be wearing his *finest* clothes. Right?

No.

The purpose of the Day of Atonement is "atonement." And, in his need of atonement, the high priest is no different than any other man. Thus, he approaches God—being stripped of all regalia . . . the bells, jewels, gold adornments, cords and ephod articles. He is not even allowed to wear a robe.

None of these regal things were permitted to enter before the ark. Therefore, as the high priest approached the ark amid overwhelming incense smoke filling the room, he would have felt naked—being deprived of his vestments, being made into a normal man of sorts.

And this is exactly what we should all feel before the Lord God Almighty—the Maker of Heaven and Earth. We should feel stripped of our normal occasions for boasting and pride—standing before our Creator, throwing ourselves humbly before His mercy seat. In that condition, we can humbly cry out, "God, have mercy on me—a sinner." (Luke 18:13).

Thus, the Day of Atonement was a most powerful event. It gave occasion for the high priest to lead God's people in self-abasement. They all witnessed the high priest approach God's presence in total sincerity—entering the smoke as a humble man interceding for the people.

The ground is level at the foot of the cross. We are all in need of atonement. And the path to atonement begins with humility before God. This behavior is likewise modeled by the Christ—who although possessing full rights as God, willingly took upon Himself the humble stature of a man (Phil. 2:5-8). Therefore, God requires the high priest to approach the ark on the Day of Atonement in Christ-like humility, being stripped of all regalia.

Year of Jubilee

Every fifty years, a "Year of Jubilee" is declared on the Day of Atonement (Lev. 25:8-55). During this year, liberty is proclaimed to all the land's inhabitants, and each person returns to his family and clan. All land which was previously sold is returned to the original families. Therefore, although the original inheritor of a parcel of land may sell it, it will return to his possession automatically at the next Year of Jubilee. And, during this year, nothing is sown or reaped.

When considering the Day of Atonement, it makes sense the Year of Jubilee would be declared on this day. During the atonement, God ransoms the sins of His people—granting them life in the place of death. Therefore, during the Year of Jubilee there is likewise declared a redemption—where the entire economy resets itself.

God's Law does not allow His people to gain ruthless financial advantages over others which can be held for successive generations. Rather, His Law demands all His people to be treated as tenets, but the land and all its inhabitants ultimately belong to Him.

Festival of Tabernacles
(Lev. 23:33-43; Num. 29:12-39; Deu. 16:13-17; 31:10-13)

The 14th Day of the 7th Month

- Preparation for Festival of Tabernacles
- All God's people complete preparations for the first day of the Festival of Tabernacles (on the 15th day of the 7th month) by gathering leafy branches from trees to be used in temporary shelters

The 15th Day of the 7th Month

- First day of Festival of Tabernacles
- **Step 1**: Trumpets sounded to gather God's people (Num. 10:10). People forbidden from working on this day (Lev. 23:24).
- **Step 2**: A scheduled representative from God's people delivers the following six items to the high priest/priest**: (1) thirteen young bulls, (2) two rams, (3) one male goat, (4) fourteen male lambs one-year-old, (5) five and seven-tenths ephahs of fine flour mixed with olive oil, and (6) 10.66 hins wine.* [*-Note: *Due to the absence of drink requirements for this day, I borrow the numbers from the proportions used during New Moon offerings—half-hin wine for each bull, third-hin wine for each ram, and quarter-hin wine for each lamb. This adds up to 10.66 hins wine.*]
- **Step 3**: The goat is set aside.
- **Step 4**: The other items are used as burnt offerings, offered by the high priest/priest at the altar as an aroma unto the Lord. When performing the burnt offerings, the bulls are each matched with three-tens ephah of flour and a half hin of wine; the rams are each matched with two-tenths ephah of flour and a third hin of wine; and each lamb is matched with one-tenth ephah of flour and a quarter hin of wine. Follow "burnt offering" procedures on page 207.
- **Step 5**: As specified in the "burnt offering" procedures on page 207, the aforementioned wine is poured out upon the bread table in the tabernacle by the high priest or a priest (see page 40 for more information on the bread table).
- **Step 6**: The above goat is presented as a sin offering by the high priest/priest (Num. 28:15). Follow "sin offering" procedures, titled, "A Leader's Sin Offering," on page 230.

The 16th Day of the 7th Month

- Second day of Festival of Tabernacles
- **Step 1**: Trumpets sounded to gather God's people (Num. 10:10).
- **Step 2**: A scheduled representative from God's people delivers the following six items to the high priest/priest**: (1) <u>twelve</u> young bulls, (2) two rams, (3) one male goat, (4) fourteen male lambs one-year-old, (5) <u>five and four-tenths</u> ephahs of fine flour mixed with olive oil, and (6) <u>10.16</u> hins wine.* [*-Note: *Due to the absence of drink requirements for this day, I borrow the numbers from the proportions used during New Moon offerings—half-hin wine for each bull, third-hin wine for each ram, and quarter-hin wine for each lamb. This adds up to* <u>10.16</u> *hins wine.*]
- **Step 3**: The goat is set aside.
- **Step 4**: The other items are used as burnt offerings, offered by the high priest/priest at the altar as an aroma unto the Lord. When performing the burnt offerings, the bulls are each matched with three-tens ephah of flour and a half hin of wine; the rams are each matched with two-tenths ephah of flour and a third hin of wine; and each lamb is matched with one-tenth ephah of flour and a quarter hin of wine. Follow "burnt offering" procedures on page 207.
- **Step 5**: As specified in the "burnt offering" procedures on page 207, the aforementioned wine is poured out upon the bread table in the tabernacle by the high priest or a priest (see page 40 for more information on the bread table).
- **Step 6**: The above goat is presented as a sin offering by the high priest/priest (Num. 28:15). Follow "sin offering" procedures, titled, "A Leader's Sin Offering," on page 230.

The 17th Day of the 7th Month

- Third day of Festival of Tabernacles
- **Step 1**: Trumpets sounded to gather God's people (Num. 10:10).
- **Step 2**: A scheduled representative from God's people delivers the following six items to the high priest/priest**: (1) <u>eleven</u> young bulls, (2) two rams, (3) one male goat, (4) fourteen male lambs one-year-old, (5) <u>five and one-tenth</u> ephahs of fine flour mixed with olive oil, and (6) <u>9.66</u> hins wine.* [*-Note: *Due to the absence of drink requirements for this day, I borrow the numbers from the proportions used during New Moon offerings—half-hin wine for each bull, third-hin wine for each ram, and quarter-hin wine for each lamb. This adds up to* <u>9.66</u> *hins wine.*]
- **Step 3**: The goat is set aside.
- **Step 4**: The other items are used as burnt offerings, offered by the high priest/priest at the altar as an aroma unto the Lord. When performing the burnt offerings, the bulls are each matched with three-tens ephah of flour and a half hin of wine; the rams are each matched with two-tenths ephah of flour and a third hin of wine; and each lamb is matched with one-tenth ephah of flour and a quarter hin of wine. Follow "burnt offering" procedures on page 207.
- **Step 5**: As specified in the "burnt offering" procedures on page 207, the aforementioned wine is poured out upon the bread table in the tabernacle by the high priest or a priest (see page 40 for more information on the bread table).
- **Step 6**: The above goat is presented as a sin offering by the high priest/priest (Num. 28:15). Follow "sin offering" procedures, titled, "A Leader's Sin Offering," on page 230.

The 18th Day of the 7th Month

- Fourth day of Festival of Tabernacles
- **Step 1**: Trumpets sounded to gather God's people (Num. 10:10).
- **Step 2**: A scheduled representative from God's people delivers the following six items to the high priest/priest**: (1) <u>ten</u> young bulls, (2) two rams, (3) one male goat, (4) fourteen male lambs one-year-old, (5) <u>four and eight-tenths</u> ephahs of fine flour mixed with olive oil, and (6) <u>9.16</u> hins wine.*
  [*-Note: *Due to the absence of drink requirements for this day, I borrow the numbers from the proportions used during New Moon offerings—half-hin wine for each bull, third-hin wine for each ram, and quarter-hin wine for each lamb. This adds up to 9.16 hins wine.*]
- **Step 3**: The goat is set aside.
- **Step 4**: The other items are used as burnt offerings, offered by the high priest/priest at the altar as an aroma unto the Lord. When performing the burnt offerings, the bulls are each matched with three-tens ephah of flour and a half hin of wine; the rams are each matched with two-tenths ephah of flour and a third hin of wine; and each lamb is matched with one-tenth ephah of flour and a quarter hin of wine. Follow "burnt offering" procedures on page 207.
- **Step 5**: As specified in the "burnt offering" procedures on page 207, the aforementioned wine is poured out upon the bread table in the tabernacle by the high priest or a priest (see page 40 for more information on the bread table).
- **Step 6**: The above goat is presented as a sin offering by the high priest/priest (Num. 28:15). Follow "sin offering" procedures, titled, "A Leader's Sin Offering," on page 230.

The 19th Day of the 7th Month

- Fifth day of Festival of Tabernacles
- **Step 1**: Trumpets sounded to gather God's people (Num. 10:10).
- **Step 2**: A scheduled representative from God's people delivers the following six items to the high priest/priest**: (1) <u>nine</u> young bulls, (2) two rams, (3) one male goat, (4) fourteen male lambs one-year-old, (5) <u>four and a half</u> ephahs of fine flour mixed with olive oil, and (6) <u>8.66</u> hins wine.*
  [*-Note: *Due to the absence of drink requirements for this day, I borrow the numbers from the proportions used during New Moon offerings—half-hin wine for each bull, third-hin wine for each ram, and quarter-hin wine for each lamb. This adds up to* <u>*8.66 hins wine.*</u>]
- **Step 3**: The goat is set aside.
- **Step 4**: The other items are used as burnt offerings, offered by the high priest/priest at the altar as an aroma unto the Lord. When performing the burnt offerings, the bulls are each matched with three-tens ephah of flour and a half hin of wine; the rams are each matched with two-tenths ephah of flour and a third hin of wine; and each lamb is matched with one-tenth ephah of flour and a quarter hin of wine. Follow "burnt offering" procedures on page 207.
- **Step 5**: As specified in the "burnt offering" procedures on page 207, the aforementioned wine is poured out upon the bread table in the tabernacle by the high priest or a priest (see page 40 for more information on the bread table).
- **Step 6**: The above goat is presented as a sin offering by the high priest/priest (Num. 28:15). Follow "sin offering" procedures, titled, "A Leader's Sin Offering," on page 230.

The 20th Day of the 7th Month

- Sixth day of Festival of Tabernacles
- **Step 1**: Trumpets sounded to gather God's people (Num. 10:10).
- **Step 2**: A scheduled representative from God's people delivers the following six items to the high priest/priest**: (1) <u>eight</u> young bulls, (2) two rams, (3) one male goat, (4) fourteen male lambs one-year-old, (5) <u>four and two-tenths</u> ephahs of fine flour mixed with olive oil, and (6) <u>8.16</u> hins wine.*
  [*-Note: *Due to the absence of drink requirements for this day, I borrow the numbers from the proportions used during New Moon offerings—half-hin wine for each bull, third-hin wine for each ram, and quarter-hin wine for each lamb. This adds up to* <u>*8.16 hins wine.*</u>]
- **Step 3**: The goat is set aside.
- **Step 4**: The other items are used as burnt offerings, offered by the high priest/priest at the altar as an aroma unto the Lord. When performing the burnt offerings, the bulls are each matched with three-tens ephah of flour and a half hin of wine; the rams are each matched with two-tenths ephah of flour and a third hin of wine; and each lamb is matched with one-tenth ephah of flour and a quarter hin of wine. Follow "burnt offering" procedures on page 207.
- **Step 5**: As specified in the "burnt offering" procedures on page 207, the aforementioned wine is poured out upon the bread table in the tabernacle by the high priest or a priest (see page 40 for more information on the bread table).
- **Step 6**: The above goat is presented as a sin offering by the high priest/priest (Num. 28:15). Follow "sin offering" procedures, titled, "A Leader's Sin Offering," on page 230.

The 21st Day of the 7th Month

- Seventh day of Festival of Tabernacles
- **Step 1**: Trumpets sounded to gather God's people (Num. 10:10).
- **Step 2**: A scheduled representative from God's people delivers the following six items to the high priest/priest**: (1) seven young bulls, (2) two rams, (3) one male goat, (4) fourteen male lambs one-year-old, (5) three and nine-tenths ephahs of fine flour mixed with olive oil, and (6) 7.66 hins wine.*
  [*-Note: *Due to the absence of drink requirements for this day, I borrow the numbers from the proportions used during New Moon offerings—half-hin wine for each bull, third-hin wine for each ram, and quarter-hin wine for each lamb. This adds up to 7.66 hins wine.*]
- **Step 3**: The goat is set aside.
- **Step 4**: The other items are used as burnt offerings, offered by the high priest/priest at the altar as an aroma unto the Lord. When performing the burnt offerings, the bulls are each matched with three-tens ephah of flour and a half hin of wine; the rams are each matched with two-tenths ephah of flour and a third hin of wine; and each lamb is matched with one-tenth ephah of flour and a quarter hin of wine. Follow "burnt offering" procedures on page 207.
- **Step 5**: As specified in the "burnt offering" procedures on page 207, the aforementioned wine is poured out upon the bread table in the tabernacle by the high priest or a priest (see page 40 for more information on the bread table).
- **Step 6**: The above goat is presented as a sin offering by the high priest/priest (Num. 28:15). Follow "sin offering" procedures, titled, "A Leader's Sin Offering," on page 230.

The 22nd Day of the 7th Month

- Eighth day of Festival of Tabernacles
- **Step 1**: Trumpets sounded to gather God's people (Num. 10:10).
- **Step 2**: A scheduled representative from God's people delivers the following six items to the high priest/priest**: (1) one young bull, (2) one ram, (3) one male goat, (4) seven male lambs one-year-old, (5) one and two-tenths ephahs of fine flour mixed with olive oil, and (6) 2.58 hins wine.*
  [*-Note: *Due to the absence of drink requirements for this day, I borrow the numbers from the proportions used during New Moon offerings—half-hin wine for each bull, third-hin wine for each ram, and quarter-hin wine for each lamb. This adds up to 2.58 hins wine.*]
- **Step 3**: The goat is set aside.
- **Step 4**: The other items are used as burnt offerings, offered by the high priest/priest at the altar as an aroma unto the Lord. When performing the burnt offerings, the bulls are each matched with three-tens ephah of flour and a half hin of wine; the rams are each matched with two-tenths ephah of flour and a third hin of wine; and each lamb is matched with one-tenth ephah of flour and a quarter hin of wine. Follow "burnt offering" procedures on page 207.
- **Step 5**: As specified in the "burnt offering" procedures on page 207, the aforementioned wine is poured out upon the bread table in the tabernacle by the high priest or a priest (see page 40 for more information on the bread table).
- **Step 6**: The above goat is presented as a sin offering by the high priest/priest (Num. 28:15). Follow "sin offering" procedures, titled, "A Leader's Sin Offering," on page 230.

Variable Numbers in Offerings during Festival of Tabernacles

When reading the above offering requirements for each of the eight days during the Festival of Tabernacles, you might have noticed the decreases in certain numbers as the week progresses. (To make it easier to spot, I underlined all the decreasing numbers found in each successive day.)

Beginning on the second day of the festival, the number of bulls decreases by one. Then every day after this, the number of bulls offered continues to decrease by one. And, as a result the number of flour-ephahs and wine hins also decrease proportionately.

Finally, this pattern culminates in the 7th day of the festival—when seven bulls are offered on that day. Interestingly, there are a total of 70 bulls offered on the 7 days ($13 + 12 + 11 + 10 + 9 + 8 + 7 = 70$). Therefore, this pattern is reminiscent of the seventy-sevens of Daniel's prophecy—perhaps serving to illustrate, as stated clearly elsewhere, that the Festival of Tabernacles is intended by God to continue without fail until the end of all ages (Zech. 14:16-21).

Then, on the last day of the festival, only one bull is offered—perhaps pointing toward the Messiah, upon whom all the festivals turn their attention. The number of lambs likewise decrease—but to the number seven, maybe pointing to the perfection of the one bull who is to usher in perfection at the end of all sevens (Dan. 9:24). Interestingly, as stated in Revelation 5:6, the Lord Jesus is the symbolic lamb of Heaven—possessing seven eyes and complete vision of all things. It might be the sequence of numbers within the offerings during this festival provide a numerical pattern which points God's people toward the Messiah—the one bull.

Moreover, just as the festival week is sustained by many bulls, so also God sustained His people throughout the ages with many *prophets* who served in the pattern of the Messiah, the ultimate *Prophet* (Deu. 18:18-19). But at the end of all things—when the seven-seven pattern is complete, it is the "one bull" who brings the completion to all things, ushering in perfection (Heb. 10:10).

Although we are left to live for a season as strangers and pilgrims in this fallen world, if we are mindful, we can see the pattern. Each day brings us closer—serving as a count-down to the final revelation of God in this age. The Lord Jesus will return from Heaven in the same way He went into Heaven (Acts 1:11). And, when He brings with Him His Heavenly kingdom, all our days as pilgrims will be rewarded. God will forever set up His tabernacle with us (Isa. 4:5; 66:18-23; Ezek. 37:26-28; Amos 9:11; Zech. 14:16-21).

Year of Cancelling Debts

Every seventh year is proclaimed as the "Year of Cancelling Debts." During the Festival of Tabernacles, the high priest/priest is to read Deu. 15:1-11 and 31:10-13 to the assembled people.

The Year of Cancelling Debts requires all people to be generous and openhearted to one another—forgiving debts they are owed. Interestingly, this is proclaimed during the Festival of Tabernacles—when all the people are humbled by living in simple dwellings made of leafy branches. And, from this sentiment of humble equality, God commands the people to carry forth simple compassion for one another—letting go of debts.

This grants us wonderous insight into the teachings of the Lord Jesus. In parable, He spoke of a man who—although forgiven much—violently oppressed another who owed him little (Matt. 18:28). And, in His wisdom, the Lord Jesus teaches us the same lesson we see within the association of Tabernacles and the Year of Cancelling Debts: In place of leafy branches, God has graciously given us homes. Following His example of kindness, we are likewise called to be generous and openhanded to our fellow man.

Festival of Ingathering
(Exo 23:14-19; 34:22-24)

At the end of the harvesting year, on the day after the sabbath

Although the Law of Moses does not discuss the specific steps of the Festival of Ingathering, it is likely the steps would mirror those of the Harvest Festival of First Fruits (see page 175).

Why?

Well, the Festival of Ingathering deals with harvesting—similar to the Harvest Festival of First Fruits.

So, how would the Festival of Ingathering differ from the Harvest Festival of First Fruits?

With the initial offering of the first fruits from their fields, all men gain for their families the right to eat that year's crops (see page 175). Therefore, the Festival of Ingathering should require no additional offering from the people—since they already offered the sheaf, lamb, flour and wine on their family's behalf.

So, what would happen on the Festival of Ingathering?

As explained in my above discussion of the Harvest Festival of First Fruits, it would have been necessary for the priests to be prepared to receive first fruit offerings throughout the entire summer and fall—because depending on what each family grew, they would reap their harvests at different times throughout the summer and fall.

Make sense?

Therefore, the purpose of the Festival of Ingathering was to wrap up the *entire* harvesting year—being the *last opportunity* for men to present any first fruit offerings for their families before the winter. Interestingly, this is why the LXX refers to the Festival of Ingathering as the *"feast of completion."*

Got it?

Thus, the steps for the Festival of Ingathering would mirror the steps of the Harvest Festival of First Fruits—as the last opportunity for men to offer any first fruit "sheaf" offerings for that harvesting year before the beginning of winter.

These are the steps for the Festival of Ingathering . . .

At the end of the harvesting year, on the day after the sabbath

- Festival of Ingathering
- **Step 1**: Trumpets sounded on the day after the sabbath (following the last week of the harvesting season in fall) to gather God's people who are ready to offer any remaining first fruits which were not previously offered (Num. 10:10). [*All males among God's people must appear before the tabernacle with their harvest first fruits (Exo. 23:17; 34:24). After harvesting his fields, every man is required to journey to the tabernacle with his first fruits—being prepared for the sounding of the trumpet on the day after the sabbath. The Festival of Ingathering is the last opportunity for men to make their first fruit offerings for that harvest year.*]
  Step 2: Upon hearing the trumpets, the men with first fruit offerings bring them to the priests. Each man with a first fruit offering must bring the following items: (1) a "sheaf"* of the first grain (or whatever he farms/grows/makes), (2) a year-old lamb, (3) two-tenths ephah of fine flour mixed with olive oil, and (4) quarter hin of wine. (*See note on page 176 for a detailed discussion of "sheaf.")
  -[Note: *Even if a man does not have a first fruit offering at this time, he is still required to appear at the tabernacle on the first day after the sabbath after the last harvesting week in the fall.*]
- **Step 3**: Upon receiving the items from each man, the priest "lifts up" the received sheaf as a "wave offering." The priest sets the sheaf aside for use by his own family (Num. 18:12-13). For more information on "wave offering," see page 236.
- **Step 4**: The priest offers the lamb and two-tenths ephah as a burnt offering. Follow "burnt offering" procedures on page 207.
- **Step 5**: As specified in the "burnt offering" procedures on page 207, the aforementioned wine is poured out upon the bread table in the tabernacle by the high priest or a priest (see page 40 for more information on the bread table).
- **Step 6**: Although unstated, it would make sense given the context of the blessing passage (Num. 6:22-27), for each priest to send away each man with the blessing.

Even if a man does not have a first fruit offering at this time, he is still required to appear at the tabernacle on the first day after the sabbath after the last harvesting week in the fall.

Additional Festivals Not in the Law

Of course, over time other festivals were added to the required ones taught by Moses. This includes the celebration of Purim in the book of Esther and also the celebration of Hanukkah which was instituted during the Intertestamental Period. However, if one ventures to simply reestablish the Law of Moses, it is important to remember that additional festivals and celebrations are not required therein (Deu. 4:2). Only the above discussed festivals and celebrations are required by the Law of Moses.

You are free to decide for yourself the validity of additional celebrations, but do so with the understanding they were not commanded by God in the Law of Moses itself (Deu. 4:2). The reader is encouraged to research such festivals separately to determine if there is adequate Biblical support to warrant their observation despite their lack of mention in the Law.

Annual Festival/Offering Minimum Requirements

If you are a stickler for details, you may wonder *how many* animals and other supplies you would need to provide for *all* the above festivals. Of course, there are some variables—especially with the Harvest Festival of First Fruits & Festival of Ingathering—depending on how much God's people choose to bring. But in the cases where we know *exact* numbers, I can provide the "minimums" required to perform the festival offerings for one year.

Earlier in Phase #3, I noted how the high priest and priest should be skilled administrators—similar to Joseph and Daniel (see page 92). This being the case, it is advisable that anyone in these positions should carefully *plan ahead for the annual calendar*—ensuring local farms carry extra stock of animals and supplies which are always available for use. After all, the tabernacle should never arrive at a calendar date to find the necessary supplies are unavailable.

Thus, I provide the following graph as a general guideline for planning efforts. (The following graph shows the numbers required in an entire year of 365 days, including 12 new moons.)

ANNUAL REQUIRED	Bulls	Rams	Goats	Lambs	Flour Ephahs	Wine Hins	Olive Oil Hins
Morning Offerings	0	0	0	365 (male or female)	36.5	91.25	91.25
Evening Offerings	0	0	0	365 (male or female)	36.5	91.25	91.25
Sabbath Offerings	0	0	0	104 (male or female)	10.4	13	13
New Moon Offerings	24	12	12 (male)	84 (male)	18	36.96	0
Passover/ Unleavened*	14	7	7 (male)	49 (male)	10.5	0	0
HFFF*	0	0	0	Variable	Variable	Variable	0
Weeks/Pent*	2	1	1 (male)	7 (male)	1.7	3.08	0
Trumpets*	1	1	1 (male)	7 (male)	1.2	0	0
Atonement	2	1	2 (male)	7 (male)	1.2	0	0
Tabernacles	71	15	8 (male)	105 (male)	34.8	66.7	0
Ingathering*	0	0	0	Variable	Variable	Variable	0
TOTALS	**114**	**37**	**31 (male)**	**1,093**	**150.8**	**302.24**	**195.5**

By using the above numbers for planning efforts, the high priest could maintain a fallback plan in the case that a scheduled representative is delayed or otherwise unable to bring a required offering on the prescribed date. By maintaining liaison with local farms near the tabernacle, the high priest could have a supernumerary representative go to a local farm to get the required supplies for the respective day's offerings. Then, upon the arrival of the delayed representative, he could simply reimburse the local farm. (For more information on this type of planning, read pages 67-94.)

*-[Note: Keep in mind that this graph only includes the required offerings at the tabernacle—not the offerings made by individuals. For example, the number of animals listed for Passover in the above graph does not include all the lambs eaten in households. Nor do the above numbers reflect the individual offerings during the Harvest Festival of First Fruits, Festival of Weeks, Festival of Trumpets or Festival of Ingathering.]

How to Keep the Law
Phase 6
Sacrifice & Offering

In the book of Ezra, it explains the priests offered sacrifices upon a newly constructed altar before even the foundation of the temple was laid. Rather than waiting for the completion of the *entire* temple, God's people chose to institute their worship calendar immediately—celebrating first the Festival of Tabernacles, then the others in order (Ez. 3:2-6).

So, just because the people of God do not have a temple or tabernacle, it doesn't mean they shouldn't observe the calendar or offer sacrifices. They simply did what they could—beginning their worship calendar on the next scheduled festival day, which happened to be Tabernacles in the seventh month. And this was a fitting way to begin their worship cycle—when considering the people were not fully established in the land. Thus, this camping festival was apropos for their situation indeed.

Why am I telling you this?

Well, to "keep the Law of Moses," one must observe the calendar and offer the prescribed sacrifices and offerings. It is incorrect for a person to say they are "keeping the Law of Moses" if the sacrifices and offerings are not presented.

Sacrifice is a profound concept. And, if you are like me, when reading discussions about animal sacrifice, you might be conditioned to think of it as wasteful.

After all, what is the point of killing and animal—just to burn it on an altar?

The straightforward answer is the sacrifices provided food portions for the priests and Levites. And, I am quite convinced these sacrifices—all of them in fact—are most useful for supernatural purposes, providing the means for supernatural things in our world. Indeed, the Holy Spirit is directly connected with the life of Earth's creatures, so it is feasible that the withdrawal of life as part of the Law could perform supernatural transfers of some kind—perhaps allowing for healing and miracles (Psa. 104:27-30). But I will not further explore such musings here.

The point of this book is for me to simply present the Law to you—not paste all my creative thoughts to it. I mention this to stir your interest in my other books—which are chock full of my own musings and theories. Since you are nearly done with this book, perhaps you could consider reading another. If you are interested, I have written other books which further interact with the tabernacle—especially how it works both naturally and supernaturally.

I say this simply to challenge your conditioning as a 21st Century human. Just because we don't fully understand animal sacrifice, this doesn't mean it is *wasteful*. It simply means we don't understand. So, if you desire to understand this topic further, I invite you to read my other books to coach you in the process of developing your own perspective.

But I digress.

In earlier Phases, you might have noticed my frequent notes—referring to *types of offerings*. In this Phase, I will present the different types of offerings. When performing the different ceremonies on the tabernacle calendar, the high priest and priests would simply conduct each specified offering as detailed below.

So, without further ado, I present you with the offerings of the Law of Moses . . .

Enjoy!

Burnt Offering
(Lev. 1:1-17; 6:8-13; 9:12-14; Num. 15:3-12;
Deu. 12:13-14; 12:26-27; 17:1; 18:3-5)

-**Step 1**: One of God's people brings the following items to the tabernacle entrance: (1) a male bull, ram, goat, lamb or dove/pigeon (Lev. 1:3), (2) flour offering*, and (3) drink offering.* (In the case of a morning offering, evening offering, or sabbath offering, female or male lambs can be offered as burnt offerings.)
–[*Note: *To determine the appropriate size of the flour offering and drink offering, match a _bull_ with three-tenths ephah of flour and a half hin of wine; a _ram_ with two-tenths ephah of flour and a third hin of wine; or a _lamb_ with one-tenth ephah of flour and a quarter hin of wine (Num. 15:3-12). The amount for a goat and a dove/pigeon is unspecified, but would be proportionate in size based on the animal. For example, if a goat is a little bigger than a lamb, then the drink offering and flour offering would be a little bigger.*]

-**Step 2**: The person offering the animal lays his hand upon its head before the priest (Lev. 1:4). Laying hand upon its head grants atonement.

-**Step 3**: Priest slaughters the animal (Lev. 1:4): <u>Bulls and rams</u> are slaughtered at tabernacle entrance (Lev. 1:3); <u>lambs and goats</u> are slaughtered on the north side of the altar table (Lev. 1:10-11); <u>dove/pigeon</u> is slaughtered at the altar table (Lev. 1:14-17). For more information on the altar table, see page 20.

-**Step 4**: Priest sprinkles blood on all the sides of the altar table—most likely on the horns and table top (Lev. 1:5).

-**Step 5**: Priest butchers the animal: <u>Bull/ram/lamb/goat</u> is butchered by (1) removing its skin, (2) cutting its body into pieces, (3) the head, fat, internal organs and legs are separated, (4) entrails, feet and belly are washed (Lev. 1:6-9; 9:14). A <u>dove/pigeon</u> is slaughtered and butchered by (1) wringing off its head, (2) draining blood from its body on the side of the altar table, (3) crop and feathers removed and thrown east of the altar where the ashes are, and (4) wings are opened as it is placed upon the wood fire (Lev. 1:14-17). The priest completes this process by determining portions as follows . . .
-*Portion for the priests**: For all bulls or sheep presented as offerings, the priests are authorized to take for themselves meat from the head, internal organs and a shoulder (which would mean a leg) (Deu. 18:3). The LXX further clarifies the specific part of the head and internal organs, explaining the priests could take the cheek meat from the head, and the great intestine. This would mean the priest would remove the cheek meat from the head before he placed it on the fire as the Lord's portion, in addition to removing the great intestine before he placed the internal organs on the fire as the Lord's portion. [Wave Offering: *Priests were also authorized to take for themselves meat from the breast and right shoulder (Num. 18:18). Whenever a priest takes for himself the breast and right shoulder (that is the entire leg) of an animal, he must "lift it up" as a wave offering with the fat upon it. Then the priest separates the pieces in his hands in different shares: the Lord's portion is the fat—which is placed on the altar table to be burned; the priest's portion is the breast and right shoulder. For more information on "wave offerings," see page 236.*] All these pieces for the priest would be cooked in similar manner to the meat of the "consecration ceremony"—near the tabernacle and most

likely boiled. Moreover, Lev. 7:8 says the priest is authorized to keep the hide of any animal offered as a burnt offering—but the LXX omits this.

-*Portion for the Levites**: Deu. 18:1 states the Levites were authorized to eat meat from the burnt offerings, but it does not specify what part. Perhaps 1 Sam. 2:13-16 is referring to a Levite as a "servant of the priest." If so, then 1 Sam. 2:13-16 may indicate the practice of Levites in being permitted to remove an unspecified portion of meat for themselves after the fat portions were butchered and placed on the altar table as the Lord's portion.

-*Portion for the one bringing the sacrifice**: The person offering a burnt offering is authorized to eat an unspecified portion of the meat once the blood and other portions are removed (Deu. 12:17-18, 27). The meat would be cooked, most likely boiled, near the tabernacle—as in the consecration ceremony—and not on the altar table itself.

-*Portion for the Lord*: The butchered animal pieces which will not be used in portions for the one bringing the sacrifice, or for the priest's portion or for the Levites portion are all devoted to the fire as the Lord's portion, including the head, fat, internal organs and legs (Lev. 1:8-9).

*-[Note: <u>Whole Burnt Offering</u>: *A "whole burnt offering" is a burnt offering where no portions are taken from the sacrificial animal. During a "whole burnt offering," the person offering it, the priest and Levites abstain from their assigned portions. Instead, the entire animal is devoted to the fire of the altar table as the Lord's portion. An example of this occurs in the "consecration ceremony"—where the first ram is offered as a "whole" burnt offering (Exo. 29:18) (see page 238). For a discussion of when priests and Levites would consider abstaining from an assigned portion, see the section titled, "When to Abstain from a Portion: A Discussion of Lev. 10:16-20" on page 235.*]

-**Step 6**: Priest adds wood to altar table and arranges it for the animal pieces and the flour offering designated as the <u>Lord's portion</u> (Lev. 1:7). –[Note: *Fire always remains burning on the altar table (except when tabernacle being relocated) (Lev. 6:12).*]

-**Step 7**: The aforementioned wine is poured out upon the bread table in the tabernacle by the priest (Num. 15:3-12) (see page 40 for more information on the bread table).

-**Step 8**: As necessary, ashes from altar table are placed in pile east of the altar table (Lev. 1:16). As necessary, to dispose of the ash pile: (1) the priest changes his clothes, putting on unspecified clothing—leaving behind his normal priestly clothes, (2) he relocates the ashes to a ceremonially clean place outside the camp, and (3) upon his return to the tabernacle area, the priest changes his clothes, clothing himself again with his normal priestly clothes (Lev. 6:10-11) (for an illustration of the priests' clothing, see page 50). It is likely this would be a duty for the priests rather than the high priest due to the high priest bearing the ephod.

-**Step 9**: Burnt offerings are left burning overnight (Lev. 6:9)

Confession (Lev. 26:40-45)

Lev. 26:40-45 offers forgiveness to the entire community of God's people who would be unfaithful and hostile toward the Lord—if only they would choose to confess their sins and the sins of their ancestors and humble themselves. This is the most remarkable proof which stands against false claims that God does not offer forgiveness for *intentional* sin. Even in this most dire example, the Lord offers complete restoration to his repentant community—and He grants it even before an animal sacrifice can be offered. In other words, God extends forgiveness *first*, *then* the community brings the guilt offering (Num.15:22-26)!

Therefore, we can conclude, when God examines the hearts of all people, if He determines them to be true, they are never beyond His reach! As long as you have breath it is *never too late* to confess your sins and ask forgiveness in humility.

Now, you might have previously thought the Law to be cold and uncompassionate. But when understanding this principle, we see clearly God's eagerness to restore the covenant to His people—no matter how far they have wandered. And it is through repentance of the heart that restoration occurs—not through sacrifice. God immediately accepts repentance and grants atonement to allow the restoration of the covenant. And, only after this extension of grace do God's people reinstitute tabernacle sacrifice out of obedience and love for Him who first loved us.

Therefore, the Law powerfully declares grace to those who are far off (Lev. 26:40-45).

Don't forget this.

So, what are the steps which the wayward community of God's people would follow? Just these . . .

-**Step 1**: Confess your sins, unfaithfulness and hostility
-**Step 2**: Receive the restoration of the covenant

If you are looking for an example of such confession and restoration, read Dan. 9:2-23. In this example, we see the angel Gabriel was prepared for the exact moment Daniel prayed on behalf of God's people. And, being faithful to His promise in Lev. 26:40-45, God *immediately* accepts Daniel's prayer on behalf of His wayward people.

In a far-off land, Daniel was separated from the house of the Lord and incapable of following the Law (as presented throughout this book—with the tabernacle, sacrifices and so on). In this foreign land, Daniel had no judge established to give him guidance under the authority of Moses. Therefore, Daniel brings his heartfelt complaint to the Lord Himself—as his Judge. Considering the importance of judges to the administration of the Law (see pages 239-250), it is significant Daniel's name means "the Lord is my judge."

Get it?

And, just like the judges established under the authority of Moses, the Lord made a ruling on behalf of Daniel's complaint—setting in motion events to restore the covenant unto them. Therefore, when Daniel had no other judge, the Lord Himself served as his Judge.

Beyond this, note the movement of the marching order of God's people after the *judge* (page 74). Upon receiving the Word of the Lord, Daniel was *happy* as he received the angel who answered his prayer. Then, in Dan. 10:2-3, he fasts and receives a series of visions as he *wrestles* with the future. Last, in the promise of his resurrection in Dan. 12:13, Daniel can offer *praise*—recognizing God has granted him as a *wage* an everlasting *habitation*, promising him an allotted portion in God's inheritance. Thus, as seen at other places in the Bible, the unfolding of events follows the marching order established in the Law.

Do you understand? Do you see it?

Drink Offering

Wine and drink is offered by being poured out upon the bread table in the tabernacle by the high priest or a priest (Num. 15:3-12) (see page 40 for more information on the bread table).

Drink & Its Significance

Drink is specifically required in many of the offerings discussed in this Phase. Additionally, it is used in many of the calendar ceremonies discussed on pages 153-204.

Why?

Similar to the flour's representation of the body, drink likewise represents the blood of the Messiah. In the Last Supper, the Lord Jesus invites His followers to drink wine—as an earthly representation of the atoning sacrifice He completes on our behalf within the Heavenly tabernacle (Luke 22:20).

Therefore, wine and drink in the Law serve a unique function in representing the blood of the Messiah—which was shed for you.

It is unstated whether or not priests and Levites were authorized to receive a portion of offered drinks.

Do you think priests and Levites should be authorized to drink a portion of the offered wine before it is poured out upon the bread table?

Fellowship Offering
(Lev. 3:1-17; 7:11-21; 7:28-34; 9:18-21; 10:14-15; 19:5-7; Num. 15:3-12)

-**Step 1**: One of God's people brings the following items to the tabernacle entrance: (1) a male or female lamb/goat/oxen*, and (2) kneaded loaves of baked bread with oil, from the appropriate amount of flour for the animal**, (3) drink offering of the appropriate amount for the animal. *The LXX states a fellowship offering animal can be an "oxen" (Lev. 3:1).

–[Note: *To determine the appropriate size of the flour offering and drink offering, match an <u>oxen</u> with three-tenths ephah of flour and a half hin of wine; or a <u>lamb</u> with one-tenth ephah of flour and a quarter hin of wine (Num. 15:3-12). The amount for a goat is unspecified, but would be proportionate in size based on the animal. For example, if a goat is a little bigger than a lamb, then the drink offering and flour offering would be a little bigger.*]

–[**Note: *The <u>loaves of bread can have yeast</u> in them, however, if the loaves have yeast they cannot be burned on the altar table as the Lord's portion (Exo. 34:25). Rather, the priests would take for their own portion any loaves made with yeast. (Lev. 7:11-13)*]

-**Step 2**: The person offering the animal lays his hand upon its head before the priest.

-**Step 3**: Priest slaughters the animal at the tabernacle entrance.

-**Step 4**: Priest sprinkles blood on all the sides of the altar table—most likely on the horns and table top.

-**Step 5**: Priest butchers the animal: <u>An oxen</u>* is butchered by (1) removing the internal organs and their fat, (2) removing the liver and surrounding fat, and (3) removing the kidneys and surrounding fat (Lev. 3:3-4). A <u>lamb</u> is butchered by (1) removing the rump, also called the "fat tail," (2) removing the internal organs and their fat, (3) removing the liver and surrounding fat, and (4) removing the kidneys and surrounding fat (Lev. 3:7-10). A <u>goat</u> is butchered by (1) removing the internal organs and their fat, (2) removing the liver and surrounding fat, and (3) removing the kidneys and surrounding fat (Lev. 3:12-15).

–[*Note: Due to the mention of "oxen" in the LXX in Lev. 3:1, it is likely the butchering instructions found in Lev. 3:3-5 are intended for an ox offering. Perhaps, due to lack of agreement between the LXX and some English versions, it would be best to opt for lambs and goats only as fellowship offerings.]

-**Step 6**: As necessary, priest adds wood to altar table and arranges it for the animal pieces designated as the <u>Lord's portion</u>. –[Note: *Fire always remains burning on the altar table (except when tabernacle being relocated) (Lev. 6:12).*]

-**Step 7**: The priest takes in his hands the breast and right shoulder of the animal and places the fat upon them (Lev. 10:15). Then he lifts up his hands as a "wave offering." [*The Lord's portion is the fat—which is placed on the altar table to be burned; the priest's portion is the breast and right shoulder. For more information on "wave offerings," see page 236.*]

-**Step 8**: The priest completes this butchering process by determining portions as follows . . .

-*Portion for the Lord*: Includes all fat (including rump/fat tail), liver, kidneys and internal organs.

-[Note: *If the bread loaves brought in Step #1 have yeast, they cannot be burned on the altar table as the Lord's portion (Exo. 34:25).*]

-*Portion for the priests*: For fellowship offerings, the priests were authorized to take for themselves meat from the breast and right shoulder (as discussed in the Step #7 "wave offering"). For all sheep presented as offerings, the priests were authorized to also take for themselves meat from the head, internal organs and a shoulder (which would mean a leg) (Deu. 18:3). The LXX further clarifies the specific part of the head and internal organs, explaining the priests could take the cheek meat from the head, and the great intestine. These pieces would be cooked in similar manner to the meat of the "consecration ceremony"—near the tabernacle and most likely boiled. The meat of the fellowship animal must be eaten on the day it is offered (Lev. 7:15).

-[Note: *If the bread loaves brought in Step #1 have yeast, they cannot be burned on the altar table as the Lord's portion (Exo. 34:25). All bread loaves with yeast are the priest's portion.*]

-*Portion for the Levites*: Deu. 18:1 states the Levites were authorized to eat meat from the burnt offerings, but it does not specify what part. Perhaps 1 Sam. 2:13-16 is referring to a Levite as a "servant of the priest." If so, then 1 Sam. 2:13-16 may indicate the practice of Levites in being permitted to remove an unspecified portion of meat for themselves after the fat portions were butchered and placed on the altar table as the Lord's portion.

-*Portion for the one bringing the sacrifice**: If they are ceremonially clean, the person offering a fellowship offering is authorized to eat an unspecified portion of the meat once the blood and other portions are removed (Lev. 7:19). The meat would be cooked, most likely boiled, near the tabernacle—as in the consecration ceremony—and not on the altar table itself.

-*Remaining meat*: Any meat remaining after the removal of the above portions can be eaten without specificity—by priests, Levites and the one bringing the sacrifice as long as he is ceremonially clean. Remaining fat found while eating is burned on altar table late in the evening, before the morning, after the high priest/priest adds firewood (Lev. 6:12).

-**Step 9**: The aforementioned wine is poured out upon the bread table in the tabernacle by the high priest or a priest (Num. 15:3-12) (see page 40 for more information on the bread table).

-**Step 10**: As necessary, ashes from altar table are placed in pile east of the altar table (Lev. 1:16). As necessary, to dispose of the ash pile: (1) the priest changes his clothes, putting on unspecified clothing—leaving behind his normal priestly clothes, (2) he relocates the ashes to a ceremonially clean place outside the camp, and (3) upon his return to the tabernacle area, the priest changes his clothes, clothing himself again with his normal priestly clothes (Lev. 6:10-11) (for an illustration of the priests' clothing, see page 50). It is likely this would be a duty for the priests rather than the high priest due to the high priest bearing the ephod.

-**Step 11**: Evening: Any remaining meat from fellowship offerings must be burned (Lev. 7:15). Remaining fat found while eating is burned on altar table late in the evening, before the morning, after the high priest/priest adds firewood (Lev. 6:12). Offerings smoldering on the altar table are left burning all night.

Freewill Offering
(Exo 35:29; Lev. 7:16-18; 22:18-23; Num. 15:3-12; Deu. 16:10)

<u>Freewill offerings can be used to gather tabernacle materials</u>: In Exo. 35:29 and 36:3 it explains how freewill offerings were used to gather all the materials for the construction of the tabernacle. In these cases, a person could simply bring forth the required item and would not be required to follow all the below steps. Deu. 16:10 indicates the Festival of Weeks was the appropriate time for God's people to bring various materials and items as freewill offerings—similar to the initial freewill offerings received to fund the tabernacle's original construction.

<u>Freewill offerings are appropriate for vows</u>: When a person desires to make a vow, he can offer a freewill offering to commemorate that vow, as explained in Lev. 22:18-23.* A person deciding to make a vow would follow the same steps below (although he should read Matt. 5:34-37 first).

If a person is bringing an animal as a part of his freewill offering, he would follow the below steps . . .

-**Step 1**: One of God's people brings the following items to the tabernacle entrance: (1) a male lamb/goat,* (2) flour offering**, and (3) drink offering.**
-[*Note: *In Lev. 22:23, some English translations permit God's people to offer deformed oxen or sheep for a freewill offering; however, the LXX <u>strictly forbids the offering of any deformed animal</u>—even citing various example of animal deformity. Therefore, it would be prudent to <u>require all animals to be completely blemish-free</u> to meet the requirements of the LXX.*]
–[**Note: *To determine the appropriate size of the flour offering and drink offering, match a <u>lamb</u> with one-tenth ephah of flour and a quarter hin of wine (Num. 15:3-12). The amount for a goat is unspecified, but would be proportionate in size based on the animal. For example, if a goat is a little bigger than a lamb, then the drink offering and flour offering would be a little bigger.*]

-**Step 2**: Priest slaughters the animal. This is most likely done at the tabernacle entrance.

-**Step 3**: Priest butchers the animal. –[Note: *Although details are absent from English translations, the LXX provides the following details in Lev. 7:19-24 regarding the "gift" portion presented to the Lord. If this is referring to freewill offerings*]. Butchering would be accomplished as follows: A <u>lamb/goat</u> is butchered by (1) removing the breast, (2) removing the right shoulder (that is the entire right leg), (3) removing the liver and surrounding fat, and (4) removing additional fat.

-**Step 4**: As necessary, priest adds wood to altar table and arranges it for the animal pieces designated as the Lord's portion.
-[Note: *Fire always remains burning on the altar table (except when tabernacle being relocated) (Lev. 6:12).*]

-**Step 5**: The priest takes in his hands the breast and right shoulder of the animal and places the fat upon them (Lev. 10:15). Then he lifts up his hands as a "wave offering." [*Then the priest separates the pieces in his hands in different shares: the Lord's portion is the fat—which is placed on the altar table to be burned; the priest's portion is the breast and right shoulder. For more information on "wave offerings," see page 236.*]

-**Step 6**: The priest completes this butchering process by determining portions as follows . . .

-*Portion for the Lord*: Includes all fat and the liver, along with the flour offering.

-*Portion for the priests*: If Lev. 7:19-24 in the LXX is a reference to freewill/gift offerings, then the priests are authorized to take for themselves meat from the breast and right shoulder (which would mean the entire leg). For all sheep presented as offerings, the priests were authorized to also take for themselves meat from the head, internal organs and a shoulder (which would mean a leg) (Deu. 18:3). The LXX further clarifies the specific part of the head and internal organs, explaining the priests could take the cheek meat from the head, and the great intestine. It would be cooked in similar manner to the meat of the "consecration ceremony"—near the tabernacle and most likely boiled.

-*Portion for the Levites*: Deu. 18:1 states the Levites were authorized to eat meat from offerings, but it does not specify what part. Perhaps 1 Sam. 2:13-16 is referring to a Levite as a "servant of the priest." If so, then 1 Sam. 2:13-16 may indicate the practice of Levites in being permitted to remove an unspecified portion of meat for themselves after the fat portions were butchered and placed on the altar table as the Lord's portion.

-*Portion for the one bringing the sacrifice**: The ceremonially clean person offering an animal with his freewill offering is likely authorized to eat an unspecified portion of the meat once the blood and other portions are removed—similar to the fellowship offerings (Lev. 7:19). The meat would be cooked, most likely boiled, near the tabernacle—as in the consecration ceremony—and not on the altar table itself.

-*Remaining meat*: Any meat remaining after the removal of the above portions can be eaten without specificity for two days (on the day it is offered, throughout the evening and throughout the following day)—by priests, Levites and the one bringing the sacrifice as long as he is ceremonially clean (Lev. 7:16-17).

-**Step 7**: The aforementioned wine is poured out upon the bread table in the tabernacle by the high priest or a priest (Num. 15:3-12) (see page 40 for more information on the bread table).

-**Step 8**: As necessary, ashes from altar table are placed in pile east of the altar table (Lev. 1:16). As necessary, to dispose of the ash pile: (1) the priest changes his clothes, putting on unspecified clothing—leaving behind his normal priestly clothes, (2) he relocates the ashes to a ceremonially clean place outside the camp, and (3) upon his return to the tabernacle area, the priest changes his clothes, clothing himself again with his normal priestly clothes (Lev. 6:10-11) (for an illustration of the priests' clothing, see page 50). It is likely this would be a duty for the priests rather than the high priest due to the high priest bearing the ephod.

-**Step 9**: Evening of the 2nd Day: Any remaining meat from freewill offerings must be burned (Lev. 7:16-18). Offerings smoldering on the altar table are left burning all night.

Are All Freewill Offering Animals Slaughtered?

When considering the purpose of freewill offerings—to provide provisions for the households of priests, Levites and also materials for tabernacle services, we are left to consider if it was necessary for all animals offered to be sacrificed.

In other words, if a person were offering a lamb, could a priest choose instead to keep the lamb because it was a freewill offering?

When viewing the Law of Moses, we would be left to conclude:

No.

Why?

Well, in the Bible passages referenced, it appears the animals brought as freewill offerings were devoted to slaughter. After all, the tabernacle system constantly provided meat for the priests and Levites— thereby making it unnecessary for them to maintain their own animals for meat. The Bible offers examples— demonstrating the households of the priests and Levites were fully sustained with the various sacrifices presented at the tabernacle (Lev. 22:12-13). And, priests and Levites were to devote themselves to the work of the tabernacle rather than maintaining their own farms and ranches (Neh. 13:10).

Grain Offering
(Lev. 2:1-16; 6:14-23; 10:12-13; Num. 18:8-10)

Grain offerings are different than *flour offerings* used elsewhere. Although flour offerings can be referred to as "grain offerings" in Scripture, there are two different types when we closely examine the Bible texts.

All the **flour offerings** associated with the different festivals and offerings were either burned by the high priest or a priest or eaten as specified (Num. 15:3-12). These are different than the "**grain offering**" mentioned here.

The grain offering discussed here is explained in Lev. 2:1-16. It is different from the **flour offerings** in Num. 15:3-12 because those **flour offerings** are attached to animal sacrifices and drink offerings. However, the **grain offerings** of Lev. 2:1-16 are presented with frankincense and salt and are independent of animals and drinks. So, this section will deal *only* with the latter type of grain offering as presented in Lev. 2:1-16.

Interestingly, the LXX in Lev. 2:1 discusses this grain offering as a "gift"—similar to the "gift" of the freewill offerings. Therefore, we can conclude the purpose of the grain offering was to allow God's people to freely approach the priests to present them with grain offerings—similar to how a person could approach the priests with other types of freewill offerings.

In other words, it is kind of like an old lady who gives you cookies. But in this case, the man from the household would be bringing the "freewill" baked goods to the priest.

Make sense?

So, if one of God's people desired to bring a **<u>grain offering</u>**, these are the steps he would follow . . .

-**<u>Step 1</u>**: One of God's people prepares a grain offering, using unleavened fine flour and olive oil.
(A) If offered <u>near the time of the Harvest Festival of First Fruits</u>, the person would prepare this grain offering by roasting crushed heads of grain in fire. *Do not use yeast or honey.*
(B) If *not* offered near the time of the Harvest Festival of First Fruits, then follow these guidelines:
-If prepared in an <u>oven/furnace</u>, make thick loaves kneaded with olive oil, or make thin loaves brushed/anointed with olive oil. *Do not use yeast or honey.*
-If prepared in a <u>griddle/flat plate</u>, mingle it with olive oil, crumble it and pour more olive oil on top. *Do not use yeast or honey.*
-If prepared in a <u>pot/stew pan</u>, simply make it with some olive oil—no further instructions are specified. *Do not use yeast or honey.*

-**<u>Step 2</u>**: The person brings the following items to the priest at the tabernacle entrance: (1) his grain offering prepared in Step #1 above, (2) salt—to add to the grain offering (Lev. 2:13), and (3) some frankincense— according to the LXX. –[-Note: *Due to the restrictions against God's people making incense according to the tabernacle formula (Exo. 30:37; Exo. 30:33 LXX), it should be understood, the person offering the grain offering is <u>only to bring frankincense</u>. They are <u>not</u> permitted to make the sacred incense formula on page 44.*]

-**<u>Step 3</u>**: The priest receives the grain offering, salt and frankincense.

-**<u>Step 4</u>**: The priest determines portions of the grain offering. The <u>priest's portion</u> of the grain offering and salt is withheld so he can eat it along with the other priests. (No mention is made of the portion for the one offering the grain offering.) The portion determined to be the <u>Lord's portion</u> is burned along with the frankincense and salt on the altar table. -[Note: *The priest <u>cannot</u> burn the offered frankincense on the incense altar (Exo. 30:9). It must be burned on the altar table with the grain offering and salt.*]

-**<u>Step 5</u>**: In some English translations it states the priests must eat the grain offering in the tabernacle courtyard (Lev. 2:16). But the LXX does not state where the grain offering is eaten. Num. 18:9-10 indicates the priest's portions were to be regarded as holy, however, so it is likely it would need to be eaten in the tabernacle area (see also Lev. 10:12-13).

The Grain Offering Made by the New High Priest

When the high priest is replaced, the new high priest to be anointed is to bring an offering on the day he is anointed (Lev. 6:20-21). The offering is one-tenth ephah fine flour, kneaded thoroughly, then prepared with oil on a griddle. Then the incoming high priest is to break it in pieces—offering half in the morning and the other half in the evening.

Unlike the other "grain offerings," where the priest could eat a portion (see page 218), this offering had to be burned completely. The priests were not authorized to eat any portion of the grain offering for the anointing of the new high priest (Lev. 6:22-23).

(To read more about the high priest's consecration ceremony, see page 97.)

Flour & Its Significance

Flour is specifically required in many of the offerings discussed in this book. Additionally, it is used in many of the calendar ceremonies discussed on pages 153-204.

Interestingly, flour can even be offered in lieu of an animal sacrifice for a "sin offering." (page 232)

So, whereas the Law grants atonement through blood, we see here the Law also grants atonement through flour!

How is this possible?

Offerings foreshadow the sacrifice offered in Heaven discussed in the book of Hebrews. And, even in the case that flour is offered rather than blood in the tabernacle, it is still blood which truly atones in that Heavenly tabernacle—where the Messiah offers Himself on our behalf.

In John 6:35, the Lord Jesus said He is the Bread of Life. Later, at the Last Supper, He invites His followers to eat the unleavened bread as an earthly representation of His body—which would be broken on their behalf, granting atonement to all who believe in Him.

Therefore, flour in the Law atones through its representation of the very body of the Messiah—given for you.

Guilt Offering
(Lev. 5:14-6:7; 7:1-10; Num. 15:22-31; 18:8-10)

Individual Guilt Offering

The guilt offering was designed to provide a person a means of atoning for unintentional sin—as determined by a judge (see note section titled, "Intentional and Unintentional Sin" on page 223. The person who sinned *unintentionally*, upon finding out about his sin, would begin the following steps . . .

-**Step 1**: The person would pay restitution in whatever they failed to do. –[Note: *The Lord Jesus comments on the importance of reconciliation in this regard by stating such a person should go first and seek reconciliation with the person they wronged <u>before</u> they come to God's house (Matt. 5:24).*] If the person wronged another person, restitution would be paid to the person before carrying out the following procedures. If the person sinned against the Lord, they would bring appropriate restitution to the priest. To determine the amount of restitution, the person would likely need to consult with a judge established under the authority of the God-appointed leader, as explained on pages 239-250. The judge would require the person to overpay with an additional penalty of one-fifth beyond their offense (Lev. 5:16).

-**Step 2**: After paying restitution to the person they wronged, or preparing restitution to be paid to the priest, the person would bring the following items to the tabernacle entrance: (1) a ram or female goat (Lev. 5:15; Num. 15:27), (2) flour offering*, (3) drink offering*, and (4) restitution payment—if ordered by a judge to pay to priest in lieu of the person they wronged (see Step #1 above).
–[*Note: *To determine the appropriate size of the flour offering and drink offering, match the <u>ram</u> with two-tenths ephah of flour and a third hin of wine. (Num. 15:3-12). The amount for a <u>goat</u> is unspecified, but would be proportionate in size based on the animal. For example, since a goat is a little bigger than a lamb, then the drink offering and flour offering would be a little bigger than the proportions set for the lamb—which are one-tenth ephah of flour and a quarter hin of wine.*]

-**Step 3**: The priest sets aside the flour offering, drink offering and restitution payment (if applicable) from Step #2. (Lev. 1:3)

-**Step 4**: The priest slaughters the ram at the tabernacle entrance, or slaughters the female goat at the north side of the altar table.

-**Step 5**: Priest sprinkles blood on all the sides of the altar table—most likely on the horns and table top (Lev. 7:2)

-**Step 6**: As necessary, priest adds wood to altar table and arranges it for the animal pieces designated as the Lord's portion. –[Note: *Fire always remains burning on the altar table (except when tabernacle being relocated) (Lev. 6:12).*]

-**Step 7**: Priest butchers the animal: <u>Ram/goat</u> is butchered by (1) removing rump (fat tail), (2) internal organs and their fat, (3) liver and its fat, and (4) kidneys and their fat. The priest completes this process by determining portions as follows . . .

-*Portion for the Lord*: Includes all fat (including rump/fat tail), liver, kidneys and internal organs.

-*Portion for the priests*: The portion for priests is unspecified, but as a standard rule the priests would be authorized to take for themselves meat from the breast and right shoulder (that is the entire leg) as a "wave offering." The LXX further clarifies in Deu. 18:3 the specific part of the head and internal organs which could also be taken as the priest's portion, explaining the priests could take the cheek meat from the head, and the great intestine. It would be cooked in similar manner to the meat of the "consecration ceremony"—near the tabernacle and most likely boiled.

-*Portion for the Levites*: Deu. 18:1 states the Levites were authorized to eat meat from offerings, but it does not specify what part. Perhaps 1 Sam. 2:13-16 is referring to a Levite as a "servant of the priest." If so, then 1 Sam. 2:13-16 may indicate the practice of Levites in being permitted to remove an unspecified portion of meat for themselves after the fat portions were butchered and placed on the altar table as the Lord's portion.

-*Portion for the one bringing the sacrifice*: No portion is specified—likely because it is not authorized due to the purpose of the offering. The one offering the sacrifice receives atonement as his portion.

-**Step 7**: The priest takes in his hands the breast and right shoulder of the animal and places the fat upon them (Lev. 10:15). Then he lifts up his hands as a "wave offering."

-**Step 8**: The priest burns upon the altar table the butchered pieces and flour offering designated as the Lord's portion.

-**Step 9**: The aforementioned wine is poured out upon the bread table in the tabernacle by the priest (Num. 15:3-12) (see page 40 for more information on the bread table).

-**Step 10**: As necessary, ashes from altar table are placed in pile east of the altar table (Lev. 1:16). As necessary, to dispose of the ash pile: (1) the priest changes his clothes, putting on unspecified clothing—leaving behind his normal priestly clothes, (2) he relocates the ashes to a ceremonially clean place outside the camp, and (3) upon his return to the tabernacle area, the priest changes his clothes, clothing himself again with his normal priestly clothes (Lev. 6:10-11) (for an illustration of the priests' clothing, see page 50). It is likely this would be a duty for the priests rather than the high priest due to the high priest bearing the ephod.

-**Step 11**: Evening: Offerings smoldering on the altar table are left burning all night.

Community Guilt Offering (Num. 15:22-26)

In the case where the *entire community* of God's people have sinned unintentionally, they would make a guilt offering by following these steps . . .

-**Step 1**: A representative from God's people would bring forth <u>a young bull as a whole burnt offering</u>, and <u>a male goat as a sin offering</u>. Follow "burnt offering" and "sin offering" procedures found on pages 207 & 228, respectively.

-[Note: *In the judge's determination of the community's sin/guilt, he should reconcile the two requirements of the community guilt offering and the community sin offering to prescribe the appropriate offering based on the offense. The judge would need to carefully consider Lev. 4:13-21 & Num. 15:22-26.*]

Intentional and Unintentional Sin

It is often said, "there is no sacrifice for *intentional* sin." And, thus, people struggle with Heb. 10:26.

However, the point of the "guilt offering" isn't to distinguish "intent" but to give the person a pathway for atonement.

When considering the sins described in Lev. 6:1-4, it might be going too far to think there is no Law sacrifice for those who sin *intentionally*. Lev. 6:1-4 describes lying, deceiving, stealing, cheating, concealing stolen property, extortion, betraying a trust and swearing falsely. These sins all involve *intent*—or specific design on the part of the offender to make unjust gains at the expense of others. Therefore, it would be good to avoid the incorrect position of stating as others have said, "there is no sacrifice for intentional sin." Lev. 6:1-4 demonstrates the guilt offering was designed to provide atonement for *intentional* sins as well as unintentional sins.

For further consideration, reflect on Num. 15:30—which says a person who sins defiantly should be cut off from among God's people.

So, here's the problem . . .

When we consider the sins described in Lev. 6:1-4—the lying, deceiving, stealing, cheating, concealing stolen property, extortion, betraying trust and swearing falsely—all of these sins could be determined as intentionally defiant. So, why does Lev. 6 allow atonement for these defiant sins, while Num. 15:30 demands such a person to be cut off? How can these be reconciled with Heb. 10:26?

The answer:

A judge, established under the authority of the God-appointed leader, would make the determination—whether or not the person would have opportunity for atonement or if they would be cut off. Frankly, by forgetting about the system of the Law itself—and the judges who rule in such matters—people who comment on the Bible allow their thoughts to go too far. Certainly, we see this is the case when reading the various interpretations of Heb. 10:26. Without the "judge system" to make determinations, people today struggle to define for themselves what is *intentional* and what is *unintentional*. And in doing so, they err.

According to the Law of Moses, an individual would not make such distinctions for himself—whether something is innocent enough to warrant atonement through a guilt offering, or high-handed enough to warrant expulsion from the community. Instead, the "system of the judges" would render such verdicts.

This is why people should not attempt to keep the Law on their own. The Law is designed as a system. It needs the system of judges to interpret the laws for individuals. People do not interpret the Law for themselves, nor is an average person authorized to rule on what is "defiant" or "intentional."

Keep this in mind whenever you hear people say things like, "*In the Law of Moses there was no way to atone for intentional sins.*" This is not true. Judges alone are responsible for making such distinctions. Average people are not authorized to do so.

This is why people likewise struggle to understand different commands delivered to people by the Lord Jesus (Matt. 8:20-22; 19:21). Some have commented—wondering why the Lord Jesus gave such commands to these specific people.

But when understanding the system of the original Law of Moses, the commands of Jesus demonstrate the personal leadership of a legitimate "judge." A judge would hear a person, then render a verdict to resolve *their* exact situation. And, that verdict was personally relevant to only the person for whom it was given—intending to guide them to restoration. In fact, the judge was prohibited from adding any of his verdicts onto the Law as "case laws" or prior verdicts—thereby compelling judges to be concerned only with exercising leadership with the person standing before them (Deu. 4:2). Thus, the Law requires simple obedience from God's people: They would go to a judge, listen to his verdict, then obey. For more information on the system of the judges, see pages 239-250.

Moreover, concerning the topic of intentional and unintentional sin, consider Lev. 26:40-45. In this passage, God offers forgiveness to the entire unfaithful and hostile community—if only they would choose to confess their sins and humble themselves. Even in this most dire example, the Lord offers complete restoration to his repentant community—and He grants it even before an animal sacrifice can be offered. In other words, God extends forgiveness *first, then* the community brings the guilt offering (Num.15:22-26)!

Therefore, we can conclude, when God examines the hearts of all people, if He determines them to be true, they are never beyond His reach. As long as you have breath it is *never too late* to confess your sins and ask forgiveness in humility.

Now, you might have previously thought the Law to be cold and uncompassionate. But when understanding this principle, we see clearly God's eagerness to restore the covenant to His people—no matter how far they have wandered. And it is through repentance of the heart that restoration occurs—not through sacrifice. God immediately accepts repentance and grants atonement to allow the restoration of the covenant. And, only after this extension of grace do God's people reinstitute tabernacle sacrifice out of obedience and love for Him who first loved us.

Therefore, the Law powerfully declares grace to those who are far off (Lev. 26:40-45). Thus, "grace" is established in the Law of Moses.

Sin Offering
(Lev. 4:1-5:13; 6:24-30; 9:8-11; 10:16-20)

The High Priest's Sin Offering (Lev. 4:3-12)
If a priest sins unintentionally, he is required to perform the following steps . . .

-**Step 1**: The high priest brings a bull to the tabernacle entrance.

-**Step 2**: The high priest lays his hand upon the bull's head.

-**Step 3**: The high priest slaughters the bull.

-**Step 4**: The high priest takes some of the bull's blood and (1) sprinkles it seven times in front of the curtain of the most holy place in the tabernacle, and (2) uses his finger to put blood on the four horns of the incense altar.

-**Step 5**: High priest pours out the remaining blood of the bull at the base of the altar table—most likely upon the grating. (For more information on the altar table and grating, see page 20.)

-**Step 6**: As necessary, the high priest adds wood to altar table and arranges it for the animal pieces designated as the <u>Lord's portion</u>. –[Note: *Fire always remains burning on the altar table (except when tabernacle being relocated) (Lev. 6:12).*]

-**Step 7**: High priest butchers the bull by removing the following pieces: (1) internal organs and their fat, (2) kidneys and their fat, and (3) liver and their fat.

-**Step 8**: High priest places butchered bull pieces upon the altar table to be burned.
-*Portion for the Lord*: Includes all pieces specified above. These are placed upon the altar table to be burned.
-*Portion for the priests*: No portion can be eaten (Lev. 6:30).
-*Portion for the Levites*: No portion can be eaten (Lev. 6:30).

-**Step 9**: The remaining bull carcass is taken by the high priest to the ceremonially clean place outside the camp where ashes are disposed. There he starts a wood fire and burns the entire carcass of the bull. <u>No one can eat any portion of this bull because it is a sin offering whose blood was brought into the tabernacle (Lev. 6:30)</u>. –[Note: *The LXX specifies this wood fire must be made on top of ashes already present in this location from the altar table.*]

-**Step 10**: Any garment which has blood from a sin offering upon it must be washed in the tabernacle area (Lev. 6:27).

-**Step 11**: As necessary, ashes from altar table are placed in pile east of the altar table (Lev. 1:16). As necessary, to dispose of the ash pile: (1) a normal priest would changes his clothes, putting on unspecified clothing—leaving behind his normal priestly clothes, (2) he relocates the ashes to a ceremonially clean place outside the camp, and (3) upon his return to the tabernacle area, the priest changes his clothes, clothing himself again with his normal priestly clothes (Lev. 6:10-11) (for an illustration of the priests' clothing, see page 50). It is likely this would be a duty for the priests rather than the high priest due to the high priest bearing the ephod.

-**Step 12**: Evening: Offerings smoldering on the altar table are left burning all night.

Community Sin Offering (Lev. 4:13-21)
If the *entire community* sins unintentionally, they are required to perform the following steps . . .

-**Step 1**: The entire assembly must appear before the tabernacle. A representative must bring forth a bull to the tabernacle entrance.

-**Step 2**: The community elders must all lay their hands upon the bull's head.

-**Step 3**: The high priest slaughters the bull. -[Note: *The high priest must perform the community sin offering.*]

-**Step 4**: The high priest takes some of the bull's blood and (1) sprinkles it seven times in front of the curtain of the most holy place in the tabernacle, and (2) uses his finger to put blood on the four horns of the incense altar.

-**Step 5**: High priest pours out the remaining blood of the bull at the base of the altar table—most likely upon the grating. (For more information on the altar table and grating, see page 20.)

-**Step 6**: As necessary, priest adds wood to altar table and arranges it for the animal pieces designated as the Lord's portion. –[Note: *Fire always remains burning on the altar table (except when tabernacle being relocated) (Lev. 6:12).*]

-**Step 7**: High priest butchers the bull by removing the following pieces: (1) internal organs and their fat, (2) kidneys and their fat, and (3) liver and their fat.

-**Step 8**: High priest places butchered bull pieces upon the altar table to be burned.
-*Portion for the Lord*: Includes all pieces specified above. These are placed upon the altar table to be burned.
-*Portion for the priests*: No portion can be eaten (Lev. 6:30).
-*Portion for the Levites*: No portion can be eaten (Lev. 6:30).
-*Portion for the one bringing the sacrifice*: No portion can be eaten (Lev. 6:30).

-**Step 9**: The remaining bull carcass is taken by the high priest to the ceremonially clean place outside the camp where ashes are disposed. There he starts a wood fire and burns the entire carcass of the bull. No one can eat any portion of this bull because it is a sin offering whose blood was brought into the tabernacle (Lev. 6:30). –[Note: *The LXX specifies this wood fire must be made on top of ashes already present in this location from the altar table.*]

-**Step 10**: Any garment which has blood from a sin offering upon it must be washed in the tabernacle area (Lev. 6:27).

-**Step 11**: As necessary, ashes from altar table are placed in pile east of the altar table (Lev. 1:16). As necessary, to dispose of the ash pile: (1) a normal priest would changes his clothes, putting on unspecified clothing—leaving behind his normal priestly clothes, (2) he relocates the ashes to a ceremonially clean place outside the camp, and (3) upon his return to the tabernacle area, the priest changes his clothes, clothing himself again with his normal priestly clothes (Lev. 6:10-11) (for an illustration of the priests' clothing, see page 50). It is likely this would be a duty for the priests rather than the high priest due to the high priest bearing the ephod.

-**Step 12**: Evening: Offerings smoldering on the altar table are left burning all night.

-[Note: *In the judge's determination of the community's sin/guilt, he should reconcile the two requirements of the community guilt offering and the community sin offering to prescribe the appropriate offering based on the offense. The judge would need to carefully consider Lev. 4:13-21 & Num. 15:22-26.*]

A Leader's Sin Offering (Lev. 4:22-26)
If a community leader sins unintentionally, he is required to perform the following steps . . .

-**Step 1**: The community leader brings a male goat to the tabernacle entrance.

-**Step 2**: The community leader lays his hand upon the goat's head.

-**Step 3**: A priest slaughters the goat at the north side of the altar table—the same location where goats are slaughtered as burnt offerings.

-**Step 4**: Priest uses his finger to put some of the goat's blood on each of the four horns of the altar table. (For more information on the altar table, see page 20.)

-**Step 5**: Priest pours out the remaining blood of the goat at the base of the altar table—most likely upon the grating.

-**Step 6**: As necessary, priest adds wood to altar table and arranges it for the animal pieces designated as the Lord's portion. –[Note: *Fire always remains burning on the altar table (except when tabernacle being relocated) (Lev. 6:12).*]

-**Step 7**: Priest butchers the goat following the same requirements of the fellowship offerings: Goat is butchered by (1) removing the internal organs and their fat, (2) removing the liver and surrounding fat, and (3) removing the kidneys and surrounding fat (Lev. 3:12-15).
-*Portion for the Lord*: Includes all pieces specified above. These are placed upon the altar table to be burned.
-*Portion for the priests**: The portion for priests is unspecified, but as a standard rule the priests would be authorized to take for themselves meat from the breast and right shoulder (which would mean the entire leg)—as a "wave offering." The LXX further clarifies in Deu. 18:3 the specific part of the head and internal organs, explaining the priests could take the cheek meat from the head, and the great intestine. It would be cooked in similar manner to the meat of the "consecration ceremony"—near the tabernacle and most likely boiled.
-*Portion for the Levites**: Deu. 18:1 states the Levites were authorized to eat meat from offerings, but it does not specify what part. Perhaps 1 Sam. 2:13-16 is referring to a Levite as a "servant of the priest." If so, then 1 Sam. 2:13-16 may indicate the practice of Levites in being permitted to remove an unspecified portion of meat for themselves after the fat portions were butchered and placed on the altar table as the Lord's portion.
-*Portion for the one bringing the sacrifice*: No portion is specified—because it is not authorized due to the purpose of the offering. The one offering the sacrifice receives atonement as his portion.
-[*Note: *The priests and Levites are permitted portions from "A Leader's Sin Offering" because the blood is only applied to the altar table, and not any of the articles within the tabernacle itself (see Lev. 6:30; 10:18).*]

-**Step 8**: The priest takes in his hands the breast and right shoulder of the animal and places the fat upon them (Lev. 10:15). Then he lifts up his hands as a "wave offering." For more information on "wave offerings," see page 236.

-**Step 9**: The priest burns upon the altar table the butchered pieces designated as the Lord's portion.

-**Step 10**: The remaining goat carcass is taken by the priest to the ceremonially clean place outside the camp where ashes are disposed. There he starts a wood fire and burns the entire carcass of the goat. –[Note: *The LXX specifies this wood fire must be made on top of ashes already present in this location from the altar table.*]

-**Step11**: The pot or container in which the portions were cooked must be broken (if it is made of clay), or scoured and rinsed (if made of metal) (Lev. 6:28).

-**Step 12**: Any garment which has blood from a sin offering upon it must be washed in the tabernacle area (Lev. 6:27).

-**Step 13**: As necessary, ashes from altar table are placed in pile east of the altar table (Lev. 1:16). As necessary, to dispose of the ash pile: (1) a normal priest would changes his clothes, putting on unspecified clothing—leaving behind his normal priestly clothes, (2) he relocates the ashes to a ceremonially clean place outside the camp, and (3) upon his return to the tabernacle area, the priest changes his clothes, clothing himself again with his normal priestly clothes (Lev. 6:10-11) (for an illustration of the priests' clothing, see page 50). It is likely this would be a duty for the priests rather than the high priest due to the high priest bearing the ephod.

-**Step 14**: Evening: Offerings smoldering on the altar table are left burning all night.

Sin Offering for Person Not Specified Above
(Lev. 4:27-35; 5:1-13)

If *anyone else*, that is someone other than the high priest or a community leader, sins unintentionally, he is required to perform the following steps . . .

-**Step 1**: The sinner must confess his exact sin (Lev. 5:5). –[Note: *This confession is most likely to a judge established under the authority of the God-appointed leader, who will interpret the Law and render a personal verdict. Why is this important? Because an individual is not expected to understand every nuance of the Law (Lev. 5:1-4), and judges like Moses and his subordinate judges were established to help people with such cases. For example, what if the individual thought he sinned, but he really didn't? Or what if mitigating circumstances would allow the individual to offer a sin offering of flour rather than a lamb or goat? Therefore, a judge is necessary. Just as individuals today do not live independent of God's authority, so also individuals did not live independent of the authority of the Law's judge system. (For more information on the role of judges, see pages 239-250.]*

-**Step 2**: As directed by a judge, the sinner brings *one* of the following items to the tabernacle entrance: a female goat, or female lamb, or two doves, or two pigeons, or one-tenth ephah fine flour *without* oil and *without* incense. –[Note: *As explained in the text, the standard expectation is for the sinner to bring either a female goat or female lamb. But if they cannot afford this, then Lev. 5:7-11 authorizes them to bring either two doves, or two pigeons or one-tenth ephah fine flour instead. So, how would an individual make such a determination? He wouldn't. Rather, in discussing his case with a judge in Step #1, the judge would prescribe the appropriate penalty for the sinner based on the offense and mitigating circumstances. (For more information on the role of judges in these legal processes, see pages 239-250.)*]

-**Step 3**: The sinner lays his hand upon the animal's head. Or, if he is offering flour, the sinner would likely lay his hand upon the flour to signify transfer of his guilt to the item offered for atonement.

-**Step 4**:
(A) *If the sinner brought a lamb or a goat*, the priest slaughters the animal in the same respective location as burnt offerings (Lev. 6:24): A lamb or goat is slaughtered on the north side of the altar table (Lev. 1:10-11)
(B) *If the sinner brought two doves or two pigeons*, the first bird is slaughtered at the altar table (Lev. 1:14-17) by wringing its head—without dividing it (Lev. 5:8).
(C) (*This step omitted in the case he is offering flour.*)

-**Step 5**:
(A) *If the sinner brought a lamb or a goat*, the priest uses his finger to put some of the animal's blood on each of the four horns of the altar table. (For more information on the altar table, see page 20.)
(B) *If the sinner brought two doves or two pigeons*, the first bird's blood is splashed on the side of the altar table, then drained at the base of the altar—most likely upon the grating. (For more information on the altar table, see page 20.)
(C) (*This step omitted in the case he is offering flour.*)

-**Step 6**:
(A-B) Priest pours out the remaining blood of the slaughtered animal (whether lamb, goat or bird) at the base of the altar table—most likely upon the grating. (For more information on the altar table and grating, see page 20.)
(C) (*This step omitted in the case he is offering flour.*)

-**Step 7**: As necessary, priest adds wood to altar table and arranges it for the animal pieces designated as the Lord's portion. –[Note: *Fire always remains burning on the altar table (except when tabernacle being relocated) (Lev. 6:12).*]

-**Step 8**:
(A) *If the sinner brought a lamb or a goat*, the priest butchers the goat following the same requirements of the fellowship offerings: A lamb is butchered by (1) removing the rump, also called the "fat tail," (2) removing the internal organs and their fat, (3) removing the liver and surrounding fat, and (4) removing the kidneys and surrounding fat (Lev. 3:7-10). A goat is butchered by (1) removing the internal organs and their fat, (2) removing the liver and surrounding fat, and (3) removing the kidneys and surrounding fat (Lev. 3:12-15).
(B) *If the sinner brought two doves or two pigeons*, the priest sets aside the carcass of the first bird which was slaughtered.
(C) (*This step omitted in the case he is offering flour.*)

-**Step 9**: Portions are determined as follows . . .
-*Portion for the Lord*: Includes all pieces specified above. These are placed upon the altar table to be burned.
-*Portion for the priests**: If birds are offered, the priests receive no portion. But if a lamb/goat is offered: The portion for priests is unspecified, but as a standard rule the priests would be authorized to take for themselves meat from the breast and right shoulder (which would mean the entire leg)—as a "wave offering." The LXX further clarifies in Deu. 18:3 the specific part of the head and internal organs, explaining the priests could take the cheek meat from the head, and the great intestine. It would be cooked in similar manner to the meat of the "consecration ceremony"—near the tabernacle and most likely boiled.
-*Portion for the Levites**: If birds are offered, the Levites receive no portion. But if a lamb/goat is offered: Deu. 18:1 states the Levites were authorized to eat meat from offerings, but it does not specify what part. Perhaps 1 Sam. 2:13-16 is referring to a Levite as a "servant of the priest." If so, then 1 Sam. 2:13-16 may indicate the practice of Levites in being permitted to remove an unspecified portion of meat for themselves after the fat portions were butchered and placed on the altar table as the Lord's portion.
-*Portion for the one bringing the sacrifice*: No portion is specified—because it is not authorized due to the purpose of the offering. The one offering the sacrifice receives atonement as his portion.
-[*Note: *The priests and Levites are permitted portions from "Sin Offering for Person Not Specified Above" because the blood is only applied to the altar table, and not any of the articles within the tabernacle itself (see Lev. 6:30; 10:18).*

-**Step 10**: If a lamb/goat was offered, the priest takes in his hands the breast and right shoulder of the animal and places the fat upon them (Lev. 10:15). Then he lifts up his hands as a "wave offering." *If birds or flour were offered, this step is omitted.*

-**Step 11**: The priest burns upon the altar table the butchered pieces designated as the Lord's portion . . .

(A) *If the sinner brought <u>a lamb or a goat</u>,* priest places butchered lamb or goat pieces upon the altar table to be burned.

(B) *If the sinner brought <u>two doves or two pigeons</u>,* the wings of the first bird are opened and it is placed upon the wood fire of the altar table. Then the second bird is slaughtered and butchered by (1) wringing off its head, (2) draining blood from its body on the side of the altar table, (3) crop and feathers removed and thrown east of the altar where the ashes are, and (4) wings are opened as it is placed upon the wood fire of the altar table (Lev. 1:14-17).

(C) *If the sinner brought <u>flour</u>,* the priest grabs a handful of it and places it on the altar table to be burned (Lev. 5:11-12). The priest *does not* add incense or oil because it is a sin offering. –[Note: *<u>To add salt or not to add salt—that is the question</u>. . . . Due to this offering of flour being presented as a sin offering it is debatable whether or not it would be proper to add salt to follow the requirement of Lev. 2:13. Considering that Lev. 4:26, 31 directly links offering procedures for this step of the sin offering to the requirements of the fellowship offerings, it might be best to do the same with the offering of flour. If so, it might be most proper for a priest to add salt to a sin offering of flour similar to how salt is added to "grain offerings.". Or it might be best to omit the salt just as oil and incense are omitted. After all, "grain offerings"—as discussed in detail on page 217 are different than offerings of flour—so perhaps that provision to add salt to all grain offerings only applies to the type described there. What do you think? Should salt be added to the flour sin offering?*]

-**Step 12**: If a lamb or goat was offered, the remaining carcass is taken by the priest to the ceremonially clean place outside the camp where ashes are disposed. There he starts a wood fire and burns the entire carcass of the offered animal. (*This step omitted if birds or flour were offered.*)

-**Step 13**: The pot or container in which the portions were cooked must be broken (if it is made of clay), or scoured and rinsed (if made of metal) (Lev. 6:28).

-**Step 14**: Any garment which has blood from a sin offering upon it must be washed in the tabernacle area (Lev. 6:27).

-**Step 15**: As necessary, ashes from altar table are placed in pile east of the altar table (Lev. 1:16). As necessary, to dispose of the ash pile: (1) a normal priest would changes his clothes, putting on unspecified clothing—leaving behind his normal priestly clothes, (2) he relocates the ashes to a ceremonially clean place outside the camp, and (3) upon his return to the tabernacle area, the priest changes his clothes, clothing himself again with his normal priestly clothes (Lev. 6:10-11) (for an illustration of the priests' clothing, see page 50). It is likely this would be a duty for the priests rather than the high priest due to the high priest bearing the ephod.

-**Step 16**: Evening: Offerings smoldering on the altar table are left burning all night.

When to Abstain from a Portion:
A Discussion of Lev. 10:16-20

In this Bible passage we see an occasion where the high priest refused to eat his portion of a goat sin offering—and Moses was upset with him for failing to eat.

At first, Moses approaches Aaron, asking him why he failed to eat his assigned portion—citing Lev. 6:30.

So, what can we know about this passage?

And, what was the purpose of this sin offering?

Who sinned?

When examining the details of this passage in Lev. 10:16-20, and the different types of types of sin offerings discussed above, we are able to learn several things. . . .

First, we see the sin offering was a "goat." This means the sin offering was not for a sin of the high priest or a sin of the entire community (because both of those sins would require a *bull* to be offered). Therefore, we know the sin referred to in Lev. 10:16-20 was committed by either a "leader" or an "unspecified" person—because those are the only types of sin offerings which authorize the use of a goat (see pages 230 & 232)

Second, we can be certain the sin of Lev. 10:16-20 was not committed by the high priest nor the community because in those types of sin offerings, the priests were not authorized to eat any portion of the sacrificed animal (see Lev. 6:30 and pages 226 & 228).

Third, we see in Lev. 10:16 a reference to the two sons of Aaron *who were left*—implying the loss of his other sons. And, with this detail, we make our final determination. . . .

The sin preceding the goat offering of Lev. 10:16-20 was likely the sin of Aaron's sons—Nadab and Abihu. These men served as priests (leaders of the people). They were destroyed by the Lord for offering unauthorized fire in Lev. 10:1-7.

So, after the sin offering was made for Nadab and Abihu's offense—most likely offered by their households in an attempt to assuage the anger of the Lord—Aaron and the other priests decided to abstain from their portions of the goat offered as the sin offering. Instead they allowed the goat to be completely burned. In other words, the goat was offered as a "whole burnt offering" (see page 238).

When questioned, Moses at first gently rebuked the high priest with a question. But the high priest explained his reason for abstaining from his portion—perceiving in himself at least a part of the guilt due to the sin being committed by his sons. And, in this, Moses agreed with Aaron's judgment. Therefore, whenever a person for whom a portion is assigned carries within themselves reluctance or a close connection with a sin, they should consider abstaining from their assigned portion.

Wave Offering

The wave offering is different from other offerings because it is not an offering unto itself. In other words, a priest doesn't just do a wave offering like he might do a sin offering, guilt offering or burnt offering. Rather, a wave offering is a component *within* various ceremonies and offerings as detailed below . . .

In the Bible, a "wave offering," simply denotes "lifting up" an item—not jiggling it back and forth as "wave" in English tends to indicate. A wave offering indicates a shared portion on behalf of the person who "lifts up" something and the Lord. In other words, when something is lifted up as a wave offering it is an acknowledgement by the "lifter" that what they are holding wholly belongs to the Lord, yet He has allowed them to hold back part of what they are holding for their own benefit.

Get it?

Wave offerings are present in the Consecration Ceremony—where the high priest and his sons receive the portions of the sacrificed animals (page 97). Also, Moses in the Consecration Ceremony receives his portion of meat as a wave offering—which he lifts up to the Lord.

The Levites themselves are also made a wave offering during the Levite Consecration Ceremony (page 135). As I explain, the Levites are "lifted up" by the high priest—most likely by him approaching them and helping each to his feet after they kneel during the ceremony. In this sense, the high priest "lifts them up" and makes them a wave offering—much as a king "knights" a soldier.

Wave offerings are presented as a step in the Harvest Festival of First Fruits (page 175) and the Festival of Ingathering (page 199). Upon receiving the items from each man, the priest "lifts up" the received "sheaf" as a "wave offering." The priest sets the sheaf aside for use by his own family.

During the Festival of Weeks, the high priest "lifts up" two loaves of bread and two lambs as wave offerings (page 179).

And, most notably, priests were authorized to take for themselves meat from the breast and right shoulder for most sacrifices (Num. 18:18). *Whenever* a priest takes for himself the breast and right shoulder (that is the entire leg) of an animal, he must "lift it up" as a wave offering with the fat upon it. Then the priest separates the pieces in his hands in different shares: The Lord's portion is the fat—which is placed on the altar table to be burned; the priest's portion is the breast and right shoulder—which he cooks, most likely by boiling it, near the tabernacle entrance.

Exo. 35:22 in English Versions

In some English versions, the translation of Exo. 35:22 differs from the LXX. In this passage, God's people are bringing various items for use in the construction of tabernacle articles. In some English translations it states these various items were presented as "wave offerings" by the people; yet the LXX omits the mention of "wave offerings."

So, what is happening here?

Remember the purpose of the wave offering. It is an offering where the person lifts up something which wholly belongs to the Lord, yet the Lord has allowed them to retain a portion of it for themselves. In other words, the person "lifts" it up in acknowledgement of God's ownership, yet is permitted to keep part of it for himself.

Thus, the English addition of "wave offering" to Exo. 35:22 does not fit with the purpose of the "wave offering"—since when the people brought gold and other items they were not retaining any part for themselves. So, they were not "waving" anything. It would be more proper to see the offerings of Exo. 35:22 as "freewill offerings"—which is how they are presented elsewhere (Exo. 36:3). Therefore, it might be best to side with the LXX's choice to omit the addition of "wave offering" in Exo. 35:22.

Similar things are found in Exo. 38:24, 29—where some English translations state "wave offerings;" whereas the LXX omits the term "wave."

What do you think?

Wave Offerings & Prayer

To help you to fully grasp the concept of wave offerings, think simply of how you might pray before a meal. Essentially, your prayer before eating is similar to a wave offering.

Think about it this way . . .

When you pray, you acknowledge what you are about to eat is granted through God's mercy. You note how the food really belongs to Him and how you are graced with the ability to eat it. You recognize at your meal that God is sharing with you His bounty.

Wave offerings are very similar. It is an acknowledgement that the thing to be "lifted up" truly belongs to God, yet you are blessed that He has chosen to share with you. So, He allows you to keep a portion for yourself—which is the portion you eat and enjoy.

So, here is my challenge . . .

If you want to understand this "wave offering" principle, consider changing your mealtime prayer: Rather than leaving your plate or bowl on the table and praying *over* it, put your hands *under* it and *lift it off the table* as you pray. When you complete your prayer, open your eyes and see the portion God has graciously placed in your hands because He loves you.

This is a good picture of a "wave offering"—something lifted up in acknowledgement of God's grace and received for your blessing.

Whole Burnt Offering

See note on page 208. The "whole burnt offering" is a "burnt offering" with some minor differences.

<u>**How to Keep the Law**</u>

Phase 7

Judges

Let's review our progress thus far . . .

In Phase #1, we discussed the importance of the *God-appointed leader*.
Then in Phase #2, we examined the *construction of the tabernacle* area.
In Phase #3, I explained how to *oversee the tabernacle*.
In Phase #4, we explored the concept of *consecration*.
Then, in Phase #5, I presented the annual *calendar*.
Finally, in Phase #6, we examined the various types of *sacrifices and offerings*.

This brings us to our present phase (Phase #7)—the establishment of *judges*.

So, what are "judges?"

The concept of judges can be traced to Exo. 18:13-26.

In this passage, we see Moses was often overworked in his obligation to provide justice to God's people. To remedy this, Moses' father-in-law recommended the establishment of the *judge system*—where many subordinate judges were appointed to hear cases. This allowed Moses to be relieved of many of his daily requirements.

The appointed judges were capable, feared God and hated dishonest gain. These judges served a vital role—hearing the complaints of God's people and providing them with guidance to remedy their situations. Thus, the system of judges made the Law *personal*—providing direct answers to the people to assist them with life decisions.

In some cases, people tend to view the Law of Moses as being cold and impersonal. However, this is false . . . completely false, in fact.

The system of judges made the Law *incredibly responsive*—where people could receive *direct* guidance for *any issue* they encountered. And, in this way, I would argue the system of judges was perhaps much more helpful and responsive than any government established since then. Thus, in its original design, the Law of Moses warmly welcomed people—providing helpful guidance throughout all life's situations.

Later in the Bible, there is a book titled, "Judges." Interestingly we see these men and women "judges" held similar functions to the judges of Moses' time—where they would oversee God's people and administer justice.

And, with the arrival of "kings," some of these leaders performed similar functions to the judges—although they were called "kings." Similar to judges, kings were called to use their knowledge of the Law to render decisions (Pro. 20:8; Deu. 17:19). In this way, a king served as a supreme judge within the nation.

As a side note, we see in the Bible that many of the judges had personal faults—Barak, Samson, Gideon and so on. But the role of a judge was not to be perfect. Rather, it was to stand in the stead of Moses—to motivate God's people to right action.

And, as I will show you, this system of judges is absolutely vital to the keeping of the Law of Moses.

Why?

Several reasons . . .

#1: The "system of judges" is vital because the Law of Moses is designed to be personal and responsive.

In the Law of Moses, we see Moses prohibits adding to, or subtracting from, the Law (Deu. 4:2). This means that although a judge could make a ruling in a case, that judge was *never* permitted to write down his findings as *addendums to the Law*. Rather, the judge would give a specific ruling that was tailored to the specific parties standing before him.

How would a judge decide cases?

Simple: He would discipline himself by studying the Law diligently all the days of his life, just as "kings" were called to do (Deu. 17:19). Then, when hearing a case, he would rely on God to grant him wisdom.

Why is this important?

Within this model is contained the concept of spirituality—where people were called to constantly look to God for *personal* guidance, rather than *impersonal* written code. Thus, the Law of Moses was designed to be administered in a remarkably personal fashion—where people would look to those under God's authority to provide <u>personal guidance</u>. In other words, Moses' system does not offer God's people answers which are one-size-fits-all.

The system of judges mirrors the system of prayer—where individuals call out to God to provide help within their *specific* situations. For example, when you pray, the Holy Spirit offers you personal guidance—which is intended especially for you! And, in this same way, God designed the Law to provide personal guidance to every person in whatever situation they faced. Therefore, we see the Law of Moses is quite compassionate—putting in place a system of judges to provide spiritual counseling and practical help for God's people.

This is why the establishment of a system of judges is necessary for anyone who ventures to follow the Law of Moses. The judges provided helpful guidance for all of God's people.

#2: The "system of judges" is needed to interpret the Law of Moses.

Frankly, within the Law of Moses, an individual is not permitted to interpret the Law *for himself*. The only people who hold such authority are judges. And, the only time in which a judge can interpret a specific law is when he is hearing a case.

As I stated before, the Law of Moses prohibits adding to it or subtracting from it (Deu. 4:2). This means a judge can render a ruling based on principles contained therein, but he is never authorized to write down his interpretation in a manner which is intended to be authoritative.

Sure, a person can write about the Law, but such writings cannot be viewed as being an authority because Moses himself strictly forbade it (Deu. 4:2). Remember, the Law of Moses is based on the Heavenly pattern (Exo. 25:40), so if judges were permitted to *add* to it, the Law would quickly fall away from its original design. Therefore, additions to the Law are strictly prohibited.

So, what does this mean of the thousands and thousands of extra rules written down as additions to the Law?

They are invalid—completely invalid. The Law of Moses declares them invalid (Deu. 4:2). Just as the answer to a person's prayer is intended to direct *only* that person, the ruling of a judge is to *only* direct the parties standing before him. No judge or leader, however great or revered, was ever authorized to add to, or subtract from, the Law of Moses. Period.

This point cannot be overstated. Within this bracketing, we see clearly the role of the judge system. Judges diligently learned the Law, then developed specific rulings which were intended to guide *only* the people standing before them. Those rulings were not permitted to be recorded as authoritative additions to the Law. All rulings of judges were intended to be treated similar as answers to prayer—bearing remarkable personal significance to the receiving individual but holding no direct relevance to others.

#3: The "system of judges" is needed to contextualize the Law of Moses.

Now that you understand the Law prohibits additions or subtractions, we find a problem.

So, what's the problem?

The problem is the situations described in the Law of Moses do not "fit" every culture. And, as I will show you, the situations described in the Law (that is the "specific rules" on page 261) were *not* designed to directly apply to all cultures.

Rather, the "specific rules" of the Law are similar to "case law"—as Moses himself recorded some of his common rulings as *examples* for future generations.

Therefore, to state this in a straightforward way: The Law of Moses contains *both* (1) the commands of God *and* (2) the commands of Moses.

How?

Well, God wanted it this way. This is clear. God wanted the Law to reflect *both* His own commands and the commands of Moses.

Where is this found?

In Matt. 19:8, when questioned about divorce, the Lord Jesus stated that although the Lord holds a specific standard for marriage; Moses permitted divorce because of the hardness of people's hearts. This is likely a reference to Deu. 24:1-3. Thus, we see clearly that God designed the Law to reflect both His standards and also the standards of Moses.

Why would God do this?

Well, think about it carefully: The Law of Moses was provided with the intention of being used perpetually—to the very end of time. Indeed, there were many prophets who taught this—pointing to the reestablishment of the festivals in the future (Isa. 4:5; 66:18-23; Ezek. 37:26-28; Amos 9:11; Zech. 14:16-21). And, since God's original intent was to provide salvation for all nations (Isa. 49:6), His Law would need to be capable of "fitting" *every possible culture throughout all human history.*

Got it?

So, how does the Law "fit" every specific culture throughout all human history?

Simple: Through the system of judges.

As long as the system of judges is in place, the Law of Moses is capable of *adapting* itself to any culture. It does this through the rulings of judges on cases brought before them. And, in this way, the constant feedback and teachings of the judges provide a means to continually guide God's people with the principles of the Law.

Here is an example . . .

Consider Exodus 21:28-36. In this passage, Moses provides instructions about bulls who cause injury to humans or other animals.

Now, within Moses' immediate culture, these commands were very relevant—offering guidance for situations which were likely faced by people within his Ancient Near East setting. However, unless you are a rancher living in the 21st Century, it is unlikely you own a bull. So, what can you do with these passages?

As I explained earlier, these types of "specific rules" were intended by Moses to provide an *example contextualization* to the Law. As such, the "specific rules" of Moses—about bull injuries and many other Ancient Near East topics—are intended only to provide future judges with examples of how the Law should be contextualized in their later society's circumstances.

To clarify further, let's imagine the Law of Moses has been reestablished in the 21st Century: The tabernacle has been re-built, the priests installed and now the system of judges has been appointed.

In this re-establishment, the new judges would provide rulings to God's people—giving them guidance in the specific situations they face. For example, although a person may not own a bull, he might own a Pitbull dog. And, although the Law of Moses does not specifically mention Pitbull dogs, it does provide rulings on somewhat similar situations in that ancient context. So, in the deciding of a case dealing with a dog attack, a judge may use a passage like Exo. 21:28-36.

In other words, the 21st Century judge would look at the *example contextualization* provided by Moses in Exo. 21:28-36—determining how Moses applied the Law to his ancient context. Then the 21st Century judge would contextualize that law to the specific case with the Pitbull dog—providing a ruling which upholds the spirit of Moses' example law.

Get it?

When you read the Bible, be careful to accept it on its own terms. Allow it to speak and do not shy away from what it is saying. Follow the passages to their conclusions and often you will see things which otherwise would escape your understanding. In this case, I interacted with the clear teaching of the Lord Jesus—when He indicated that the Law contains both the commands of God and the commands of Moses (Matt. 19:8). And, in doing so, we were able to see the function of the Law in providing cultural examples to future judges.

Thus, in the reestablishment of the Law of Moses, the future system of judges will need to examine the Law with a similar understanding. The Law of Moses might not require all people to become ranchers and own bulls, but it does contain within its system the ability to render decisions on strictly 21st Century issues—such as automobile accidents, credit card fraud, etc.

In whatever case is presented before a judge, the judge would simply leverage his wisdom gained through many years of diligent study as he provided an interpretation fitting for the parties before him—using the cultural contextualization of Moses as his guide. Then, after rendering his specific ruling to the specific parties before him, the judge's interpretation would only hold authority over the exact parties to whom they were rendered. The rulings of a judge *would not* be recorded (Deu. 4:2).

Simple, right?

So, I will leave you with this thought . . .

As an individual, you do not possess the authority to interpret the Law of Moses for yourself. In all cases where you need interpretation, guidance or help, the Law of Moses would direct you to seek the counsel of an established judge who is under the authority of the God-appointed leader. Then that judge would help you.

Even if you are a judge, you would still avoid making your own decisions. Rather, you would seek counsel with a judge who has been appointed over you—whether a judge who presides over a larger group, or with the person whom God has appointed to serve in the place of Moses (Exo. 18:25-26).

Indeed, the absence of the judges today is the cause for a great deal of confusion. Today there are many who venture to interpret the Law of Moses and the Bible. Yet, within the Law itself, no one is permitted to do this apart from being designated by Moses or the Prophet to do so (Deu. 4:2; 18:18-19). And, since God's people have allowed the practice of the Law as described in this book to vanish from the Earth, people are abandoned to their own wavering interpretations.

This may be harsh, but it is true. Deu. 4:2 prohibits Law interpretation apart from the God-appointed system of judges.

This is why it is altogether impossible for a single person to "keep the Law of Moses." The Law itself moves us to the recognition that we need the help of God's leaders. Without submission to this judge system it is impossible to live righteously. This is why anyone who ventures to "keep" the Law of Moses must reestablish the tabernacle and the system of judges. Without these things, there is no such thing as "following Moses."

How Judges are Appointed

It is important to note how judges are appointed to highlight how far we have drifted in the 21st Century.

We discussed Exo. 18:13-36 above. Pay specific attention to Exo. 18:25—which shows how the judges were selected. We see here the judges were not "voted in" by the people. Nor did they attain their offices as rights. Rather, they were selected through Moses—who was appointed by God Himself.

Likewise, we see throughout the Bible, that judges and prophets were not appointed by the authority of the congregation. Rather, the Spirit of God called them. Also, when Christ selected His disciples, He did so through His own authority.

This means *"judges" were not subordinate to the congregation*—because their appointments were not dependent on the congregation. Therefore, the pattern of judges resembles the office of "prophet"—where these individuals were selected *independent* of the established priestly system and the congregation. Thus, they bear a transcendence somewhat similar to Moses (Deu. 18:18-22).

Judge Pattern in New Testament

In the New Testament we see clearly the Lord Jesus teaches a continuation of the Law. He told His disciples that in the restoration of the kingdom they would sit on twelve thrones as judges for the twelve tribes (Matt. 19:28). This same thought is extended further—with 1 Cor. 6:3 stating that New Testament believers will serve as judges even over angels. And, in the book of Revelation we see the fulfillment of this reestablished order of judges after the pattern of Moses' Law (Rev. 4:4; 5:8).

Indeed, the presence of such passages shows us although the Law has fulfilled its purpose as a schoolmaster to bring us to faith, the Law will nonetheless play an incredible role as Heaven is merged with Earth (Matt. 6:10). The Law itself was given as a shadow of the heavenly pattern—so the things contained within it will continue to guide the operation of Heaven for all eternity (Exo. 25:40; Heb. 8:5).

Therefore, the New Testament believer would be wise to avoid levying criticism on the Law. Although it has faithfully completed _one_ of its purposes in leading us to faith, the Law is not complete in its work. It has much to teach us. And, if we want to prepare ourselves for eternity, perhaps the best place to look is within the Law—where we are offered a glimpse of the Heavenly economy of atoning sacrifice.

Don't dismiss things because they are hard to understand. Pray for wisdom. Be diligent. Discipline yourself in study so you can see clearly. God is always faithful to guide us.

Judges and the Calendar

Earlier in Phase 5 of this book, we discussed the calendar and the various festivals. And, in my discussion of the calendar I presented each festival in its simplicity—carefully laying out what the Bible says.

However, if you ever researched one of these festivals on your own, you may have noticed the many additions which have been made to them over many centuries—nearly making them unrecognizable from the commands of Moses. Indeed, if you set out to follow all the "added commands" in regards to Passover, it is likely you would be overwhelmed. And, in keeping all the added requirements, you might even err altogether from the spirit of the event itself.

So, how should this be resolved within the Law?

As explained over and over, the Law of Moses absolutely forbids anyone adding to or subtracting from what Moses wrote (Deu. 4:2).

Make sure you understand this, because through this principle we nullify all "added" teachings. In an instant, this principle causes all "added" things to vanish because the Law is immutable.

And, by declaring this to be the case, we can return to sanity—letting go of all the traditions which have been pasted, stapled and pasted to Moses. Over the centuries, many have wearied Moses, piling stacks of books and papers into his arms—burying him under an immense load of additional rules. It is no wonder why God sent His angel to guard Moses' body immediately after his burial (Jude 1:9). History teaches us, it seems, that people are ever seeking to pile their own teachings atop Moses—even though he forbade them from doing so (Deu. 4:2).

However, I digress.

In the case of the calendar—and all its festivals—the point was never that individuals would be deciding for themselves on such matters. Rather, when the Law is diligently reinstituted as outlined in Phases 1-10 of this book, then there are judges under the authority of the God-appointed leader to make such decisions. The God-appointed leader would be led to make declaration of the exact dates of certain festivals, and people would follow his leadership.

But without completing the requirements in Phases 1-10 of this book, there is no authoritative basis to claim anything specific about festivals.

In this we see the unity of the Law. It is not something to be mused upon nor trifled with. Rather, when it is put in practice *in its entirety*, the system of the Law provides for its own administration through the God-appointed leader, the high priest and judges.

The reason why no one completely understands the festivals is because the Law's own system of administration no longer exists on Earth. So, in its place we are left to only hear the opinions of unauthorized individuals who speak apart from the endorsement of Moses and the Prophet (Deu. 18:18-19).

For this reason, I most enthusiastically point you to the words of Moses. Who cares what other people think about the Law's provisions when the Law itself forbids their additions? Therefore, simply read what Moses wrote and implement it *in its simplicity*. And, in its full implementation, the Law will provide you with a high priest and judge to rule over such matters (Deu. 18:18-19; Heb. 8:1).

The Morphing of the Judge System

Notable, when we consider the development of Scripture, the office of judges is quite interesting.

Let me explain . . .

Within the tabernacle system, Moses—as the God-appointed leader—transcended the limits which were even placed on the high priest. For example, whereas the high priest was not permitted to approach the Ark, and when he did so on the Day of Atonement, he could only do so through a thick veil of smoke, or when hiding behind the shielding curtain to prepare the ark for transport; yet Moses freely walked into the Most Holy Place *at will*—appearing before the Lord face-to-face.

In other words, the Law grants complete transcendence to the supreme human judge—as a picture of Messiah, the God-man, who moves freely before the presence of the Father (Heb. 9:12).

Then, as the history of the Old Testament develops, we see similar transcendence being placed upon the office of judges—as in the book of Judges. Although the system of priests continued to exist, the office of "judge" became one very similar to the pattern of Moses, where individuals selected as judges by the Lord freely took upon themselves the mantle of authority independent of the priestly system.

Get it?

Then, with the coming of the *prophetic* offices, we see a unique class of individuals who exist *independent* of the priestly system—speaking directly for the Lord to redirect the system of worship, much as Moses directed the high priest from his transcendent position.

Therefore, in all these things we see the vital importance of the judge system—especially as it morphed to contain within it the office of "prophet" (Deu. 18:18-22). Through it, God established a means for Him to redirect and control the established priestly system—because it was a known fact that God would continue to grant transcendence to outside individuals, much as He originally granted transcendence to Moses (Deu. 18:18-22).

Thus, the high priest was called to always expect a judge or a prophet to speak with transcendence from the position of Moses. And, with the arrival of such faithful and called judges and prophets, the priests were required by God to render obedience (Matt. 21:33-46). Whereas the priests held the high charge of maintaining the Lord's tabernacle; the judge/prophet in the position of Moses was charged with directing the nation and speaking directly to the circumstances of God's people.

Have you ever wondered at that thought? Without being consecrated, Moses freely walked into the tabernacle and the Most Holy Place to appear before the Ark; but the high priest—who was consecrated, anointed and bore the Ephod could not. And, in Moses' final dialogues, he told God's people to prepare themselves to receive the Prophet who would arrive after this same pattern of transcendence (Deu. 18:18-22). Although there were many "prophets" who served in lieu of Moses, the ultimate "Prophet" is the Lord Jesus. That Prophet is the Messiah—who throughout all history has lent His authority to many men and women after the pattern of Moses. But the pattern of transcendence itself is both founded in the Messiah and culminates in Him (Num. 12:7-8).

This is why, in my discussion of the Law, I am careful to avoid adding to it or declaring my own thoughts. When we understand the Law of Moses *exactly as he wrote it*, we uphold the vital importance of the system of judges. Without the judges, no individual should venture to take upon himself the mantle of interpreting the various laws for himself.

The Law was designed to contain both *official leadership through the priesthood* and *transcendent leadership through the Mosaic judges/prophets*. It is no wonder why people are so disillusioned and confused by the Law—when they no longer have these two systems to guide them.

Therefore, to interpret the Law, you need the God-appointed leader after the pattern of Moses and the priesthood. Frankly, without reestablishing the *entire* tabernacle system, there is no such thing as "keeping the Law."

In other words, "keeping the sabbath" is not "keeping the Law." And eating a certain way is not "keeping the Law."

Rather, the Law demands a reestablishment of its *entire* system. Only then can God's people gain the judge system needed to guide them in keeping all the commands.

Thus, to keep the Law, start at Phase #1, then fulfill all phases *in order*. Do not be deceived into thinking you can live unto yourself as a "Phase 8 & 9 observer"—holding only to *some* of the rules within the Law. You need the entire system of the Law. And the judges are a crucial part of that system.

How to Keep the Law

Phase 8

General Rules

General Rules & Specific Rules in the Law

In the previous Phases, we discussed the following in detail:
(1) the importance of the God-appointed leader who stands in the position of Moses,
(2) the construction of the tabernacle,
(3) how to oversee the tabernacle
(4) the consecration of the tabernacle, priests and Levites
(5) the ceremonial calendar
(6) offerings, and
(7) judges

In this Phase I present the next step—which involves how to keep the *personal* commands of the Law. In discussing this topic, I refer to the Ten Commandments—and similar passages—as the "*general rules*" of the Law, because they are universally applicable to all human societies. And, in Phase #9, I will discuss the other personal rules contained within the Law—which I refer to as "*specific rules*."

Unfortunately, in many cases when people refer to the Law of Moses and how to "keep" it, they are often making a limited reference only to some of the general rules (the Ten Commandments), and *some* of the specific rules—which are convenient to keep, such as those governing diet.

However, this is a terribly inaccurate way to approach the Law of Moses because Moses taught the people to do all the other things to establish tabernacle worship. And, without the system of tabernacle worship, one cannot keep the Law. As you read further, this will become clear. And you will see the absurdity of referring to the Law of Moses as only the Ten Commandments.

This Phase will challenge you to see the Law of Moses in its wholeness—and if you are intent on keeping it, you will be challenged to keep it in its *entirety* (Phases 1-10).

General Rules

By saying "general rules," I am referring to these passages, which essentially carry within them the *universal code of conduct* which could be applied cross-culturally:

General Rules
-Ten Commandments (Exo. 20:1-17)
-Reflection of Ten Commandments (Lev. 19:1-4, 11-13, 16-18; 26:1-2; Deu. 5:6-21)
-Loving God (Deu. 6:4-6)

This above list is very short, so I invite you to look up the passages for yourself. It is interesting to see the repeated emphasis the Law places on the Ten Commandments.

But in my discussion, I will not delve into the Ten Commandments. I am doing this to illustrate my point. . . .

Often the Ten Commandments are misconstrued as being the Law themselves. They are not. Thus, in this book I have chosen to focus instead on the *neglected* portions of the Law.

If you desire an in-depth analysis of the Ten Commandments, the only legitimate place you will find it is through the judge system of the Law—as discussed in Phase #7. Frankly, individuals are not authorized to paste their own thoughts to the Law of Moses—and the only people authorized to interpret the commands are judges established under the God-given authority of Moses or the Prophet (Deu. 4:2; 18:18-19).

Speaking personally, it grieves me deeply to consider there are so many who believe in the God of the Bible, yet His special place of worship is completely absent from the Earth. Therefore, it would be much better for readers to deeply reflect on the details of Phases #1-7—allowing those thoughts to dwell within their minds, rather than simply reexamining what they already know about the Ten Commandments.

So, rather than revisiting the details of the Ten Commandments, I invite you to carefully re-examine Phases #1-7 of this book instead—doing so until you develop a heartfelt reverence for God's worship as the Law itself teaches.

Keeping the Entire Law

In my below discussions of the "general rules" and "specific rules" of the Law, I will be careful to stress the importance of the "judges."

In the Law of Moses, we see the tabernacle system consists of many parts. In other words, it is not possible for an individual—no matter how hard they may try—to keep the Law unto himself. Frankly, the individual needs the God-appointed leader, the tabernacle, the priests and the Levites to maintain the system on his behalf. And, even in the attempt to "keep" rules, such as the Ten Commandments, the individual is altogether incapable of keeping anything for himself.

Why?

From the very beginning, Moses was called to establish a system of judges—who would hear the people and guide them in applying the various commands to themselves. You see, the individual who strives to keep the Law needs judges to tell him how to keep the rules contained therein. This is discussed in detail on pages 239-250. In other words, an individual cannot operate solo within the Law of Moses. He must be under the authority of a judge who has been appointed by the God-appointed leader.

An individual is not authorized in the Law of Moses to interpret commands for himself. Rather, he is instructed to bring any questions to a legitimate judge—who will make decisions on his behalf.

And, within this system, not even the interpretations of the judge bear authority beyond the individual for which they are prescribed. The Law of Moses forbids anyone adding to the Law or taking away from it (Deu. 4:2). So, a judge is not permitted to print his own thoughts—adding them as an addendum to the rules contained in the Law itself. This is because God designed His legal system to be responsive and personal—speaking directly to individuals, giving them face-to-face responses, rather than an exhaustive code of added commands from men.

So, why am I telling you this?

Because this impacts how I will discuss the "general rules" and "specific rules" of the Law. Rather than expounding upon each of the Ten Commandments in detail—adding my own thoughts to each, I will instead challenge you to *seek answers through the Law itself*. I will challenge you to reestablish the entire Law system described in this book. Then, you will have "judges" who will guide you in your own application of the "general rules" and "specific rules."

Therefore, if you desire to live according to the Law, do not start by attempting to "keep the Ten Commandments." Rather, start from the basics: Follow the God-appointed leader who serves after the example of Moses. Then do your part to see the tabernacle rebuilt, the priesthood reestablished and the Law calendar reinstated. Only then will you have a foundation upon which you can rightly make an attempt to keep the "general rules" and "specific rules."

I will ask you, what sense does it make for one to "keep the sabbath" in the midst of a world where there is no true tabernacle, no priesthood and no offerings?

Or, what sense does it make to avoid "eating pork" in a world where there is no Ark, no Bread Table, no Incense Altar and no Day of Atonement?

Today in the 21ˢᵗ Century, many offer lip-service to the Law of Moses when they speak of the "Ten Commandments"—but by doing so they are merely speaking of the antenna on the roof of an immense skyscraper. Surely, the sabbath, diet and Ten Commandments are important things *within* the Law—but they are incredibly *small* pieces of the Law. So, I encourage you to avoid the foolhardy position of claiming to "keep the Law" while the tabernacle, priesthood and sacrifices remain altogether absent from the world.

Thus, I encourage you to start from the beginning. If you desire to keep the Law of Moses, my challenge is for you to implement carefully—step-by-step—everything I have discussed in this book, in order. Then you will be a true disciple of Moses—doing things exactly as *he* prescribed.

As it is now, however, every single man and woman who claims to follow Moses is in complete error.

Do the *entire* Law—from start to finish. And, upon its complete reestablishment, then turn your attention to the "general rules" and "specific rules"—looking to the judges to guide you in all your ways.

Sure, it is easy to "keep the Law" when misleading teachers tell you that you must merely keep the sabbath or live by a certain code.

But do you have the great faith to "keep the Law" exactly how Moses delivered it—as I outline in the exhaustive Phases of this book?

Answer that question.

If your answer is "no," then you are not a disciple of Moses.
If your answer is "no," then you are proven to be in complete error by the Law of Moses.

If you are looking to the Law of Moses for your righteousness, and you do not keep the Law as exactly as written, then the Law declares you "unrighteous." Any actions you perform in its *partial* fulfillment are inadequate and you have been proven as falling short of its standard.

If you want to live by the Law of Moses . . .

-Reestablish the one who serves in the likeness of Moses (pg. 1)
-Re-construct the "tabernacle" and its articles (pg. 9)
-Re-establish the system of oversight for the tabernacle (pg. 67)
-Re-consecrate the tabernacle, high priest, priests and Levites (pg. 95)
-Reestablish the ceremonial calendar (pg. 153)
-Reestablish tabernacle offerings (pg. 205)
-Re-appoint judges (pg. 239)

And, only after you complete these above steps will you be prepared to properly "keep the sabbath," remove pork from your diet and live by a Mosaic moral code. Don't listen to teachers who tell you, apart from Moses' authority, that you can shortcut this process—neglecting the tabernacle, priesthood, judges, ceremonial calendar and sacrifices.

You cannot.

If you don't believe me, listen to Haggai—who likewise spoke to people who *claimed to follow Moses* while the Mosaic system was absent from the Earth . . .

Haggai said to the sabbath-keepers and the diet-keepers . . .

"Is it time for you to be living in paneled houses while (the house of the Lord) remains a ruin?" (Hagg. 1:4)

All Generations

Whereas it is easy for people in the 21ˢᵗ Century to live under a spell of misunderstanding, the words of Haggai break the spell (Hagg. 1:4).

If, in fact, the God of the Bible is your God, then you should not be satisfied living in a world which has been stripped completely of His special worship. Your God instituted the Mosaic system to be maintained without fail for all generations (Exo. 20:6; Matt. 5:17-18). The Bible tells us, quite clearly, the tabernacle contains within itself a shadow of Heaven, being established after the Heavenly pattern (Exo. 25:40; Heb. 8:5). Yet, countless people who worship this same God live unashamedly in nice houses—while the house of God Most High remains a complete ruin (Hagg. 1:4).

This is not good.

It is no wonder why people avoid reading the Old Testament—because it rebukes us most sharply . . . showing at our core we are most unfaithful in elementary things. When one claims to follow God, they should seek to worship Him *as He commands.*

This makes sense, right?

When God commands His worship to be done *a specific way*, those who worship that God should do things as He commands.

This is basic stuff: *If God is God, then those who follow God should seek to do things as He commands.*

Yet, countless people gloss over His special worship—choosing only to see what they desire to see within the Law . . . imagining it to only be a list of idle rules for living.

So, in the 21ˢᵗ Century, people are indeed under a spell. The spell has rendered God's people incapable of grasping elementary truths. People do not care about the difference between the "temple" and the "tabernacle," and within this obfuscation their minds cannot comprehend what I am talking about (Heb. 5:11-12).

Rather than drumming on, I will digress. If you are looking for a pathway to understanding, pray and reflect on Haggai 1:4. The answers are there for the one who desires to gain wisdom. Earnestly seek and desire understanding and God will show you the Way. If the Law of Moses is instituted exactly as God commands, the tabernacle would serve to constantly point the world toward Christ. But without the tabernacle, the entire world misses out on the witness it would provide—drawing us to continual reflection on atonement. Thus, in the absence of the tabernacle, God's people have chosen to have "nothing" in its place. And, as a result, all people have suffered immensely.

Why is the tabernacle so rejected, when the tabernacle speaks only of redeeming sacrifice and atonement?

The tabernacle points people directly to Christ. So, having the tabernacle would be a good thing—perhaps the best thing God's people could do to serve as a witness to future generations, guiding all people to be ever mindful of their atonement.

Confusion

Many people are confused by the Law. And by following *illegitimate teachers* that confusion continues to multiply.

Stick with me as I explain . . .

What do I mean by saying "illegitimate teachers?"

Within the Law, Moses was appointed by God. So, he had authority from God—which made his teaching legitimate. So, Moses was worthy of reverence. If Moses told a person to do something, they could trust what Moses said—because he spoke for God.

Does this make sense? Read it again if you must, but please make sure you understand this.

So, since Moses was a legitimate teacher, he had a means of passing on his legitimacy—approving specific people to render decisions on his behalf, which is God's behalf.

Still tracking?

Well, we see when the burden was too great for Moses, his father-in-law, then later God, directed him to give portions of his interpretative authority to specific people—called judges (Exo. 18:13-36). Therefore, the judges established under Moses' authority were likewise legitimate—being empowered and directed by God to serve specific roles in interpreting the Law for God's people.

Why is this important?

Because much confusion has been caused and promoted by the loss of this "legitimate" means of Law interpretation. In other words, today there are many men and women who teach things about the Law of Moses, yet the authority to do so has been broken. Since Moses declared no one can add to or take away from the Law, this means all added writings on the Law are illegitimate (Deu. 4:2). They do not bear the approval of Moses and are therefore foreign to God's commands.

This leads to all sorts of problems—many of which we have experienced. People say so many things about the Law, tossing people back and forth under every wind of doctrine. Thus, for the person who desires to follow the entire counsel of God, we await for the reestablishment of His kingdom on Earth as it is in Heaven.

Sure, some people today might say interesting things about the Ten Commandments, but none of it is authoritative. They are all illegitimate teachers according to the Law—lacking the authorization to add to it (Deu. 4:2). Only Moses and the Prophet are authorized to speak on the Law authoritatively (Deu. 18:18-19). And the high priest is simply left with the business of carrying out the Lord's commands as given through Moses or the Prophet.

Therefore, even though it is a repeated point, the only way for a person to attempt to "keep the Ten Commandments" is through reestablishing the judges. The judges are the only legitimate means of guidance capable of helping individuals to live out the commands. Thus, in our discussion of the Ten Commandments, we uphold the vital importance of Phases #1-7 in this book. And by doing so, we see that the Ten Commandments are inseparably linked to *everything* in the Law. To have the Ten Commandments, you must have the entire system of the Law (Matt. 5:18-19; Luke 16:17).

How to Keep the Law

Phase 9

Specific Rules

In the previous Phase, I discussed what I refer to as the "general rules" of the Law—which mostly consist of the Ten Commandments. In that Phase I devoted my attention to upholding the importance of the *entire* Law as a system—stressing the interpretive importance of the judges.

Likewise, in this Phase, I will briefly present the Bible passages I refer to as "*specific rules.*" But I will be careful to avoid pinning my own thoughts to the commands themselves—reverently awaiting the Day when the Lord will reestablish His worship on Earth. Frankly, believers need the tabernacle and they need the prescribed system of worship described in the Bible. Believers today do not need another teacher who pins his own thoughts to the commands—which were chiseled in stone.

Therefore, I will simply present you with the various "specific rules" found throughout the Law.

So, what is a "specific rule?"

When venturing to understand the Law, think simply of the "*general rules*"—or Ten Commandments—as bearing the ability to be *universally applied to all cultural settings*.

However, the "*specific rules*" found in the Law bore specific relevance to God's people in Moses' *specific cultural setting*.

In other words, the "specific rules" of the Law prescribe behavior for citizens who lived agriculturally and pastorally in the ancient world. So, in applying these "specific rules" to your current setting, it may be difficult because you might not be a farmer nor a rancher. Therefore, you would need a Moses-appointed judge to interpret the various laws *for you.*

For example, let's say you crash your car into another car. The Law of Moses does not specifically discuss automobiles; therefore, you would be unable of determining your responsibility by looking at the laws themselves.

So, what would you do in this situation?

You would simply go to your judge, and he would help you develop a plan to resolve your automobile situation.

How would the judge do this?

The judge could follow these steps to resolve your case . . .

- **Step 1**: The judge would listen to you.
- **Step 2**: The judge would consult the various "specific rules" written by Moses. The judge would find similarities between your case and the "specific rules" of the Law (see page 261).
- **Step 3**: The judge would consider mitigating factors—such as how much you could afford to pay in restitution (see page 220).
- **Step 4**: The judge would determine intent (see page 223).
- **Step 5**: The judge would give you a course of action to follow—whether it involved you paying restitution to an injured party, commanding you to go to the priests to offer a sacrifice, or another thing.

When understanding the above format, we see clearly that the Lord Jesus' interactions with people followed this same "judge" pattern. When people encountered Jesus, He gave them certain instructions that were intended *only for them*—whether telling them to show themselves to the priest, to wash in a certain pool, sell all their possessions, etc.

Even when the Lord Jesus told Lazarus to walk out of the tomb, He did so as a judge presiding over Lazarus! And, in this case, as in others, Lazarus was faithful to obey the instruction of his Judge.

In all these things, we see clearly the Lord Jesus served in the likeness of Moses, calling people to certain steps of obedience (Deu. 18:18).

Likewise, to address all problems among God's people, the Law of Moses provides a system of judges—who hear cases brought before them, helping people to best apply these ancient "specific rules" to their own situations in the modern world (Exo. 18:13-26).

So, what are the "specific rules" contained within the Law of Moses?

Below I will present a list of the "specific rules." . . .

Specific Rules
-**Animals** (Exo. 23:12; Lev. 19:19, 26; 24:18-21; 27:9-13, 26-27; Deu. 15:19-23; 22:1-4, 6-7; 22:10; 27:21)
-**Camp** (Num. 5:1-3; Deu. 23:9-14)
-**Childbirth** (Lev. 12:1-8)
-**Circumcision** (Gen. 17:9-14; Exo. 4:24-26)
-**Cities of Refuge** (Num. 35:6-34; Deu. 4:41-43; 19:1-13)
-**Clothing / Adornment** (Lev. 19:19, 27-28; Num. 15:37-41; Deu. 6:4-9; 14:1; 22:5, 11-12)
-**Dedicating / Devoting** (Lev. 27:1-29; Num. 18:14-19)
-**Diet** (Lev. 7:22-27; 11:1-47; 17:1-16; 19:26; 20:25; Deu. 12:15-16, 20-25; 14:3-21)
-**Discharges** (Lev. 15:1-33; Num. 5:1-3; Deu. 23:9-14)
-**Exclusion from Assembly** (Deu. 23:1-8)
-**Fallen Religions** (Exo. 34:12-17; Lev. 19:26, 31; 20:1-6, 23, 27; Deu. 4:15-31; 6:14-15; 7:25-26; 12:2-3, 30-31; 13:1-18; 16:21-22; 17:2-7; 18:10-11, 14; 23:17; 29:16-18)
-**Farming** (Exo. 23:10-11; 34:21; Lev. 19:9-10, 19, 23-25; 25:1-7; Num. 18:12-13; Deu. 11:18; 22:9-10; 23:24-25; 24:19-22; 25:4)
-**Firstborn** (Deu. 21:15-17)
-**House** (Deu. 6:4-9; 11:20; 22:8)
-**Inheritance** (Num. 36:7-9; Deu. 25:5-10)
-**Injury** (Exo. 21:12-36; Lev. 24:19-20)
-**Justice and Mercy** (Exo. 23:1-9; Lev. 19:15; Deu. 10:17-19; 21:22-23)
-**King** (Deu. 17:14-20)
-**Marriage / Engagement** (Deu. 22:13-30; 24:1-5)
-**Mold** (Lev. 13:47-59; 14:33-57)
-**Nazirite** (Num. 6:1-21)
-**Parenting** (Exo. 13:14; Deu. 6:4-9, 20-25; 11:19; 29:29)
-**Property Protection and Restitution** (Exo. 22:1-15; Num. 5:5-10; Deu. 19:14)
-**Rebellious Son** (Deu. 21:18-21)
-**Sabbath** (Exo. 23:10-13; 31:12-17; 34:21; 35:1-3; Lev. 23:3; Num. 15:32-36)
-**Servants** (Exo. 21:2-11; 23:12; Lev. 19:20-22; Deu. 15:12-18; 23:15-16)
-**Sacrifices** (Lev. 22:17-30)
-**Sex** (Lev. 18:1-30; 19:20-22, 29; 20:10-21; Deu. 27:20-23)
-**Skin Disorders** (Lev. 13:1-46; 14:1-32; Num. 5:1-3; Deu. 24:8-9)
-**Social Behavior** (Exo. 22:16-31; Lev. 19:12-14, 16, 32-36; Deu. 23:19-20, 24-25; 24:6-7, 10-18; 25:11-16; 27:18-19, 24-25)
-**Ten Commandments and Enforcement** (Lev. 20:9; 24:15-17, 19-22)
-**Unfaithful Wife Test** (Num. 5:11-31)
-**Unsolved Murder** (Deu. 21:1-9)
-**Vows / Oaths** (Num. 30:1-15; Deu. 6:13; 12:26-27; 23:8, 21-23)
-**War** (Deu. 20:1-20; 21:10-14; 24:5; 25:17-19)
-**Witnesses** (Deu. 19:15-21)
-**Worship** (Deu. 12:4-7)

"Case Law" Examples

Within the Law, the "general rules" represent universally applicable, cross-cultural principles, but the "specific rules" speak directly to the immediate cultural environment.

So, how does the Law of Moses apply to modern society?

In some cases, we might have heard people say the Law of Moses doesn't apply to us at all. And, in other cases, you might have heard teachers tell you only the Ten Commandments count.

Of course, during the time of Moses, the "specific rules" *directly addressed* the common grievances within their society. Indeed, it is quite likely many of these specific rules were recorded by Moses after he heard a complaint which presented that issue. For example, the Lord Jesus tells us Moses wrote commands about divorce in response to a specific situation where the people were hard-hearted (Deu. 24:1-3; Matt. 19:6-8).

In other words, the "specific rules" likely record many of the rulings Moses issued during his years as a judge (Exo. 18:13). Therefore, Moses would have included these "specific rules" as "case law" within the Law itself—providing "sample verdicts" to help future judges to render decisions. Thus, the more verdicts Moses included, the better "feel" future judges would have for the overall spirit of the Law.

So, why did Moses prohibit anyone else—especially judges—from adding onto the Law with their own verdicts (Deu. 4:2)? Wouldn't the Law be made stronger if judges pasted their own verdicts into it?

No. The Law would become muddied by differing opinions from different judges. Moreover, the Law would become *liberal* in its interpretation—sliding further away from its original form. By including *only* the specific rulings of Moses, it required all future judges to preserve the original form of the Law. No matter where a judge served—however far into the future—Deu. 4:2 would require the judge to "travel" back to Sinai. The judge would need to see the Law through the eyes of Moses—in its original setting. Thus, God designed the Law to be *conservative*—holding fast to its original form by prohibiting additions (Deu. 4:2). And, this is vital because the Law itself is based on the pattern of Heaven (Exo. 25:40; Heb. 8:5). So, to alter the Law *in any way* would immediately cause it to lose its Heavenly pattern.

Think about it this way: It was part of God's design that the Law *only* contain: (1) the basic start-up information needed to establish the tabernacle, (2) the "general rules" (that is Ten Commandments), and (3) one set of "specific rules" included by Moses.

By looking at Moses' "specific rules," future judges could see an "example" of how the Law was applied to a certain cultural context. This would help each judge in the administration of his own judgeship— as he/she ventured to do the same. Each judge would simply follow Moses' example—evaluating the original context of his commands and their own cultural context. Then the judge would issue only personal rulings to guide individuals toward reconciliation with God and others.

The Mosaic system appointed judges for the purpose of being personable and responsive to individuals; not to sit in ivory towers interpreting, re-interpreting and musing on their own thoughts. This is why the system of the *entire* Law is vital for the administration of the commands. Without the *entire* Law system, the commands cannot be fully followed.

In other words, when one follows a command, he is only following his own illegitimate interpretation of that command. Because Moses barred any addition to the Law apart from himself, the judges and the Prophet, nothing one adds to the Law is approved by the Law itself (Deu. 4:2). If, in our example, the illegitimate man was to speak with a legitimate judge, the judge may call him to a higher level of obedience—demonstrating his view of the specific command in question was incorrect (ex. Matt. 19:16-21). Therefore, judges were entrusted with the work of helping people to spiritually blossom and grow—rather than remaining captive within their own limited perceptions.

So, what would it be like to interact with a judge or prophet who followed after the pattern of Moses?

Well, we could expect a judge to listen to us with concern and compassion. And we could expect devotion—as the judge would join with us in whatever challenge we faced. Then, on our part, the judge would require obedience—calling us to perform certain steps to resolve our situation. At times, a judge might tell us to do something arbitrary, but in the assignment of an arbitrary task we might learn much about the attitude of our hearts (2 Kings 5:10-15).

Responsiveness

Interestingly, the system of the Law mirrors the function of the Holy Spirit and how He guides us through prayer. When using the judges within their established role, the individual believer receives a *personal action plan*—helping him to better relate to God and others in his *exact* situation.

Think about it this way . . .

First, when a person experiences a problem, they go to a judge.

Second, the judge carefully listens to everything the person says.

Third, the judge looks into the rules of the Law to find an answer for the person.

Fourth, the judge discusses the specific laws with the person—helping them to understand.

Fifth, the judge gives the person specific steps to fulfill to remedy their situation.

Sixth, the person leaves from the judge and obediently carries out his/her instructions.

The above is how the Law is designed. The Law itself was never designed for people to sit alone, interpreting the rules for themselves. It is no wonder why people are so confused by the Law and avoid reading it—*we don't have the system of judges to help us!*

It is good to see how the Law was designed. Whereas many wrongly criticize the Law as being a cold list of commands; we see instead the personal-responsiveness of the judges—where they would enter into problems with individuals, offering personal coaching and specific steps on the path to reconciliation.

How often have you heard people say, "*I wish I knew what God wanted me to do?*"

Frankly, this is a problem believers face today *because* the Law has been forsaken. If the tabernacle system were in place, you would have judges who were empowered by the Holy Spirit, under Moses' authority, to coach you through whatever circumstance you face. But apart from that prescribed system of worship, humans are sadly left to themselves.

Think about it.

People today lack direction because we have forsaken the system of judges which offers direction.

How to Keep the Law

Phase 10

Becoming God's People

Finally, "keeping the Law" requires us to make a personal decision.

In the Bible, God's people are not based on a bloodline, but rather the seed of Abraham (Gal. 3:29). Regardless of nationality, a person can choose to be grafted in among God's people (Acts 13:26; 17:4).

Interestingly, in the writings of Paul, he refers to this grafting of the Gentiles as the "mystery of the gospel" (Rom. 11:25; Eph. 3:3-9; 5:32).

Therefore, in order to "keep the Law," one must make a personal decision to become one of God's people.

Now, it may seem backwards for this to be discussed as the 10th Phase, rather than the 1st Phase.

After all, shouldn't a person "make the decision" to follow God *before* the entire process detailed above?

No.

When understanding the Law of Moses, we see the design was for all future generations to be born into a world with the tabernacle, priesthood and sacrificial calendar *already* in progress. In other words, the tabernacle itself—and all the accompanying phases described in this book—should have remained throughout all generations on Earth. Then, as new people are born into the Earth, the tabernacle would *already* be functioning (Exo. 12:14, 17, 24; 27:21; 29:9; Lev. 16:29, 31, 34; 23:14, 21, 31, 41; 24:3; Num. 10:8; 15:15; 18:23; 19:10, 21).

Thus, the personal decisions of individuals to follow God should come *after* the entire tabernacle system is reestablished.

When considering the vast numbers of people who believe in the Bible, it is most bizarre that God's established pattern of worship has been permitted to disappear from the Earth. Generation after generation passes away—with none being stirred to reestablish the exact patterns God instituted.

Since the God of the Bible is our God, the first order of business should be His worship. We should seek first to worship Him in the prescribed way. This is the first task of anyone who believes—to approach God in the manner He requires.

However, in our fallen world, we are left to grapple with things as they are. We are left to consider why things appear as they do. And, finally, we are left to cope.

Are we satisfied living in a world where our God is not worshipped in the way He demands?

No matter where you find yourself in your spiritual journey, I hope you will reflect on this question. We are called to be pilgrims on this Earth. And we do not need to accept things as they are.

In this final phase of the Law, I leave you with this thought . . .

We are all left to make decisions. What decisions will you make?

How to Keep the Law

Conclusions

Violations of Deu. 4:2 in Bible History

Following the death of Moses, God's people rapidly fell away from the Law established by Moses. Although the Law of Moses was set up as a shadow of the eternal pattern of Heaven—and thus immutable and eternal—God's people nonetheless changed *nearly every aspect* of this pattern (2 Kings 18:12). Therefore, at the arrival of the New Testament, the "Law" practiced was a corrupt version.

This is why the Lord Jesus had such strong criticisms for the priests—because although the priests stated they followed the Law of Moses, in fact they did not.

So, how can I explain this in a way you will understand?

Since you have a thorough understanding of the Law of Moses from reading this book, I will show you the many ways God's people fell away from the original Heavenly pattern. And, as we examine various passages from the Bible, it will become clear that God's people quickly lost sight of the good Law after Moses' death. Although the people "thought" they were following Moses, the religion they practiced became more and more divorced from the original pattern.

So, what's the big deal?

Well, if you understand this, then the New Testament criticisms of the Law will make sense. In other words, the Lord Jesus and Paul the apostle were not criticizing the original "Law of Moses." Rather, the Lord Jesus and Paul were criticizing the false version of the "Law" which existed during their earthly ministries.

You must understand, the Law of Moses is eternal—being a pattern of the Heavenly tabernacle. As such, that perfect Law is never going away. It will remain relevant throughout all eternity (Isa. 4:5; 66:18-23; Ezek. 37:26-28; Amos 9:11; Zech. 14:16-21). Therefore, New Testament criticisms of the Law are not criticisms of the "Law of Moses," but rather criticisms of the *corrupt version of the Law*—resulting from the changes added to it by generations of fallen men.

To begin this presentation, consider these four points . . .

#1 The Law of Moses contains both the commands of God and the cultural commands of Moses (See pages 243 & 259-262).

#2 The Law of Moses is a replica of the Heavenly tabernacle itself (Exo. 25:40; Heb. 8:5).

#3 The Law of Moses is immutable—with no one being permitted to alter it (Deu. 4:2).

#4 The Law of Moses will be reestablished in eternity (Isa. 4:5; 66:18-23; Ezek. 37:26-28; Amos 9:11; Zech. 14:16-21).

Understand those four principles. Re-read them because they affect your understanding of the New Testament. For, when we understand that the Law of Moses: (1) contains God's commands, (2) reflects the patterns of Heaven, (3) are immutable and eternally in force, *then* this means that the Law of Moses (in its pure form) is *never abolished*.

Therefore, whenever the New Testament interacts with the Law in a pejorative fashion, it is NOT criticizing the pure Law of Moses. Rather, the New Testament criticizes the corrupt version of the Law. So, it is not that the authors of the New Testament are criticizing Moses. Rather they are criticizing the corruption of the priests—who highjacked the Law of Moses, changing it in violation to Deu. 4:2.

In other words, from the time of Moses up to the New Testament, people altered the Law of Moses in violation of Deu. 4:2—adding and subtracting many things. Thus, the Law of Moses became something completely different and lost its purity as established. Thus, with the arrival of the New Testament, the authors had criticisms of the Law—but their criticisms were not for the "Law of Moses" itself; rather their criticisms were for what the "Law" had become under the corruption of men.

In order to provide you a clear contrast between the two systems, I will show you how the original "*Law of Moses*" completely differs from the practice of the Law common during New Testament time. To do so, I will refer to this second, corrupted version of the Law as the "*Commands of Men*."

Below I will present New Testament passages which interact with the Law. I will also present the various ways in which the Law of Moses was altered throughout the Old Testament. And, I will show you how New Testament criticisms were directed at the "Commands of Men" rather than the "Law of Moses."

So, without further ado, let's discuss the ways Deu. 4:2 was violated by God's people in the Old Testament . . .

How the "Law of Moses" was Entirely Corrupted into the "Commands of Men"

To prepare for this section, I recommend reading 2 Kings 18:12.

This Bible verse makes it clear that God's people quickly swayed from the commands of Moses after his death. And, by doing so, their religion lost its original pattern (Exo. 25:40).

Having completed this book, you have knowledge of the *exact* requirements delivered by God on Mount Sinai. Now I want to lead you to use the knowledge you gained.

So, let's evaluate God's people in the Old Testament based on the *exact requirements* of Moses' Law.

Below you will find a series of charts. Each chart presents a certain area of the Law of Moses—detailing what God commanded in His perfect Law and how His people failed to keep His commands. Each chart contrasts the original pattern with the unauthorized changes made by God's people throughout Bible history.

The charts are each organized based on a different aspect of the Law as discussed in this book. The charts below will make it clear that the "Law" practiced by the people became radically divorced from the original pattern of the Law of Moses. So, pay careful attention to the differences in each comparison . . .

The God-Appointed Leader

Law of Moses	Change
The Lord Himself leads His people by directing Moses (the God-appointed leader) (see page 1-8).	People reject the Lord as their leader (1 Sam. 10:19).
The God-appointed leader, like Moses, must be called by God—then permitted to serve (Deu. 18:18-22)	The boy, Samuel, who was a descendant of Ephraim, was appointed as a priest, and before he was called by the Lord. He was permitted to sleep before the ark and minister in the Lord's house (1 Sam. 3:20)
The God-appointed leader is selected based on God's will.	Although Samuel is serving as the God-appointed leader in the place of Moses, the people demand a king (1 Sam. 8:5-9). The Lord grants their request because they are obstinate.
God-appointed leader/Prophet: The office of prophet is based on the pattern of Moses and prescribed in Deu. 18:18-22. It is a high office, intended to serve alongside the high priest to direct the work of the tabernacle and the nation.	The prophetic office degraded to the point that ordinary citizens began referring to themselves as "prophets," although they bore no resemblance to Moses (1 Kings 13:18).
God-appointed leader/Prophets are called and empowered by the Holy Spirit to provide guidance to the high priest, priests, people and tabernacle (Deu. 18:18-22). Moses told the people to expect prophets whom the Lord would send.	Prophets consistently rejected throughout all Bible history (ex. Amos 7:10-15). The Lord Jesus told us how many prophets were rejected by the priests and the people alike (Matt. 21:33-46). This widespread rejection of the prophets is encoded in the Festival of Tabernacle's seventy-one bulls (see page 192).

Tabernacle

Law of Moses	Change
Tabernacle must have the ark, and is in a single location with the high priest serving at the altar.	A city named Nob maintained a separate "house of God"—where presumably rival tabernacle furniture was placed, including a rival bread table with showbread (1 Sam. 21:1-4). Perhaps this is the reason why David's men were permitted to eat the consecrated bread—because this "house of God" in Nob was *not* the official tabernacle (see Luke 6:2-5).
Tabernacle set-up: Conducted by the Levites—with the Merarites setting posts; Gershonites setting curtains and coverings; and Kohathites setting the holy articles. (For complete details, see pages 57-61).	David was involved with the set-up of the ark's tent (2 Sam. 6:17). Moreover, the ark required the specific tabernacle items to be in place for its arrival, so a common tent according to the Law of Moses is insufficient. The tabernacle had specific coverings (see page 28-32).
Tabernacle is a portable tent (see page 28-32). Perhaps this is one of its most notable traits because if the tabernacle remained, it could be relocated on a circuit throughout all Israel by the priests and Levites. And, most relevant to Israel's history, if the tabernacle remained it would have been immune to capture (as enemies threatened a certain location, the tabernacle could be easily moved to a safer location).	David desires to build a permanent temple and God is reluctant at first, then concedes (2 Sam. 7:2-7). As history will reveal, permanently placing the ark and other holy articles in one location made them vulnerable to enemy capture. Therefore, we are left to consider if the Lord permitted His people to do this simply because they were obstinate—similar to when He permitted them a king (1 Sam. 8:5-9). Consider 1 Kings 3:1-4. Also, in 1 Kings 9:3-9 it seems the Lord allowed the temple in order to provide a means to test His people's faithfulness. Either way, we can be certain the temple was not the original pattern but something added (Deu. 4:2). What do you think?
Tabernacle: Priests guard the tabernacle at all times. In the Law of Moses, the priests were responsible for preventing citizens from approaching the tabernacle area—unless they were bringing an offering.	Priests wrongly permit Adonijah to physically grab and hold onto the horns of the altar (1 Kings 1:51). Then they wrongly allow a second group of men to approach the altar to retrieve Adonijah (1 Kings 1:53). See also 1 Kings 2:28-34.
Tabernacle: Its dimensions were based on the size of the coverings (see pages 28-32).	Temple made to replace the tabernacle had different dimensions—which would have wrongly impacted the placement of the articles within it (1 Kings 6:2).

277

Tabernacle: God directed the tabernacle to have specific layers of coverings.	The temple made to replace the tabernacle was made with walls rather than the coverings God directed (1 Kings 6:5).
Tabernacle has no windows.	Temple has windows (1 Kings 6:4). LXX says "secret" windows.
Tabernacle contains only two areas: the area with the bread table, incense altar and lampstand, and the most holy place with the ark. There are no extra rooms.	Temple was made with chamber room structures outside (1 Kings 6:5).
Tabernacle construction precludes additions (Deu. 4:2). One could say the three articles in the holy place are symbolic of the Trinity—so additional items would off-balance this Heavenly pattern.	Temple introduced unauthorized furniture and articles—including gold chains, pillars, cherubim carved of wood, another basin (sea), floor coverings, door frames, dressed stone (1 Kings 6).
Tabernacle does not contain a treasury.	Temple contains a treasury area (1 Kings 7:51).
Tabernacle capable of relocating—making it nearly immune to enemy capture.	Shishak, king of Egypt, attacks Jerusalem and plunders the temple (1 Kings 14:26). Similar occurrences are found in 2 Kings 12:18; 14:14; 16:8; 18:14-16; 24:13; 25:8-17! We are left to consider: What articles were taken and what did each plundering leave behind—if anything?

Ark

Law of Moses	Change
Ark designed to remain *in the Tabernacle*—being perpetually shielded behind the veil.	It is possible the Ark was still outside the Tabernacle during the days following the Jericho campaign (Josh. 7:6). In Josh. 8:33 it appears the Ark is placed on display before the people.
The Ark designed to remain in the Tabernacle—being moved only when the Tabernacle is transported (see page 36).	Ark used as a military weapon—being taken onto battlefields (Josh. 6:4 & 1 Sam. 4:3).
Ark separated within the tabernacle by the shielding curtain. Only the God-appointed leader, in the place of Moses, appears before it, and the high priest or his son on the Day of Atonement.	The boy, Samuel, was permitted to sleep near the ark (1 Sam. 3:3). David permitted to go before the ark in the tent (2 Sam. 7:18).
Ark cannot be looked upon—not even by the Levites who carry it (see page 36 & 57-61).	Citizens look at the ark (1 Sam. 6:19).
Ark: The ark belongs within the tabernacle—behind the shielding curtain.	The ark was left in a person's house in Kiriath Jearim for twenty years—rather than the Levites bringing it back to the Lord's house (1 Sam. 7:1-2).
Ark: The ark belongs within the tabernacle.	Israel "consecrates" a man so he can keep the ark in his house (1 Sam. 7:1-2). See also 2 Sam. 6:10-11.
Ark: "Before the Lord" is a phrase meaning before the Ark—where the Lord would appear to Moses above the mercy seat, or before the tabernacle entrance.	"Before the Lord" used ethereally—independent of the Ark because it is not in Gilgal (1 Sam. 11:15; 12:7). The ark was in a different location in Kiriath Jearim (1 Sam. 7:1-2). See also 1 Sam. 21:6—where the "presence" of the Lord is stated to be within the house of God in Nob, although the ark is not at Nob. (Additional instance occurs in 2 Sam. 5:3.)
Ark: Transported by being covered by the priests with the shielding curtain, and carried by shoulder with the carrying poles by the Kohathites of the Levites (see pages 57-61 for full details).	Ark wrongly transported by ox cart (2 Sam. 6:3-6). Ark wrongly carried independent of the tabernacle and other articles (2 Sam. 15:24-29).
Ark contained the jar of manna, Aaron's staff that budded and the two tables of the Law (Heb. 9:4).	The ark contained only the two tables (1 Kings 8:9). What happened to the jar of manna and the staff?
Ark: The ark cannot be viewed idly by anyone—even the high priest on the Day of Atonement or the Levites who carry it (see page 185).	The ark is placed in a way where the carrying poles (which always remain inserted in the carrying rings of the ark) are visible to random priests from outside the most holy place (1 Kings 8:8).

Lampstand

Law of Moses	Change
Lampstand must never go out—except when prepared for transport (see page 42 & 57-61)	Lampstand permitted to go out/quenched as regular practice (1 Sam. 3:3).
Lampstand: The lampstand is the only source of light within the tabernacle (see page 42).	LXX states Solomon placed ten additional candles within the temple (1 Kings 6:49*). (*English translations found in 7:49*)

Trumpets

Law of Moses	Change
Trumpets: Priests use the sacred trumpets to rally God on behalf of His people when marching to war.	Gideon uses his own trumpet because the priests fail to rally the nation with the sacred trumpets (Judg. 6:34; 7:18-20). Later in repeated battles throughout the Old Testament, God's people fail to use the sacred trumpets as required.
Trumpets to be used before battles within the land (see page 48)	Military campaigns throughout Old Testament often neglect mention of the trumpets—with the exception of the battle of Jericho.
Trumpets used to signal setting out of God's people in order—east, south, west and north.	No mention of trumpets used to signal the setting out of camps (Josh. 3:3).
Trumpets used for specific purposes (see page 48)	Zadok the (high?) priest uses trumpet to signal the appointing of Solomon as king—although using the trumpets for political appointments is not prescribed in the Law of Moses (1 Kings 1:34).

Altar Table

Law of Moses	Change
Altar table is located next to the tabernacle (pg. 20).	Sacrifices made at rival altar (1 Sam. 10:8)
Altar table is located next to the tabernacle.	While the tabernacle was in Bethel, the people of Israel set up a rival altar (Judg. 20:26-28; 21:4). Why not just use the altar which was already at the tabernacle?
Altar table is located next to the tabernacle.	Samuel sets up another altar in Ramah (1 Sam. 7:17).
Altar table is still located next to the tabernacle!	Rival altars used (1 Sam. 11:15; 13:9; 14:35), while the Ark wrongly is kept away in Kiriath Jearim (1 Sam. 7:1-2). See also 2 Sam. 24:18; 1 Kings 3:1-4.
Altar table: Horns were used for the placement of blood.	Priests wrongly permit Adonijah to physically grab and hold onto the horns of the altar (1 Kings 1:51). See also 1 Kings 2:28-34.
Altar table: The tabernacle has *one* altar table outside of its entrance—and upon this altar table sacrifices are presented.	King Ahaz tells the priest, Uriah, to make another altar to replace the altar table (2 Kings 16:10-15). Then they move the prescribed altar table north so the new altar can take its place.

Anointing Oil

Law of Moses	Change
Anointing oil in Law of Moses reserved for the high priest, priests, the priestly garments and tabernacle articles (see page 86). Judges and prophets not needing to be anointed because they are anointed/empowered by the Holy Spirit.	People obstinately demand a king—and to accomplish this Samuel anoints Saul with oil (1 Sam. 9:16). Later the practice of anointing kings—with olive oil, continues (1 Sam. 16:13; 1 Kings 1:39).
Anointing oil made from prescribed formula (see page 86).	Anointing is done with *olive oil* (1 Sam. 10:1)
Anointing oil: Container unspecified	Anointing oil begins being placed in horn (1 Kings 1:39).

Water of Cleansing

Law of Moses	Change
Water of cleansing to be used for all troops returning from battle (see page 80).	Water of cleansing is never used—not even for David. Priests neglect this duty. Perhaps the only noteworthy reference to the water of cleansing is found in Heb. 10:19-22—where the author uses it to heighten our awe of the Lord Jesus' *bodily* resurrection. For, since the Law of Moses required sprinkling on the 3rd and 7th days after contact with a deceased body, those who draw near to the body of Christ would require cleansing on the 3rd day after His death. But on the 3rd day He was risen! Thus, the body of Christ shows within it fulfillment of the Law concerning the water of cleansing—because on the 3rd day their remains *no need* for cleansing.

The High Priest

Law of Moses	Change
High priest responsible for maintaining the ephod, in addition to overseeing the tabernacle area as prescribed by Moses (see page 50)	Ahijah, the priest, is apparently serving as the high priest because he is bearing the ephod in the LXX, yet he fails to reestablish the tabernacle by neglecting to bring the ark back from Kiriath Jearim (1 Sam. 14:18). Here the high priest, Ahijah, is roving with Saul's army—independent of his other priests, Levites and the tabernacle (1 Sam. 14:41). This demonstrates neglect of his primary duties as high priest—to guard and to oversee the tabernacle.
High priest must be consecrated, in addition to making a grain offering when anointed (see page 97 & 218).	With the death of Eli (the former high priest) and both his sons, it is presumed the high priest position is vacant. Then it appears a priest named Ahijah has taken upon himself the high priesthood (1 Sam. 14:18). A similar situation is presented in 1 Sam. 23:6—where Abiathar takes the supposed ephod of the high priest without being consecrated to do so. No mention is made of the required consecration steps—or whether he was officially clothed with the ephod according to the Law of Moses.
High priest is accountable only to the God-appointed leader—the prophet in the place of Moses (Deu. 18:18), with the Lord Himself serving as the supreme authority.	The high priest office is degraded into a political billet subordinate the king (2 Kings 12:7). In lists of court officials, the high priest is often listed as a mere member of a king's court.

Ephod

Law of Moses	Change
Ephod stones to be used to manifest truth, in addition to the prophet in the place of Moses interceding before the Ark in the Most Holy Place.	Elders neglect use of ephod and intercession (Josh. 9:14)
Ephod is a holy article worn by the high priest—containing within it Manifestation and Truth (see pages 52-53).	Rival ephod placed on display (Judg. 8:27; 17:5)
Ephod is worn by the high priest who serves at the tabernacle. There is only one ephod.	English translations state the ephod is on display in the house of God in Nob—however the LXX omits mention of the "ephod" (1 Sam. 21:9). English translations imply the priests made rival ephods at multiple locations. Later, a priest brings this ephod to David (1 Sam. 23:6; 30:7).

Priests

Law of Moses	Change
Priests offer sacrifices on behalf of God's people	Due to the absence/inaction of priests, citizens begin offering their own sacrifices (Judg. 6:19-25; 13:19). Gideon offers goat, bull and builds an altar See also 2 Sam. 24:18-25.
Priests are distinct from Levites	The distinction between priests and Levites is lost (Judg. 17:9-10).
Priests required to remain at the tabernacle—even camping outside of it to guard it.	Priests freelance—assigning themselves to random households in the countryside (Judg. 17:9-10; 18:18-20; 1 Sam. 22:23; 30:7; 2 Sam. 20:26)
Priestly garments are sacred—with even priests being unable to touch priestly garments for themselves before they are consecrated (see page 50).	Citizens take it upon themselves to make and handle priestly garments for priests (Judg. 17:9-10; 1 Sam. 2:19; 2 Sam. 6:14).
Priests *must* be descendants of Levi	Samuel was from the lineage of Ephraim, and through adoption, was permitted to become a priest—because at this point he was not yet called by God as a prophet (1 Sam. 1:1, 28; 3:1).
Priests responsible for guarding the tabernacle—ensuring it is not misused.	Although the "house of God" at Nob was a rival tabernacle—and not the one tabernacle—nevertheless the basic responsibility of the priests is neglected (1 Sam. 22:11): All the priests leave the house of God—which would have left it unguarded. Other examples include the (high?) priests Abiathar and Zadok are used as political informants and messengers (2 Sam. 15:35-36)—when they should remain at the tabernacle.
Priests serve at the one tabernacle.	Priests are dispersed—living in various cities in Israel (1 Sam. 21:1-4; 1 Kings 2:26).
Priests: The sons of the high priest were to be consecrated and serve at the tabernacle as priests (see page 97).	Ahimaaz, the son of the Zadok, the high priest, served as a military messenger rather than a tabernacle priest (2 Sam. 18:19-22). It is unlikely physical defect barred him from priestly service due to his ability to outrun other messengers.

Priests: Priestly duties primarily occur at either the altar table and tabernacle entrance. They are only required to go *into* the tabernacle few times—once in morning and once in evening to tend the bread table, incense altar and lampstand, and also limited times during festivals, and when pouring out drink offerings on the bread table.	Priests precluded from performing services *in* the tabernacle due to the presence of the Cloud (1 Kings 8:11). Did the priestly duties at the temple require additional tasks from the priests which required them to *remain* in the tabernacle for extended periods of time? Certainly, the Law of Moses did not require priests to remain *in* the tabernacle.
Priests supervise the tabernacle and oversee everything.	Here we see a scribe/secretary is assigned to manage the temple (2 Kings 22:3).
Priests are from the tribe of Levi.	At rival worship locations priests were selected from various tribes (1 Kings 12:28-31).

Procedures

Law of Moses	Change
Nazirites required to follow specific procedures (see page 261).	Nazarite procedures unfollowed (Judg. 13). Priests do not support people who become Nazirites.

Blessing

Law of Moses	Change
Blessing: Num. 6:24-27 prescribes the *exact* way the priests are *required* to bless God's people.	Eli the priest sends away Hannah with different words (1 Sam. 1:17; 2:20). The priests had the responsibility of blessing the people (2 Sam. 6:18).

Levites

Law of Moses	Change
Levites: The Levites were responsible for relocating the tabernacle.	With the establishment of the stationary temple, the Levites became obsolete—being assigned instead as musicians (1 Kings 10:12), or more likely being pushed away from their duties.
Levites responsible for movement of tabernacle—making it necessary for them to remain near the tabernacle (see page 57-61).	Levites given land possessions which are widely dispersed—making their direct connection with the tabernacle impractical (Josh. 21; Judg. 17:9).
Levites: The Levites are assigned the responsibility of carrying the tabernacle and its articles.	The establishment of the stationary temple renders the assigned ministry of the Levites obsolete. In 1 Kings 8:1-4, the "priests" are presented as carrying the ark and other articles—which is improper.
Levites: The Levites were responsible for maintaining the posts, bases, crossbars, curtains and all structural items of the tabernacle and the courtyard. If craftsmen were needed to replace anything, the craftsmen should be filled with the Spirit as were Bezalel and Oholiab—which would allow a non-Levite to serve as a craftsman.	Many contractors were hired to repair the temple—with no mention of specific names, lineage or Spirit-empowerment for their tasks (2 Kings 12:11-16). This is certainly different than the great care taken in the selection of Bezalel and Oholiab. Alas, all temple repairs were pointless because the king cleared out the temple in 12:18. A similar occurrence is found in 22:4-7.

Festivals

Law of Moses	Change
Festivals: The Festival of Unleavened Bread comes after Passover, with prescribed offerings being made daily for a week (see page 167).	No mention of the Festival of Unleavened Bread following Passover (Josh. 5:11). No mention of the required sacrifices during the week they marched around Jericho.
Festivals: The Law of Moses states in the seventh month the Festival of Trumpets, the Day of Atonement and the Festival of Tabernacles are to be observed along with their *precise* offerings.	In the seventh month, Solomon oversees a festival which lasts for seven days. Although this is likely the Festival of Tabernacles, there is no mention of the required offerings on those days—only the *excessive* offering of 1 Kings 8:63.
Festival Offerings: Are to be conducted *exactly* as specified in the Law of Moses.	In the seventh month (which has several festivals), God's people did not follow the *exact* prescribed festival requirements, but sacrificed animals *without number* (1 Kings 8:2-5, 63). Although sacrificial excess is laudable in the eyes of people, the Law of Moses precludes excess in favor of simple obedience.
Festivals are prescribed by the Law of Moses.	An unauthorized festival was designated on the 15th day of the 8th month (1 Kings 12:32-33).

Offerings

Law of Moses	Change
Offerings: In the Law of Moses, offerings are specific in purpose—which would preclude excess in offerings. In other words, a person simply offers the prescribed sacrifice and nothing further.	Solomon offers one-thousand animals as sacrifices at an unauthorized location (1 Kings 3:4). Yet the Law of Moses does not demand such excess—and even in the case of freewill offerings, excess is turned away (Exo. 25:1-8; 35:4-29; 36:3-6). See also 1 Kings 8:5.
Offerings: Priests make offerings on behalf of the people (see page 133).	King Saul makes burnt offering although he is not permitted to do so (1 Sam. 13:9). See also 2 Sam. 6:13, 18—where David makes burnt offerings. Solomon does similar in 1 Kings 3:15.
Offerings are to be made at the tabernacle.	David mentions an annual sacrifice held by his family in Bethlehem (1 Sam. 20:6). Neither the tabernacle or the ark is located in Bethlehem.
Offerings: Presented upon the altar table.	Due to the excessive offering of 1 Kings 8:53, the priests had to burn offerings in an area of the courtyard. Although we may be inclined to view this as a "good thing," we must recognize that it departs from the exact pattern prescribed (Exo. 25:40).
Offerings: Portions are assigned to the priests and Levites for many offerings.	The verse in 2 Kings 23:9 indicates the priests shared their portions with unauthorized individuals who presided over rival ritual locations.
Drink offering: Authorized drink offerings to the Lord are poured out upon the bread table in the tabernacle (see page 40)	Citizens pour out unauthorized drink offerings of water on the ground (1 Sam. 7:6).
Freewill offering: Census and freewill offerings were the recognized means of procuring resources for the tabernacle.	An unauthorized money chest was placed in a room of the temple to take money offerings from God's people (2 Kings 12:9).

Freewill offering for vows: Procedures are set for how a person makes a vow—by presenting a freewill offering (see page 214). Perhaps by requiring an official offering to commemorate a vow, it may have deterred people from making hasty vows (see Matt. 5:34-37). In other words, the Law of Moses implies one should not swear an oath unless he was serious enough to commemorate it with a specific freewill offering.	Saul makes a hasty oath without a freewill offering (1 Sam. 14:24, 39, 44). Later David and Jonathan make a covenant, yet they do not offer the prescribed freewill offering (1 Sam. 23:18). See also 1 Sam. 24:22; 25:22.
Sin offering is required for those who sin (see page 226).	Although Saul confesses sin, and is accepted by Samuel, he is not ordered to make a sin offering as the Law of Moses commands (1 Sam. 15:24-31).
Sin offering: In 1 Sam. 7:3-4, the appropriate sacrifice for the congregation would have been a *bull* (see "Community Sin Offering" on page 228).	Samuel offers a *lamb* as a burnt offering for the people (1 Sam. 7:9)
Sin offering is required for sins (see page 226).	Samuel does not require a sin offering from the community when they confess their sin (1 Sam. 12:19-21). Nathan does not require a sin offering from David after he confesses his sin (2 Sam. 12:13). David is not required to offer a sin offering, but rather makes a burnt offering and fellowship offering in 2 Sam. 24:25. See also 1 Sam. 23:18; 26:21.
Fat of sacrifices was strictly reserved as the Lord's portion to be burned on the altar table (see page 149).	Priests take their portions and do not cut off the fat to be burned upon the altar table (1 Sam. 2:15).

Behavior

Law of Moses	Change
Behavior: The Law of Moses prohibits idolatry and the worship of other gods.	Innumerable occasions of worshipping other gods—resulting in synchronization and corruption of their religion (see 2 Kings 23:4-7; Ezek. 8:1-18). A summary of this history is found in 2 Kings 17:7-23.
Behavior: The Law of Moses commands certain behavior (see pages 252 & 261).	Israel became lawless—with everyone doing as he saw fit (Judg. 17:6; 21:25).
Worship of other "gods" prohibited.	Beginning in Judg. 2:11-19, Israel continually fell into the practice of worshipping other "gods" throughout the entire Old Testament. These led to *synchronization*—where the original Law of Moses was corrupted through the import of other practices/beliefs. One such instance of synchronization occurs in Judg. 17:3.
Additions to the Law forbidden (Deu. 4:2)	Samuel, the prophet in the place of Moses, writes down rules for the kingship (1 Sam. 10:25). Yet Deu. 17:14-20 contains the only rules for a king—according to the Law of Moses. The Law requires no additional rules, nor would it necessitate the recording of additional rules for the kingship (Deu. 4:2).
Additions and Subtractions: The Law of Moses forbids additions or subtractions to its pattern (Deu. 4:2; Exo. 25:40; Heb. 8:5).	God's people failed in all things to maintain the Heavenly pattern contained in the Law of Moses (2 Kings 18:12). Therefore, *no one after Moses* ever witnessed the actual Law of Moses. The "Law" was no longer the "Law of Moses." The false practices of the corrupt Law were infuriating—and Paul was right to get angry. But he was not angry at the original Law of Moses—because no one after Moses *ever* experienced or practiced it.

The above charts are not exhaustive. There are *many* more examples which could be listed where the Law of Moses was violated. Armed with your knowledge from this book, you could easily go through books like Ezra, Nehemiah and later New Testament books to identify examples where God's people strayed from the Law of Moses.

Perhaps such an exercise would serve as a helpful opportunity for you to put in practice what you learned—evaluating your ability to identify religious practices which wandered from the original pattern. If you are interested in undertaking such a project, simply start with a book in the Bible and read what the priests were doing. Ask yourself, *"Does it match what Moses commanded?"* Or, take a look at how the festivals are celebrated today in comparison to how they were instituted. Or, compare religious ceremonies. Regardless of what you plan to research next, I challenge you to see these things *for yourself.*

So, after reading all these charts, what should we conclude?

We should agree with 2 Kings 18:12—which says the many generations of God's people failed in *all* the commands of Moses. In *every* area of the Law, the people failed to observe the prescribed patterns. Therefore, the religion they practiced was *entirely divorced* from the original Heavenly pattern of the Law (Exo. 25:40).

Thus, we can agree most heartily with Paul in Galatians when he stands in criticism of the "Law" he observed. After all, as stated in 2 Kings 18:12, God's people failed in all areas of the Law—and this is exactly what my charts demonstrate.

In this way we see the problem is not the original pattern of the Law of Moses—for that Law is perfect and based on the Heavenly pattern (Exo. 25:40; Heb. 8:5). And, that perfect Law will be reestablished in the last days (Isa. 4:5; 66:18-23; Ezek. 37:26-28; Amos 9:11; Zech. 14:16-21). Our problem instead is with all the corruptions added unto the Law in violation to Deu. 4:2—resulting in a corruption which is wrongly referred to as the "Law."

In my own study I hold fast to the original patterns taught in God's Word. I am not interested in the many additions people made to the Law—whether temples, altars, high places, pillars, seas and innumerable gold and silver articles. While others may seek after the glimmer of gold upon the rocks of the temple, I seek only the simplicity of *exactly* what God's Word commands: the tabernacle "tent" administered faithfully by prophet and priest.

My dear friend, in all cases I encourage you to let go of what the world esteems. Do not be enticed by thoughts of grandeur—for what is highly esteemed in the eyes of men is despised by God. Keep your sight on the Teacher, not a temple (Mark 13:1-2). Prepare your heart by being mindful of the original form of perfection. And seek only to be found there. In this way you can avoid being led astray. You will make yourself immune to enticement, standing firmly upon the Rock.

Of course, when reading the above charts, you may have mixed feelings—thinking perhaps some of the "changes" were positive and done for good purpose. For example, you might think it was good for the tabernacle to be transformed into the temple. Or you might think it was good Israel used the Ark during military campaigns. You are free to decide for yourself.

Who knows? Some of the changes might have been done at the will of the Lord alone, or they may have been *reluctantly* commanded by the Lord—similar to how the Lord permitted Samuel to give the people a king, even though He did not really desire to do so (1 Sam. 8:6-9).

For example, let's think about how the Ark was marched around Jericho. It might be that God knew the people were obstinate and unwilling to march out unless He sent the Ark out ahead of them. If this is the case, then it means although the Lord commanded this change, He did so only to coax His people from their obstinance. But in doing so, any change to the Law of Moses—regardless of motive or who gave the direction—would have had the effect of marring the Heavenly pattern contained in the Law.

In other words, since the Ark is based on the Heavenly Ark—and its function mirrors that of the higher copy, then to do things with the Ark which are not founded in the Law would be to remove the Ark from its Heavenly pattern.

Get it?

And, we know the Heavenly Ark is not being used as a weapon—being paraded around enemy cities to cause walls to fall. Since this is the case, we can be certain—that although the Jericho story is inspiring—it represents a pulling of the Ark away from its original pattern and holiness. But I digress.

The above chart is clear in its purpose: It demonstrates the Law of Moses was gradually changed from its original, Heavenly form. And, upon the arrival of the New Testament, it is clear the "Law" practiced by the Pharisees and Sadducees was *completely different* from the original pattern instituted by the Lord Himself on Mount Sinai (Exo. 25:40; Heb. 8:5). So, in all cases where the New Testament offers criticism for the Law, this should be recognized—that the New Testament authors are commenting on the pervading corruptions which seeped into the perfect Law over many generations, high-jacking it with repeated violations of Deu. 4:2.

In other words, the "Law" at the time of the New Testament was no longer the "Law of Moses."

And, even more remarkable, as demonstrated in this book, we could argue quite persuasively that *no human after Moses ever saw the Law operating in its original Heavenly form.* As the chart above demonstrates, God's people repeatedly pushed, pulled, yanked and prodded nearly every facet of the Law—forcing it to conform to *their own patterns* throughout time. Thus, the Law was no longer the Law of Moses—but rather the commands of men. It is no wonder why the Lord Jesus—who established the original pattern with Moses—was so infuriated by the false Law promoted by the religious teachers during His earthly ministry.

And, when Paul writes the book of Galatians, he is commenting on his perception of the "Law"—based on what *he observed in his lifetime.* However, as I demonstrate above, Paul *never witnessed* the true "Law of Moses." Rather, Paul observed only the corrupted version of what the Law had become after many generations of changes. So, when you read Galatians, realize Paul's criticisms are not for the "Law of Moses," but for the "Law of the Pharisees and Sadducees."

It is clear the Lord Jesus is in full agreement with Moses. After all, Moses appeared to Jesus on the mount of transfiguration—thereby endorsing the ministry of the Lord. Likewise, the Lord endorsed the Law of Moses at the beginning, appearing to him on Mount Sinai and at many other times (Exo. 33:11; Num. 12:8; Deu. 34:10). Therefore, the only way in which New Testament criticisms of the "Law" can be reconciled is through understanding that New Testament criticisms of the "Law" are not directed toward the *original Law*, but toward the *corrupted version of what it became*. After all, the Lord Jesus Himself endorses the Law of Moses (Matt. 5:17-18).

In fact, we can prove God *still* approves of the Law of Moses because it will be reinstituted throughout eternity (Isa. 4:5; 66:18-23; Ezek. 37:26-28; Amos 9:11; Zech. 14:16-21). And surely, we believe these prophets! Thus, we believe once all the corrupted dross is purged, God will reestablish His Law as it was in its original Heavenly form. And in that moment, when we are in that Heavenly congregation with Paul, we will all praise God—realizing in that moment Paul's criticisms were not for the perfect Law, but rather for the corruptions which pervaded it during his lifetime.

So, our challenge is to understand the Law—in its original form . . . as I have carefully laid out in this book. Because, when we understand the original Law of Moses, we see how it rebukes the same corrupt practices. In other words, when Paul criticizes the Law in his writings, the Law of Moses stands on Mount Sinai in total agreement with Paul! . . .

Paul proclaims, "Circumcision should not be the primary concern of the Law!"

Mount Sinai calls out, "Paul, you are right! My chief concern is the tabernacle system."

Paul adds, "The priests should not be running around policing circumcision and the private parts of citizens."

Mount Sinai agrees, "I told the priests to stay at the tabernacle—supervising the Levites. I never told them to take such an overwhelming concern with the private parts of citizens."

Paul offers further, "The Pharisees and Sadducees . . ."

Mount Sinai interrupts: "Who are the Pharisees and Sadducees!? I never commanded such divisions among priest and Levites!"

Paul continues, "Well, they are having us observe 'special days and months, seasons and years!'"

Mount Sinai replies, "Paul, I never authorized additional fasts or extra observances—only the ones I describe in this book as a direct pattern of Heaven. In fact, I commanded against all additions in Deu. 4:2!"

Paul proclaims further, "The priests are teaching against grace."

Mount Sinai replies, "Paul, I uphold grace! Read again Lev. 26:40-45 to see how I extend complete forgiveness without sacrifice to entire nations—just when they choose to pray! And, I am faithful to do it. Ask Daniel (Dan. 9:2-23)! Or ask Nehemiah. What bigger picture of grace is there than that—save the grace of the cross?"

Paul states further, "Mount Sinai puts all people under bondage."

Mount Sinai replies, "Paul, as you said, the Law must serve as the schoolmaster to bring people to faith (Gal. 3:24-25). And unless they sense the weight of their sin, they cannot accept grace in its fulness (Luke 7:47). So, the full weight of the Law ushers the believer to the grace of the cross." Mount Sinai concludes, "Paul we are in agreement. The problem is not me. I have been highjacked by those who have changed my Heavenly pattern. I uphold the cross and I uphold grace. Your problem is not with me; rather your problem is with the false version of me as taught by the priests—who you call the Pharisees and Sadducees. They have violated me and I am a victim of their falsehoods (Deu. 4:2). I am also angry about this!"

Consider further . . .

If an Engineer were to design the "perfect car," and if you removed parts from that car, it would no longer be the "perfect car."

Or, if an Architect were to design the "perfect house" and if you knocked out its walls and put in new rooms, it would no longer be the "perfect house."

And, finally, when you make a copy of a key, if one extra cut is made or neglected, the key no longer "fits" the intended lock.

Likewise, we understand that <u>any change</u> to the Law of Moses resulted in the loss of its perfect Heavenly pattern. The Law of Moses was immediately and irreparably changed from its "perfect Heavenly pattern" following the death of Moses. Therefore, <u>Paul in Galatians is not criticizing the original Law of Moses—because he never witnessed it</u>. In fact, no person after Moses ever witnessed the perfect Law— because it was long ago marred from its original pattern.

My final recommendation concerning Deu. 4:2 . . .

If you desire to keep the Law of Moses, keep it *exactly as it was instituted by Moses*. Its original form is patterned after the Heavenly tabernacle. Therefore, strip away all things which violate Deu. 4:2 and follow it *exactly* as it was received from the Lord Himself. Although a "change" may seem good for the time, realize that any change—however slight—has the effect of completely marring the Heavenly pattern contained within the Law of Moses (Exo. 25:40; Deu. 4:2; Heb. 8:5).

A key with just one extra cut no longer fits in its original lock.

Compromises & Keeping the Law Partially

If you are like me, you may look at the Law of Moses and feel overwhelmed. And, when realizing it would be impossible to keep it in its entirety—tabernacle, priesthood, sacrifices, etc.—you might be enticed to "do your best."

Sure, I think such things.

It might be good—although I cannot build the tabernacle and re-establish the priesthood—to at least *do my best* to keep the ceremonial calendar, and *try* to follow the Ten Commandments.

But, let me tell you, this attempt would not be "keeping" the Law of Moses. The Law is a unified whole—and it must be wholly kept (Jam. 2:10-11).

So, if you are inclined to merely "do your best," let me offer the following . . .

In the 6th Century B.C., there were many people who attempted such a compromise. They called themselves "God's people" and made personal attempts to "do what they could" to follow the Law.

But Haggai, the prophet, challenged their priorities.

He asked them if it was time for them to be living in nice houses while the house of their God remained in ruins (Hagg. 1:4).

This question was piercing for God's people. It quickly stirred them to correct their behavior—making God their first priority.

And, likewise, if we ponder Hagg. 1:4, I am convinced it can have a similar effect in our hearts. The tabernacle—which our God commanded to offer sacrifices *daily*—is absent from the Earth. Just as they did in the 6th Century B.C., the words of Haggai leave us to consider our priorities today. . . .

Why should we live in nice houses while the tabernacle of our God is abandoned?

After all, if the God of the Bible is our God, then how can we be satisfied living in a world where His established, holy place of worship has been destroyed?

Indeed, when serving our God, we should venture first of all to uphold Him as God—with reverence and honor. Thus, the words of the prophet Haggai continue to challenge us today . . . How indeed can we say we worship the God of the Bible while we allow His holy place of worship to remain absent from the world?

It is intriguing to ponder, and I simply pose the question for your own deliberation.

You are free to decide for yourself.

If you have never considered these things, I invite you to read the following Bible passages—which declare God's will for the tabernacle and the Law as an enduring, eternal pattern (Exo. 12:14, 17, 24; 27:21; 29:9; Lev. 16:29, 31, 34; 23:14, 21, 31, 41; 24:3; Num. 10:8; 15:15; 18:23; 19:10, 21).

We must be mindful that although Christ is the fulfillment of the Old Testament, the pattern of all those things are His own (Exo 25:40; Heb. 8:5). The Law of Moses is the Law of God.

So, it is with a heavy heart, I pass onto you the challenging words of Haggai 1:4.

Reflect and ponder for yourself . . .

Is it satisfying to live in a world which has been bereft of the holy worship of our God?

Is it okay for us to offer lip-service to God while the tabernacle—which He instituted as a perpetual pattern—is absent from the Earth?

And, although we may have simple buildings which we dedicate as "churches," how could this ever replace the command to maintain forever the holy place—the tabernacle—where God's people are called to appear?

Frankly, all these things place us in a most bizarre position. We live in a world where God's holy pattern has vanished from among us. Whereas it is commanded to be near us and known—instead we await the final day when God will once again emblaze His Law pattern upon the Earth (Isa. 4:5; 66:18-23; Ezek. 37:26-28; Amos 9:11; Zech. 14:16-21).

Reflect on those passages.

Although the Law has fulfilled one of its many purposes as explained in Galatians, it has many yet to accomplish throughout the endless march of ages.

Blessing

Until we meet again, my friend.

May *Praise* will be the *wages* of your *habitation. Behold the Son!* *Hear Him with acceptance* and He will grant you *fortune.* The Lord will grant you a *double-portion* and you will *forget all your troubles* with the *Son at your right hand.* The Lord will serve as your *judge*—leading you to *happiness.* As you *wrestle* with hardship, break free by beginning anew with *praise!*

"The Lord bless you and keep you;
The Lord make His face shine on you and be gracious to you;
The Lord turn His face toward you and give you peace" (Num. 6:24-26)

Bible Passages Referenced

For more books from Genesis Pilgrim, check out www.GenesisPilgrim.com!